Meditations

among
deep
hair

Meditations

The Assorted Prose *of* BARBARA GUEST

Edited with an Introduction by
Joseph Shafer

Foreword by
Marjorie Welish

Wesleyan University Press
Middletown, Connecticut

Wesleyan University Press
Middletown CT 06459
www.wesleyan.edu/wespress

Manufactured in the United States of America
Designed and composed in Monotype Bulmer by
Chris Crochetière, BW&A Books

Library of Congress Cataloging-in-Publication Data
Names: Guest, Barbara, author. | Shafer, Joseph, 1984– editor. |
Welish, Marjorie, 1944– writer of foreword.
Title: Meditations : the assorted prose of Barbara Guest / edited with
an introduction by Joseph Shafer; foreword by Marjorie Welish.
Description: Middletown, Connecticut: Wesleyan University Press, 2025. |
Includes bibliographical references. | Summary: "A collection of Barbara Guest's essays, lectures, reviews, and profiles of poets and artists, as well as forms of fiction, biography, poetic prose, drama, comics, and other mixed-genre pieces" — Provided by publisher.
Identifiers: LCCN 2025000359 (print) | LCCN 2025000360 (ebook) |
ISBN 9780819501738 (cloth) | ISBN 9780819501745 (ebook)
Subjects: LCGFT: Literature.
Classification: LCC PS3513.U44 M36 2025 (print) | LCC PS3513.U44 (ebook) |
DDC 818/.5409—dc23/eng/20250107
LC record available at https://lccn.loc.gov/2025000359
LC ebook record available at https://lccn.loc.gov/2025000360

5 4 3 2 1

Contents

Mysteriously Defining the Foreword

MARJORIE WELISH

Barbara Guest is a poet, first and foremost. And so, when reading her writings otherwise, it is with this vocation in mind.

A celebrated New York School poet, Guest assumes that daily life, the intimacy of conversation, and friendship real or imagined are ever at hand. Presupposed also is the cultural life of the city: cafés, painters' studios, bookshops—at least as New York was in the 1950s, 1960s, and 1970s. But she sees all these as prompts for writing through an imaginative style that invents worlds she knows are out of reach as projected fantasies of another time and place, and yet worth the challenge: the challenge to make of style a palpably lived atmosphere.

Atmospheric sentences are sought and invented. A lifetime of occasions prompts Guest to comply with a request to write; yet, however this occasion arises, it is a prompt for a creative composition for which lyric suggestiveness is the standard. So, on reading through *The Assorted*, we soon conclude: writing transfigures life: and this is presupposed in everything worth doing.

To read her writing is to learn how subject matter is transfigured. Liberties are taken with setting, which may or may not correspond to actual place configured as a fairy tale or more generally romance.

> The poet in us heard singing birds, saw gardens of pruned oranges and ornamental peacocks, heard water fall. The merchants were even guileless in their bargaining, as were we in our astonishment. We bought some of the silk and took it back to our ship and we sailed on with a memory of a simple grandeur, as unlikely a mixture as could be found anywhere except in poetry. The silk was turned into curtains and thus began to lead a tamed, domestic existence, their history asleep in our house, much as a poem enters into an anthology.

Romance which improves upon actual life by ignoring it, and rather invites the imagination to take charge: this is how Guest establishes a poetics for her prose. Place names populate the imagination with no explanations given—this, the prerogative of the sentences that we read in Guest's writing. As in the above excerpt from "Mysteriously Defining the Mysterious," life is the pretext for writing as such; an awareness that, as Mallarmé put it, was all meant to be turned into a book. Guest writes life in confidential sentences. *Seeking Air*, Guest's novel, was a way of addressing a friend in intimacy—intimacy of shared experience and conversation she wishes would never end.

Another way transfiguration occurs in her writing is through *passage*, as she has often said. Passage alters experience by a moving through, over or under from one place and time to another one, and yet traveling, yet not only thematically going forth in poetic movement. A favored compositional device, this traveling is a kind of modulation from one key to another, and, more broadly, a writing by association. To associate is to drift as an end in itself, to take leaving and arriving in simultaneous flux. As Guest configures it, "Prague Walking" is an accomplished instance of fiction and reality mingling their artistic and political intensities past and present: part fairy tale, part cultural vanguard. Her portrait of Prague is evocative even as Guest pays tribute to the considerable accomplishments in the modern arts of film, writing, and other avant-garde practices. Guest says, "Prague presents us with the fairy tale made real by ideas; there is the conundrum no politics can erase—Prague is a romantic city created by a vigorous intellect." For her, Prague carries memories with affective past experience, yet also anticipations.

Epiphanic phrasings frequent the page as poetry: ". . . as were we in our astonishment." Epiphanies and their avatars—*amazement* · *astonishment* · *awe* · *bewilderment* · *consternation* · *curiosity* · *disappointment* · *jolt* · *miracle* · *revelation* · *shock*—all these characterize Guest's encounter with the poetry of others she admires and speaks of, certainly throughout the poetry of Anne-Marie Albiach's in "A Talk on 'Startling Maneuvers.'" This talk about poetry that inspires her would persuade us that a theory of poetry brings about phrases striking, remarkable, singular. Although she is fascinated with the poetics of fancy as the antipode to imagination,

Guest takes pains with conceiving an essay or a talk as the invitation for a composition alive to the work-in-progress in some considerable tension with a thought.

For her part, Guest's advocacy of arts is not meant to impress with high polish. Unlike some writers, whose correspondence—if not all else—is written as for the mausoleum, these writings by Guest are driven to speak their thoughts as caught on the fly, through assemblies and clustered accumulation, severally and "at the same time," as she writes. Epiphanic though her phrasings may be, they are instruments of writing that will not take any sentence for granted—certainly not to fall back on the utility of standard English by which verse or prose perpetuates rote thought. Which is why her "Motion Pictures" is hilarious: a freely drawn caricature of film industry cliché.

Iterability and Irritability, and Kind Words, these are to be found in Guest's written temperament and method. Conspicuous is her choice of H.D. as a subject for biography; even at the expense of writing poetry. Her research drew her into the orbit—should we say vortex?—of Bryher, H.D.'s friend, a dominant force in their lives. Guest writes, "I interviewed a reluctant Bryher who refused to come to my assistance in my exploration of H.D.'s life, fending off my questions with extraneous remarks. I hope I conveyed a kind of despotic magnetism I experienced in Bryher's presence." As for H.D., she was no less difficult as a subject to pin down.

> Why had a few critics called her presence in her own books and mine, elusive? I would be the person who should be able to answer that. On this first day of spring, 1985, one year from her hundredth birthday, could I define her more fully?

For Guest, H.D. represents the singularity of identity, the identity of the type we call a poet. Not the *career* of a poet, which has social cachet; rather, in H.D. Guest identifies a literary life as something quite independent of the mechanisms of fame:

> Horace Gregory, the late noted critic and poet whom I was able fortunately to interview, said that H.D. could never have become a

> member of an "establishment," literary or otherwise. And she preferred it that way. She wanted to be left alone to weave her private web, just as she made her tapestries in her own room with their isolated romantic echoes.

This kind of singularity configured and projected as myth allows Guest to do what she herself does in her poetry and prose alike.

Introduction

JOSEPH SHAFER

In the summer of 2004, Barbara Guest signed two contracts with Suzanna Tamminen, the editor at Wesleyan University Press. One was for a collected poems and the other for a collected prose. The projects were actually proposed together five years earlier in 1999, after Wesleyan published Guest's *Rocks on a Platter: Notes on Literature*, a turn-of-the-century quasi-manifesto in the spirit of Stéphane Mallarmé's *Un coup de dés*. But several years went by between that initial proposal and the eventual signing because Guest and Tamminen were busy publishing *Miniatures and Other Poems* (2002). Once those contracts were filed, conversations about what either a collected prose or poems would entail had to be postponed as their attention was directed back toward the release of *The Red Gaze* (2005). Thus, when Guest passed away on February 15, 2006, neither a collected poems nor a collected prose had taken shape.

It was left to Hadley Haden-Guest to finish editing *The Collected Poems of Barbara Guest* (2008), as Hadley had already begun assisting her mother with editorial tasks when the two lived in Berkeley during those final years. Hadley would sometimes respond to mail on her mother's behalf, take dictation, relay information, although similar roles can be observed in 2002 when email correspondences since archived show Hadley updating editors at two small presses in particular. Guest was finalizing and sending a frequently shifting assortment of material for two books that could at last feature some of her prose, both published in 2003.

Forces of Imagination: Writing on Writing was solicited by Rena Rosenwasser and Patricia Dienstfry at Kelsey Street Press. Guest first selected "Wounded Joy" for its title, after an essay about the negotiations between a poet's joy and that of the poem's, and "Wounded Joy" is the most drafted piece of those prepared for Kelsey Street, yet editors understandably thought another essay carried a more attractive title. *Forces of Imagination* consisted of fourteen creative essays on art and poetics dating from the late 1980s to 2002. Most were previously published in journals or transcribed from talks while others of this sort were omitted in order for dissimilar types of "writing on writing" to comprise that selection. Interlaid between these essays were briefer reflections in visually experimental poetic prose. The poem "The Blue Stairs" was slipped in as well, along with four nearly blank pages with minimal designs of brushed lines of watery ink on paper.

The second book was *Dürer in the Window* with Roof Books, edited by Africa Wayne in collaboration with Guest and published by James Sherry. This assemblage of prose, poetry, and visual art had a former subtitle, *American Art in the Fifties and Sixties*. It was to be what Richard Tuttle deduced, in a December 2001 letter to Guest, "a book about your art writing," or a book about her writings on art from the fifties and sixties. That subtitle was then changed to *Reflections on Art* and Guest requested a passage from Theodor Adorno's *Aesthetic Theory* for an epigraph: "the subjective paradox of art: to produce expression by way of reflection, that is through form; not to rationalize form, but to produce it aesthetically, in blindness, 'to make things in ignorance of what they are': this is art's enigmatic character." This quotation, the bulk of which is taken from Adorno's chapter on "Semblance and Expression," is indicative of ongoing negotiations. It may have been inspired by her discussions with Robert Kaufman but was no doubt another trace of an interest in philosophy that only increased over the 1990s and 2000s while delivering a plethora of talks and essays on the nature of Art, aesthetics, and poetry. To witness an expression in presented materiality, while reflecting on it in a mode that does not overshadow that presentation, is a paradox in her prose and poetry. The word "ignorance" also seems chosen by Guest to amplify what Adorno's own internal quotation conveyed in the original German or standard English translation: "To make things of which we do not know what they are" [*Dinge machen, von denen wir nicht wissen, was sie sind*]. And despite Guest having added the closing clause from Adorno's drafted Introduction, "this is art's enigmatic character," she removed the epigraph and her subtitle, *Reflections on Art*, for the simpler request that an "x" appear in *Reflexions*.

Dürer in the Window: Reflexions on Art is largely an homage to artist friends and former collaborators, with eleven older and recent profile essays spotlighting painters and sculptors close to her: Helen Frankenthaler, June Felter, Mary Abbott, Grace Hartigan, Robert Goodnough, Tuttle, and others. These less formal than poetic retrospectives exhibit some of the styles in Guest's other written portraits over the decades. Sixteen *ARTnews* reviews from 1952 to 1953 were scattered inside with two of several comic-strip collaborations with Joe Brainard. Six poems, like "Homage," then speak to relations with a painter or painting, placed among the twenty-five photographs sprinkled throughout of sculptures or paintings by artists such as Louise Bourgeois, Richard Stankiewicz, Rice Pereira, Piet Mondrian, Alfred Leslie, and Leatrice Rose.

Dürer in the Window and *Forces of Imagination* are two artistically arranged books which offer eye-opening glimpses into Guest's varying prose forms, her influences and profound belief in an emancipatory imagination. They could not, however, reveal the full extent of her prose. *Meditations: The Assorted Prose of Barbara Guest* gives a picture of that extent while keeping the somewhat selective and collagic qualities uncommon to any "collected prose" in the traditional sense. *Meditations* contains previously published and unpublished writings from 1951 to 2003, and, in addition to Guest's lectures, essays, art criticism, profiles, literary and art reviews, including over a hundred *ARTnews* reviews from the 1950s, this miscellany samples her fiction, biography, poetic prose, drama, comics, and other mixed-genre pieces.

Content could then be organized into four sections. "Lectures, Essays, & Poetic Pieces" gathers talks, essays, and reflections on art and poetry in an array of poetic styles and voices. "Profiles" has twenty different portraits, each written in a personalized or individualized manner. Many of these profiles focus on occasions shared, as with Allen Ginsberg, James Schuyler, Charles Olson, Robert Duncan, Nell Blaine, Robert de Niro, and Tibor de Nagy, while others were formally composed for a certain audience, as with Bryher, Jeanne Reynal, or Dorothy Richardson. On the other hand, anything about H.D. is found under "H.D." Clearer examples of Guest's fiction are showcased in "Other Fiction." Among them is an excerpt from her novel, *Seeking Air*, because, like the inclusion of "Part Five" from Guest's biography in the "H.D." section, there wasn't a need to republish whole books in a collection that benefits from simply acknowledging the uniqueness of those forms in relation to others. "Other

Fiction" is titled so, moreover, on account of Guest's personal essays and poetry tending to involve fiction, as explained in "Poetry the True Fiction," just as "Lectures, Essays, & Poetic Pieces" speaks to the recurring presence of poetry within Guest's reflective prose. Lastly, reviews of a single book, poem, or exhibition fall under "Reviews."

Apart from the *ARTnews* reviews, which are chronicled by month and year, the material in these sections is not presented chronologically. Too many pieces, including a few from *Forces of Imagination*, do not have publication or composition dates, although approximations are often ascertainable. Such details concerning every item in this collection are provided in the Notes. Nor could this content be arranged in the order Guest approved for *Forces of Imagination* and *Dürer in the Window*. Those selections interspersed poems and photographs with designs that cannot be replicated in a collection which combines the prose from both books with still more published and uncollected material. Nor does evidence suggest Guest would have preferred a bibliographical, biographical, or logical ordering. Unlike single poetry collections, with their content already sequenced artistically and thus safeguarded to degrees from chronologicalization in a collected poems, Guest's prose pieces exist as standalones or in montages like *Forces* and *Dürer*. For these reasons I have tried to objectively embrace the subjective factors of curation. Sections are instructional with their explicitly loose categorizations while subtle or not-so-subtle topics, arguments, motifs, etc. may connect or carry readers from one piece to the next within those sections. The opening "Byzantine Proposals" steps into the nave of "Gothic Elevation" and on to "Radical Poetics and Conservative Poetry." Her article "The Intimacy of Biography" in the "H.D." section precedes "Part Five" of Guest's biography, *Herself Defined: H.D. and Her World*. A conversation with Duncan about H.D. scholarship, in "Profiles," slides into "The Story of Bryher," before "Dorothy Richardson: A Letter from Cornwall," and so on. That said, the order may feel shuffled, in search of a rhythm where lines of thought can wander the intersecting pathways with breaks now and again.

The collection also affords more than its parts or their sum for a figure as elusive as Guest. Her life story is arguably shrouded in as much mystery as her poetics and the two, especially for criticism, often go hand in hand. A collection of prose assists on these fronts. It invariably grants insights into her difficult poetry while teasing out narratives for what may very well prove to be an impossible biography. Basic questions lack answers. How did Guest get to New York and when? How did she appear on the so-called scene as a lauded poet and leading art critic? Where did she acquire the experience? How did she meet those with whom she is most associated, Frank O'Hara, James Schuyler, John Ashbery, Helen Frankenthaler, Joan Mitchell, for instance? When did her prose writing begin or ever pause in any decade after 1940? Where was she living during her formative years? Where is the history of someone so historical? How did she navigate that surreal life of a removed yet prominent vanguardist, neither in nor outside the communities she generated, whose name has always bore the irony of a woman famous for being perpetually marginalized? Why can readers of Guest not separate her poetic life from the prosaic, or reality from fiction?

Guest told Mark Hillringhouse in 1992 that she hadn't starting writing poetry until "very late, in my twenties," as "I began writing prose earlier." That makes sense, if by "prose" she is referring to undocumented essays or fiction written while living with an aunt and uncle in California to attend Beverly Hills High or while roaming after college graduation, for her undergraduate years were spent studying, writing, and publishing poetry. UCLA classmate and longtime friend Nancy Robbin remembers Guest (then Barbara Ann Pinson) having high aspirations as a poet, a goal that drove Guest to make connections with faculty over fellow students and to dismiss publishing opportunities with the department's humbler poetry anthology until submitting two stanzas of a longer "Abelard and Heloise" for its final 1942 issue. This reputation, by age twenty-one or twenty-two, was rebelliously validated when she transferred out of UCLA, because they "wouldn't teach modern poetry," to attend a junior college (now unknown) where modernists including Eliot and Joyce were taught and where she could learn from a professor (also unknown) whose wife considered herself to be such a poet. After a brief return to UCLA, Guest enrolled at UC Berkeley for her senior year and had teachers like Josephine Miles, who commended her paper on the Metaphysical poets.

She was twenty-three when she returned to Los Angeles in 1943. She landed a few odd jobs (like qualifying World War II veteran pilots for welfare at a social work office) but somehow managed a stint in New York City. En route, passing through Chicago, she caught pneumonia and phoned a family that could set her up temporarily in New York City. She would stay with a girl named Janie on Eighth Street while Janie's roommate was away; then Janie, as recalled in Guest's "Piet Mondrian" essay, helped her find another spare room in the apartment of a young Frieda Egger from Austria on East Ninth Street, directly across from the Hans Hofmann School. Frieda was an artist who survived by painting copies of famous works such as Mondrian's for the Museum of Modern Art, and it was Frieda's bedbug-ridden apartment that exposed Guest to the lives of artists, to MOMA, and to contemporary painters. But we also know Guest retreated to Los Angeles. She would become the personal typist of Henry Miller when he was living in Beverly Glen.

The timeframe in which she could have worked for Miller is narrow and apparently lasted until he left for Monterey in February of 1944 and for Big Sur that March. Miller advertised the position on a UCLA bulletin board and, since Guest knew his *The Cosmological Eye*—a collection of short shorties, three pieces on avant-garde film, an "Open Letter to Surrealists Everywhere," another letter on *Hamlet*, and personal essays—she knocked on his door and was hired to type his manuscripts, letters to editors, and correspondence with other writers. While working for Miller, she also started dating his housemate, John Dudley, a talented young painter and sculptor whom she'd soon marry. Anaïs Nin said Miller worshipped Dudley. Miller discovered him in Kenosha, Wisconsin, during a tour of the US in 1940, where Dudley had written a surrealist narrative or treatise to his friend Lafayette Young about a dive bar figure of God, the piano man, guiding him through a nightmarish wasteland of images. Miller said, in a book chapter Guest likely typed, "Letter to Lafayette" in *The Air-Conditioned Nightmare*, that Dudley's fiction provided "the flood and ark both." The two men had proceeded to enjoy the same New York circles, they each had affairs with Nin, they suffered the same annoying visits from Salvador Dalí at Caresse Crosby's Virginia home and in the city, so when Miller secured rent-free accommodation in Beverly Glen in June 1942, he invited Dudley. A typist was obviously needed.

Miller had drafted several books between 1940 and 1942 but felt incapable of writing anymore. He and Dudley instead turned the house into a messy painter's studio. Danish painter Knud Merrild described a spare yet chaotic apartment where manuscripts and letters were kept in kitchen drawers. Miller was living off a new love of painting: his watercolors were displayed in a Westwood art-supply store and he had sixty works hang at the American Gallery of Contemporary Art on Hollywood Boulevard. In Guest's interview with Hillringhouse, she explains that, prior to her post with Miller, she "needed something to free me," being stuck imitating poets like Robinson Jeffers, so "I became freer here." She was an educated modernist and metaphysical California poet from a working-class family in North Carolina and Florida (though her mother's family was from West Virginia, and her father was born in Kentucky) whose career commenced by immersing herself into the precarious underworlds of surviving visual artists and countercultural prose writers. She also credits Miller as being the first to seriously advise she move to New York.

It is of course her position as art reviewer and editorial associate at *ARTnews* that critics might think of when Guest said she was writing prose before the poetry of her twenties. But when Thomas Hess offered her that job, in the spring of 1952, she was thirty-one. Her first reviews appear in December 1952, a few months after *Partisan Review* printed what many consider her first published poem, "Now You Remembering Nights Awake." Her role as editorial associate began earlier, with the June-July-August issue of 1952, and she held that role well into 1954. One might even say her arrival at *ARTnews* constituted the beginning of an era, and how she got there is quite a tale. She and Dudley had traveled east as far as Kansas, where his parents lived, and where Guest worked in a factory before leaving him for New York and divorcing in 1946. She didn't wait long in New York before rendezvousing with a sculptor she met back in LA, Tony Smith. He and his wife Jane would raise her, as Guest put it, "aesthetically speaking," and Smith remained one of her most influential mentors. He was teaching painting at New York University, insisted his students study *Finnegans Wake*, and introduced Guest to close friends, including Barnett Newman, and to the motives behind artists such as Jackson Pollock. In 1947, she met Stephen Haden-Guest, a translator of mostly French historical fiction and a personal acquaintance of the poet H.D. They married in 1948. From this marriage, a Mrs. Barbara Haden-Guest would craft the penname, "Barbara Guest."

The couple was sharing an apartment in Greenwich Village when she separated from Stephen in 1949. Their daughter, Hadley, was born while Guest stayed with family in North Carolina. Hence the narrative in her "Piet Mondrian" is questionable. It claimed she came to New York from LA "in the 1950s," leading to Janie and Frieda. That may be true, in part. She did rejoin Stephen in New York after separating from him in 1949. To say she arrived in the 1950s more accurately conveys her celebrated entry into the New York School, 1950–1952. Likewise, when Guest next described her poor early days in "Piet Mondrian" on Eighth Street and East Ninth, as a single young girl "lost" in the arts, one might understand this scene less chronologically than poetically, since Guest has transposed her inaugural experience of modern art from the mid-1940s into a picture of her entering the New York art scene.

Often when following Guest's biographical traces there is a sense of doubleness, as if she or her identities are in two places at once. The conundrum rather resembles a central trait in her 1984 biography of H.D. In the chapter "Lausanne-Lugano 1947–53," the scholar Eliza M. Butler leads H.D. to envision how the spectrality of a woman poet from Pennsylvania can be Helen at Troy and Helen in Egypt at the same time. As it happens, the "Piet Mondrian" essay is a work of poetry in that regard. It foremost recollects Guest's perception of a Mondrian painting from different moments in her life. It begins by reflecting on how Mondrian's 1922 painting, *Composition with Blue, Black, Yellow, and Red*, has been reproduced in a 2000 *New York Times* article. This work, she goes on, belongs to an earlier period in Mondrian differentiated from his "middle" period—the period seen in Frieda's apartment. That memory is then juxtaposed with Mondrian's late period, which Guest sees in his ultimate rendition of New York in *Broadway Boogie Woogie* from 1941 to 1942. What, therefore, has Guest given us in the end? A prose piece from her late period is reproducing an image of her New York induction, yet those perspectives are superimposed onto an older relationship with Mondrian's paintings. The piece—part portrait, self-reflection, fiction, and poem—winds up resembling a Mondrian with her own boogie woogie.

It turns out she was already living in the West Village when Philip Pavia opened The Club at 39 East Eighth Street in September 1948. The Club held Friday night debates with those who formulated an "Abstract Expressionism," members like William de Kooning, Franz Kline, Milton Resnick, Landès Lewitin, Clement Greenberg, Robert Motherwell, Isamu Noguchi, with approximately sixty members by 1951. Honored lecturers were frequent, from Mondrian, Harold Rosenberg, Jean Arp, e. e. cummings, John Cage, to Hannah Arendt, and countless guests attended The Club's exhibitions and parties. Soon Guest was reading her poems at The Club and absorbing wisdom from Bill de Kooning. These were the days so formative they nearly precede her iconic friendships with Frankenthaler, Abbott, Hartigan, Mitchell, and Jane Freilicher, or the great wealth of money she witnessed flowing into the arts in her "Art in America: The Nineteen Fifties and Sixties (Viewed in 1999)." Her collage *East Ninth Street, New York* memorializes her time around the debut of Abstract Expressionism at the Ninth Street Exhibition in 1951. And it was upon her sofa in 1952, at 102 Christopher Street, that Robert de Niro Sr. sat when asking whether she'd like to write for *ARTnews*. In her "Robert de Niro" essay, she remembers Hess calling the very next day. He was interested in hiring a poet: making her the first to exercise the pseudo-poetry criticism Greenberg despised in *ARTnews* two years before Guest welcomed O'Hara as an associate in 1954. Schuyler and Ashbery joined in 1957.

Given that Guest's *ARTnews* reviews are seldom consulted, it's not entirely rhetorical to wonder what insight might be gained from collating them, from December 1952 to Summer 1954? Those reviews may only be paragraph-length and one hundred thirteen of them may be found in the last section of this collection, but what they lack in length is made up for in concision and abundance. They were not always assignments chosen by Hess either. Due to her interests and métier, Guest covers pros and cons of artists in a manner that cannot fully mask her underlining views of aesthetics or a poetics never far off; insights perhaps less evident in her pointed critiques, periodic dislikes, or tempered praise than in resonances across the lot. For one, she disfavors an almost unavoidable appeal in the 1950s to fad, to the value of recognized experimentation, to new currencies like abstract expressionism, action painting, shock value, even surrealist imagery, that is, unless these intentions are matched by opposing senses. Her inclination is to determine whether a work moves too consciously or too unconsciously through a sensorium and history of ideas. Think of her poem "Leaving MODERNITY," or those in *Archaics*, where she honors "the tombsman who had accompanied the discoveries," or the 1990 essay "Radical Poetics and Conservative Poetry."

In 1952–53, for example, abstraction seems to pair better with Impressionism than a painter's action or expression, and not because Guest is behind the trend. To the contrary, she says Joseph Meert "can perhaps be termed an Abstract Impressionist," a term barely used or found in print previously. Hess later said Elaine de Kooning coined "Abstract Impressionism" in 1951 at The Club, although Elaine is not seen applying the term until her review of Philip Guston in 1955. The "Abstract-impressionism" of Kandinsky is passingly referenced in Pavia's 1952 essay on how Abstract Expressionism got its unwanted name, in "Part 1: The 'Hess-Problem' and Its Seven Panelists at The Club," but Guest qualifies her terms as well. Meert had progressed from his New Deal murals into abstraction by working from subconscious impressions of landscapes, by registering the visible world and transmogrifying it. Abstract Expressionism is countered by the remaining presence of ordinary scenes nevertheless whisked by the metaphysical and metamorphic surface of rippling color. Meert's conscious use of color variegation, however, keeps his metaphysical exercises from their "move into poetry."

Critics usually pin Guest herself to Abstract Expressionism, to identify some roots, and she does look back fondly at Abstract Expressionism in later talks and essays, at the cultural movements it inspired: how the economy of New York City was reorganized socially, financially, and infrastructurally through the arts. Yet her distancing might be best captured in the 1962 book *Goodnough*, cowritten with B. H. Friedman. Friedman wrote the first half on Goodnough's "Background" and Guest the second on "The Work." Kathleen Fraser once said the book intimated Guest's own rogue poetics. The "work" is that of a loner and pioneer: the labor power in Goodnough's paintings on the American frontier "economy," "in a society which believes that labor provides the means." Pioneering efforts literally mark the energy exerted onto a canvas—the labor of each brushstroke. A hunt is underway for animals hidden in a thickening scape of color-shapes. Strokes appear to quicken, close in, to chase the animals out. That movement works against pure abstraction since figures in abstraction are destined to disappear, while Goodnough's strokes are forcing creaturely forms back into existence. Except, one heeds the discovery Cézanne made when confronting the unmarked canvas beside his dabs: nature should not be disturbed by the artist. Therefore, when these movements intensify and agitate, when creatures are finally stepping out, the hunter retires as the scene paints itself.

By 1953, Guest was laying the groundwork for future poet-critics at *ARTnews* and reshaping the poetry landscape through *Partisan Review*. Only Ashbery had published in *Partisan* before her, with his "The Picture of Little J.A. in a Prospect of Flower" in 1951, so her appearance in the September/October 1952 issue made her a commodity. Despite being on a "New Poets" panel at The Club with O'Hara, Ashbery, and Schuyler on May 14, 1952, arranged by Elaine de Kooning and moderated by Larry Rivers, Ashbery remembers spotting Guest at a street café outside his Oxford University Press office to properly introduce himself only after seeing her poem in *Partisan*. He next ushered Guest into the company of O'Hara and Freilicher. This encounter, mentioned in Karin Roffman's *Songs We Knew Best*, coincides with separate accounts of O'Hara and Freilicher looking her up after that publication before meeting her serendipitously at The Cedar Bar. Guest's 1952 and 1954 poems in *Partisan* were so well received, in fact, that its editor, Philip Rahv, gave her the role of poetry editor. After Delmore Schwartz quit in the winter of 1954–55, Rahv relied on Guest's recommendations and knowledge of arising poets, which was extremely fortunate for her new friends.

One of the many poets she asked to submit was O'Hara, and she solicited translations of international poets, including Boris Pasternak. She kept her role as poetry editor through 1958, when Ashbery's "Ode to Joy" was published, the same year Hettie Jones was hired as editorial assistant. Jones later said it was Guest who encouraged her to apply and Guest who supported her advancement. O'Hara was thankful, too. They had edited three issues of *ARTnews* together in 1954, and in 1955 O'Hara is seen sending Guest not only frequent gossip on MOMA notepads about their recent soirées, upcoming events, and collaborations with artists, but also packets of poems for her feedback and referral, with postscripts on how "I also enjoyed your reviews in ARTS," or how "I wrote a short story last summer which I sent to *The New Yorker* for the fun of it and had it returned. If I submit to *Partisan*, should I send it to you or to Philip Rahv?" She had quickly become a source and conduit for poets wanting to write art reviews, publish poems, collaborate with painters, or push their fiction. She did this while almost singlehandedly raising her daughter and, after marrying the World War II military historian Trumbull Higgins in 1954, their baby boy, Jonathan.

By the mid-1950s the theater had allowed New York poets to expand their collaborations with artists, set designers, actors, directors, etc. When Ashbery's breakout play *The Heroes* had its second showing at Myers's Artist's Theatre in 1953, it was on a triple bill with Guest's *The Lady's Choice* and James Merrill's *The Bait*. Freilicher designed the set for *The Lady's Choice*, a three-scene, one-act play written in Victorian verse, although Guest's least experimental. Its roughly thirty-year-old heiress must decide whether to sacrifice her independence with marriage or suffer social death alone. The lady instead mixes a "love potion" by adding deadly poison to her cocktail and drinks it while declaring her love to her suitor, but not before a butler unknowingly replaces her cocktail. Guest would write over a dozen plays between 1952 and 2000. Most are one act, abstract, and experimental. Five were staged. Three of those five were published posthumously in a special issue of *Chicago Review* in 2008: *The Lady's Choice*, *The Office: A One Act Play in Three Scenes* (directed by Johnny Dodd at Café Cino in 1963), and *Port: A Murder in One Act* (which Myers directed and staged at New York's American Theatre in 1965). The one included here, *Chinese Ghost Restaurant* from 1967, is another example of the politics in Guest's aesthetic play. Scenes leap from English customers in a Chinese restaurant with ghost waiters, Mao's China, the bedroom of a British ambassador and his wife while the Red Guards chat outside, collectors at a British museum, chanting Chinese gymnasts exercising in a gymnasium, a Himalayan mountain outside Nepal, and a dream-sequence by the poet Tu Fu from the Zang Dynasty. With each setting, revolutions keep spinning, like dishes immediately swapped or hierarchies kept overturned: in the gymnast's flopping and flying "hair" ("Mao" 毛 means "hair"), the ambassador honoring Her Majesty on high as his wife moves to the floor, divisions of class, East/West, or an elder mountain man teaching the young hiker that to summit is to reach the sea. The lowest is highest and vice versa.

In 1960, Guest appeared as one of four women in Donald Allen's *The New American Poetry: 1945–1960*, and, during the 1960s, she wrote most of her plays, published books like *Goodnough*, comic strips with Brainard, poetry collections *The Location of Things*, *Archaics*, *Open Skies*, *The Blue Stairs*, *I Ching*, and, as the "fifth point" in what Schuyler called "the five-pointed star" of founding New York school poets, she was featured in John Bernard Myers's *The Poets of the New York School* (1969). Thus her surprising exclusion from Ron Padgett's and David Shapiro's *An Anthology of New York Poets* in 1970 was such an injustice the omission has become canonical. Unconvincing excuses circulated for decades about how certain individuals (persuaded by Kenneth Koch, it was later revealed) could so casually remove a cornerstone of the history they sought to construct, and rumors trailed as to why a man would suddenly want the woman in their inner circle to herself face rejection. Meanwhile, as the 1960s closed, Guest produced several more poem-paintings with Abbott and began preparing a novel dedicated to Abbott. Black Sparrow Press wouldn't print *Seeking Air* until 1978, but she worked on it for years. The last years probably dragged on as several publishers communicated their regret over how this uncategorizable work seemed unmarketable. Once published, many considered it a revelation. Susan Howe revered its research on historically overlooked women, for instance Jonathan Swift's Stella (Esther Johnson), and, according to Fraser, the novel was a watermark in the arts, having combined the ideogrammatic use of white space in Olson and Duncan with the painterly white patches in Agnes Martin and Joan Mitchell. This Guest did through 103 chapters.

The novel's epigraph is from a letter Swift wrote to Vanessa (Esther Vanhomrigh), and Swift's relationship with Stella is the subject of chapter twelve. The plot, however, concerns a male writer, Morgan, struggling to advance literary theory through a project called "Dark" while also trying to make time for his partner, Miriam, seen as "White." When Sun & Moon Press printed the second edition in 1997, Guest's preface affirmed that her "fearless" Miriam was adopted from Dorothy Richardson's *Pilgrimage* novels but set in the political climate of 1970s New York. The title, *Seeking Air*, is suggestive too. Guest wrote the novel in an apartment designated for her writing, separate from the one she shared with Trumbull at 1158 Fifth Avenue. The balcony of that working-apartment supplied her another supplemental space to breathe and reflect, "when I wanted a change of air," her preface notes. In the novel, Morgan moves his writing desk onto this balcony where it stays well into winter. Being part outdoors and part of the apartment's interior architecture, the balcony is a refreshing workspace for Miriam to play as well. For when what is outside 'the work' of art is simultaneously inside, all kinds of experiences are possible. This was a rather implicit response to Gertrude Stein's maxim on aesthetics in *Paris, France*, that "painting has no air." Stein's line was used as an epigraph and redressed in the poem "Roses" in Guest's *Moscow Mansions* (1973), and as early as chapter one of *Seeking Air* we see hints of that which lies outside an artwork entering it, whether in a studio or a museum.

The novel's connection to Richardson is telling in a broader sense as well. Guest's adoration of Richardson apparently exceeded her admiration for H.D., the subject of her biography. While the years spent on *Seeking Air* led to five more writing *Herself Defined*, Richardson's life in modernist prose, and the toilsome, domestic conditions under which Richardson persevered, were most inspirational (in a letter around 1990, Guest told a fan, "I am a closet politico" against "the subordination of women," which has been "very, very hard on me," particularly in matters of labor, which is why Britain's Suffragists coming to power made 1905 "my favorite year," and why Richardson is "my favorite writer"). Bryher was held in similar regard. As the matron of H.D. and Richardson, of innumerable artists, theorists, modernist presses, and institutions, Bryher's influence is detected behind pre-World War II socio-political events and movements across the arts. In the preface to *Herself Defined*, Guest admits that this "difficult genius" born Annie Wilfred Ellerman became the figure of intrigue, and Bryher's story repeatedly threatens to commandeer a narrative that at one juncture devotes a chapter to "The Bryher Path." Guest read and spoke with those close to H.D., had probed H.D.'s papers at the Beinecke, was sharing an apartment with H.D.'s daughter Perdita at 149 West 16th Street from the mid-1980s to 1993, yet it was through studying and interviewing Bryher in Switzerland that Guest grew closest to H.D. and her world.

In addition to her biography, criticism, reviews, and lectures on H.D., her 1980 poetry collection *Biography* and writings on Imagism, Guest published a substantial essay in *The Iowa Review* in 1986, "The Intimacy of Biography." How intimate was that project? H.D.'s ghost appears at her bedside. Bryher is heard in dreams. The biographers in whom Guest confided said they too exhibited the behavior of their subjects. Guest notices an increase of selfishness and spelling mistakes. But the vulnerability and doggedness of a biographer, and the amount of time it stole from Guest's poetry, makes it all the more stunning that she proposed a second biography on Bryher. The narrative in her proposal for "The Story of Bryher" is a model of committed scholarship and intimacy: "A personage of boundless energy, a feminist all her life, a salvager of the homeless, if a martinet on her own ground, she is a stalwart, uncompromising figure." Guest was familiar with Bryher's archived correspondence at Yale and would be one of the first to examine the private papers and photographs shipped to a special library in East Hampton after Bryher's death.

A second biography was never completed. A prolific period rolled in with the 1990s as Guest produced nearly two dozen collections and a trove of essays between 1988 and 2003. A portion of these essays are profiles. A few were published as retrospectives of an artist's work, some were read at memorial services, and published or not, a couple were written for invited talks or a special issue on a friend, and others were typed, proofed, and filed with the rest. "Robert Duncan, As Once I Viewed Him," for example, dated 1998, is relatively cryptic and pithy, to the extent of seeming unfinished, yet it feels all too appropriate for those who know Duncan or his disquisitions. Poets familiar with him and Guest have long speculated about their relationship, or lack thereof, since Duncan's correspondence with H.D. and his *The H.D. Book* ostensibly claimed ownership of H.D.'s legacy while Guest was writing the biography. In her "view," she regrets not seeking Duncan's advice more actively, wishing she had shared her own secrets about H.D., but "biographers are zealous guards of their secrets."

Another group of essays belongs to "Lectures, Essays, & Poetic Pieces." This section opens the collection because it addresses wider topics like poetry, poetics, Art, or art movements. Being mostly written in the 1990s and early 2000s, these essays likewise come at a time of great reflection.

With it comes a surge in cited philosophers (e.g., Hegel, Kant, Adorno, Benjamin, Barthes, Derrida) and an urgency to defend aesthetic freedom against restrictions in contemporary theory. In an aside made during her talk at St. Mark's Poetry Project in 1986, Guest had the audacity to question the popularized method of deconstruction. The *New York Times* had just published J. Hillis Miller's "How Deconstruction Works" the month before her talk and she uses it as a counterexample. Miller's synopsis did demonstrate the crux of deconstruction by interpreting a line from *Paradise Lost.* That procedure maintains an asymmetrical or hierarchal relation, as between Adam and Eve, in Milton's "Not equal, as their sex not equal seemd." The trick of deconstruction is to sustain this asymmetry while reversing the roles of each thing. Eve, first interpreted as a subjected feminine thing of nature, supportive, substratal, and external to Man, is then realized to be the source of poetic power. The initial asymmetry is understood to be inverted. This schema, Miller asserted, renders any one meaning indeterminate. Guest disagreed. The real mystery of poetry or art in the lead-in to "Mysterious Defining the Mysterious"—whether its subject is a female Turkish merchant or a commodity, something foreign or ordinary, ancient or modern—is upheld when opposing characteristics appear in any one thing "at the same time":

> If there is any difference: clearly abstract and clearly concrete at the same time. If there is any difference of opinion here between East and West it may have to do with our different concepts of time. I personally am devoted to the idea of *at the same time.* Now we have arrived at the borders of other things.

This aside and two others were cut from the previously published version of "Mysteriously Defining the Mysterious: Byzantine Proposals of Poetry." Such omissions were why the essay was described as "excerpts" when first printed in *HOW(ever)* in 1986, and those excerpts were then reprinted in *Forces of Imagination.* But that is not the version in this collection. The paper presented here still lacks the spoken asides made at St. Mark's, but it includes the written portions prepared and delivered. The verbal comments omitted from this fuller version, and the contexts surrounding each separate version, are provided in the Notes.

This is noteworthy because the advantages of substituting an original or lengthier version for one already published are seized several times. *Forces of Imagination* can keep the shorter version of "Mysteriously Defining the Mysterious" because the paper containing additional lines is used here. Three profiles in *Dürer in the Window* were not duplicated either. Since the "Robert Goodnough" essay in *Dürer* was an abridged adaptation of the chapter in *Goodnough*, I opted for the latter. "Why has Louise Bourgeois finally become the Artist of the Moment?" in *Dürer* was altered from the 1993 publication in *Denver Quarterly* now included here. And the *Dürer* version of "Helen Frankenthaler: The Moment & The Distance" deleted material from its 1975 state in *Arts Magazine*. In any case, the Notes will identify any substitutions, changes, originals, or copytexts, and a list of items considered for inclusion but ultimately omitted, through consultation with an evolving group of advisors, is also provided.

Rena Rosenwasser and Patricia Dienstfry at Kelsey Street Press, and James Sherry at Roof Books (an imprint of Segue Foundation, Inc.), were most gracious with their contributions. Archivists at Yale University's Beinecke Rare Book & Manuscript Library, staff at the University of California–San Diego Library, and librarians in Stanford University's Department of Special Collections were instrumental. Tom McCormik, from the Estate of Mary Abbott, helped me track down and publish certain paintings by Guest and Abbott. A special thanks goes to Susan Gevirtz, Robert Kaufman, Mei-mei Berssenbrugge, Charles Bernstein, Peter Gizzi, Rachel Blau DuPlessis, Marjorie Welish, Brenda Hillman, Ron Padgett, Garrett Caples, and Daniel Katz. Finally, this collection would not exist without Norma Cole, Hadley Haden-Guest, and Suzanna Tamminen.

Lectures, Essays, & Poetic Pieces

Mysteriously Defining the Mysterious: Byzantine Proposals of Poetry

We once took a ship from Beirut and sailed along the coast of Turkey, which I shall here call Byzantium, as once Constantinople was the center of art, learning, poetry, and under the great Constantinople held the barbarian at the gates and saved a civilized world, that of the Venetians, to whom we are so much closer with its own relics of religion. We think of St. Mark's in Venice with its Byzantine domes, as one thinks of the perpetual filming of Venice which brings us the Byzantine optics of wealth and plague as we watched in *Death in Venice*. The Byzantine in Venice is slowly dying and is a major death, yet this demise shows itself in fragments, just as the poet slowly dies in the poem making sure there are fragments remaining of the empire which created the poem, the empire of a poet's soul.

The ship on which I sailed was on its way to Greece, but first it came into the harbor of Turkish Mersan. In order to enter the harbor we dropped anchor near a Russian freighter, and there were all the signs of excitement on our ship of nearness to a stranger, possibly a barbarian, not the lowly Mersan but the permanent stranger, Russia, who dominated our imagination.

We were curious about this port, so we left ship and entered the dingy, sandy town with its scarce trees, like a suburban oasis. But no sooner were we inside the gates than we entered a bazaar. It was an open bazaar—an exciting image—unlike the closed, narrow, sky-covered and awning-covered bazaars of Morocco and Damascus. A supposed simple place where country people had brought their stuffs, as they did in *Jude the Obscure*. The object of these country folk here was a small town of Mersan with one-storied houses, a few attempts at the modern world with decorated café umbrellas, but little else.

It was curiosity that had brought us there and the boredom of a confining ship. Our curiosity was rewarded, for suddenly we were in an open square of pilgrim's wares. Before our eyes were laid golden, silken stuffs of such serious and sophisticated spinning and weaving only to be viewed at expensive shops of the West. There they lay as if mute rags, palatial silks. Yet to these folk they were the ordinary treasures of a modest life. The poet in us heard singing birds, saw gardens of pruned oranges and ornamental peacocks, heard water fall. The merchants were even guileless in their bargaining, as were we in our astonishment. We bought some of the silk and took it back to our ship and we sailed on with a memory of a simple grandeur, as unlikely a mixture as could be found anywhere except in poetry.

The silk was turned into curtains and thus began to lead a tamed, domestic existence, their history asleep in our house, much as a poem enters into an anthology. The unheard sounds of their sleep are very close to this ode of Keats who transfigures the smallness of his personal environment, the narrowness of his private life into magic and vision. In one of his early poems we are led into an unexpected encounter with beauty, as the silks of Mersan greeted us, and although translated into another form, they yet retain their magical secrets. This island-bound poet, restricted to sofas and country lanes, or an occasional jaunt to London, wrote:

> Much have I travell'd in the realms of gold,
> And many goodly states and kingdoms seen;
> Round many western islands have I been
> Which bards in fealty to Apollo hold.
> Oft of one wide expanse had I been told
> That deep-brow'd Homer ruled as his demesne;
> Yet did I never breathe its pure serene
> Till I heard Chapman speak out loud and bold:
> Then felt I like some watcher of the skies
> When a new planet swims into his ken . . .

This experience Keats has shared with me I shall call Byzantine. And we can define Byzantine as that which is convoluted, difficult to track down, complicated. Underneath its apparent surface there is the presence of 'something else.' You can think of this 'something else' as a woman behind a veil. Or you can think of it as architectural complexity disguised as mathematics, as the dome of a Byzantine church. I can appeal to your Byzantine thought with words such as corridors, plots, disguise, whispers, atmospheric treaties with civilization expressed in the abstract. Underlying this rather sinister, and almost indelicate movie plot, under this disguise is the word I would like to discuss, a word that is as necessary to poetry as the oasis to the traveler, "mystery."

I would like to borrow from Mallarmé an enduring phrase, an introduction to mystery, "Not the thing, but its effect." This "effect" is what I have been leading to with my curtains from Mersan. The "Thing" is the poetic process which gives off without notice an effect which is the poem. Each, the process and the effect, go about in disguise, they must be uncovered, found out, Chapman's Homer must be opened by the poet.

In reading the Byzantine Poe, we discover that "things are not what they seem to be." This discovery was introduced much earlier in Shakespeare, where people go about in disguise, until someone, finally, in *Twelfth Night* whispers, "Things are not what they seem to be."

This phrase would have a great appeal to Mallarmé and Baudelaire who conscientiously introduced this concept into their poetry, adding a dimension to their work that exceeded the use of symbols. "Not the thing, but the effect it produces." The "effect" lends a labyrinthine element to the fundamental simplicity of the statement of a poem. It is necessary to follow a circuitous path into "realms of gold" or those realms remain highways leading to a garage door.

In our own time, Wallace Stevens called a poem a "finikin thing of air." A poem may when first glimpsed float a thing tail, like the tail of a kite in crisp air, like the first note of the Emperor's bird, and "Emperor" was a word that came easily to Stevens, as he drew his pedigreed birds in chill colloquial air. In Byzantine guise he called a poem a "purple bird" that must sing to the poet to console him for being rare; he arrives in a mysterious color that is made of several colors, an extraordinary bird who suggests the extravagance of being rare.

In whatever guise reality becomes visible to the poet, he withdraws from it into invisibility. In his cloak of Byzantine colors he spins his secret life. The poem is the unburdening of the ghosts which have come to haunt the poet after he has made his trip to the labyrinth. These are ghosts, not words, they are the effulgencies of the mystery that surrounds and decorates the poet like a halo rescued from life. And it is the poet's halo that we must see within the poem, not the full dress of rhyme or structure, or vers libre. Not the artifice of landscape or the hotels of verse. Shelley liked to think of spirits hid in clouds, and Byzantine poets imagined genies escaping from bottles, and Blake drew angels.

T. S. Eliot indicated the necessity for mystery when he offered a tribute to Walter de la Mare, whose frequently banal poetry was sometimes lifted by a mysterious presence, as in this stanza quoted by Eliot.

> The whispered incantation which allows
> Free passage to the phantoms of the mind?
> [. . .]
> By the delicate invisible web you wove—
> An inexplicable mystery of sound.

The poet doesn't come easily upon this mystery or more poets would recognize its step, and if this were so I wouldn't need to present my Byzantine proposals. Auden said that "Every poem is rooted in imaginative awe." And Marianne Moore said that what must be present in poetry is "an impassioned interest in life's creative secret." "Awe" and "Secret" are brought to us by that Spirit "hid in a cloud."

In *My Emily Dickinson* (I am fond of that "My"), Susan Howe has quoted Dickinson as confessing about reading a poet (who might have been Elizabeth Barrett Browning, a poet who sought mightily in her work for that "awe," who although passionate was singularly unimpassioned, and whose work is flawed by the heaviness of her search for mystery): "Did you ever read one of her poems backwards, because the plunge from the front overturned you? I sometimes have – A something curious overtakes the Mind." There speaks the true critic, and for my purposes I note that Dickinson took a very Byzantine turn, to reach the poem's kiosk. "A curious something overtakes the Mind."

Painters, in particular abstract or non-objective painters, were seriously concerned with the existence of mystery in their work. Kandinsky states this problem which can apply to poetry as well. Kandinsky wrote that "a problem all art imposes is the evaluation of its distance from its source." It is within the convoluted travels of distance to its dramatic center, the plumb line, that we trace the aura that distinguishes his painting. Kandinsky also had a concept of "inner sound." This sound intimidates the creative condition of the artist and controls the temperament of the painting. Every "vibration" that urges communication to be formulated "out of inner necessity, every element should be creatively inserted in the work in order to evoke that inner sound. The work of art becomes a means for spiritual communication between the creator and the viewer." Kandinsky was here invoking the Bauhaus principles of spirituality with its roots in theosophy. It is most informative that Bauhaus, which was dedicated to reducing art and architecture to "less is more," should rely on the spiritual as a reductive agent. A reach toward a minimal mystery. The cube defined the mystery and confined it, arriving through hazardous passages to total abstraction. This is compatible with the Byzantine insistence on abstraction in decoration and mosaics, properly defined as "facelessness."

The "inner sound" is what the poet hears. Mandelstam called this "sound spilling into fingers."

The mysteriousness of which I write conceals no mystery. I am urging the consideration of imagination, spirit, and "nostalgie pour l'infini."

The Byzantine aspect is a preference for abrupt connections with the remote in order to establish a concrete interior or coastal connection. It longs for a poetry of regions, not regionalism, for a poetry that can embark on ships and find its way to a settlement where a commodity such as silk is respected, and with an ability to exchange its contour for a curtain without losing an identity imposed by the bartering of one idea for another. There is nothing mandarin in this search for the instinct, or "inner sound," which withholds itself from the promises of merchants and permits a common marketplace to examine its value.

The inner sound of the poet protects the poet. Delacroix wrote that painters of marine life do not represent the sea satisfactorily: "They want to show too much science, make portraits of waves, as landscapists make portraits of trees." His argument was that these seascapes do not concern themselves with the effect on the imagination, as they are absorbed by details which 'turn the mind away.' Why? Because this mind filled with details, this poet whose sole urgency is his subject matter neglects the immensity of the depth to be rendered by Art. The depth is the mystery.

Silk, which has made sacrifices to art by concealing its leopard beauty, recognizes its value. The silk understands the merchant desire to display everything, and, with a Byzantine preference for the hidden noise of fabric, lowers its eyes, gazing into the mysterious deep.

Gothic Elevation

The Gothic elevation and extension of the veritable

Nave of the Poem delights me.   As does the implicit

idea of *renewal.* Amsterdam (site of the stares)

and its Dutch Masters might well have been hosts

to those dwellers in Magyardy whose balsam scents our *blue.*

Sympathy with Ovid

I am always in sympathy with Ovid. How little the literary life supports us. Banishment causes memory to thrive. One can also construct one's own set of circumstances. I look at the purple sunset and then a wild dawn over the Pacific. Remember, when La Comète was in the sky?

Radical Poetics and Conservative Poetry

Everything we loved, emulated was attached to the lyric modernism of Baudelaire's and Mallarmé's later writing. Walter Benjamin wrote in the late 1930s that *Les Fleurs du Mal* was the last lyric work that had a European repercussion.

In the not too far off future, the curtain will be drawn on Modernism as it enters history. Already the shades are listing as Modernism begins to cross the border, exulting in a new freedom called the past. The forms of poetry, too, are restlessly releasing themselves. Having feasted on Modernism they are readying for a new patrol into less inhibited—and what is glimpsed as a more fractured—territory.

Meanwhile the battle lines are still drawn between radical and conservative poetry, as if no one had discovered that long ago Mallarmé had solved that issue. It is said that conservative poetry is the only guide from which one can look backward, rather than forward. Its strength lies in repetition as a long line of flow assembles between the lampposts of the past, the landscapes of the past and the neighborliness of what are called "loved" objects.

Because of its ability to recognize a subject not for its substantive value but for its definition, conservative poetry takes issue with reality as it assembles itself in a poem. For instance, a planted tree is seen as planted with roots in the ground, perhaps a nearby trowel and a parent or child further off to the left watching the clearly delineated leaves, and the moral is an esteemed one placing value on the absoluteness of growing things.

The radical tree might be made of bones and the only clue to its recognition is that the poet has called it a bone-tree. And yet this tree is about growth and these are the eminent qualities of bones. But the radical poet draws no moral from the assemblage. The moral is in the hands of the reader.

In conservative poetry the poets live in a complementary world, without being aware of what surrounds them. They exist in a space hemmed in by other trees that are called "real trees." This poetry offers the promise of reality, yet in a defined space the poem, itself, is never free.

The radical poem suffers from a few of the same difficulties, but in the defenestrating process of saying something new the structure of the poem suffers and the poet becomes engaged in a search for supports that will hold together the poem; and these supports are so new themselves, like spandex, they must be marketed to realize their future. And this uses up invaluable creative time.

Meanwhile the conservative poet is comfortably ensconced in the tried leather of a poem and the voice whether from Odessa or London or Cairo is welcome, because although the sensibility may be tired the words when they arrive are refreshingly old and they look like cherries or lilies and can be understood. The poem projects meanings or values; it creates an atmosphere of security and that is like velvet.

I don't believe we need worry about the conservative poem with its borrowed ancestry. Although the heritage of the radical poem is even longer, I want to reassure myself about its immediate contests.

A diversion was created when Art was given the vulgar guise of Postmodernism. This art had nothing to do with Modernism, of course. An invented term betrays the ethos of the society that accepts it. And perhaps there are practitioners who might be called Postmodern in their vandalism. But in order to accept this term we have to believe that Modernism, itself, is finished. Like throwing a bathing cap into the divine flux.

The conservative artist would like nothing better than to believe in the demise of Modernism. It is a subject that haunts this artist continually. The life of the conservative artist is preoccupied with avoiding the hurdles of Modernism.

The radical issues of a poem are infinite and this accounts for the immodesty of the poet who confronts endless space. This imposed immodesty needs to be protected in the closed environment in which an artist lives, subject to regulation and mandated law. The modesty of the conservatives is confined to the background of their work. In the forefront, in public, they are vociferous, as if they read with many tongues. Actually they are engaged in temporary struggles, with the use of the sledgehammer against ice.

Lest I be accused of warfare with metaphors I would like to include a personal comment on the reception of Václav Havel in the United States Senate, where he was welcomed with open arms as if he possessed the magic to release its practitioners from mendacity, as if Cicero once more had appeared to castigate the rogue Catiline, "O tempora O mores!"

It is a subject for fiction, even hallucination, to suppose that an American artist would have been permitted to impose such radical opinions on the American Senate. And yet Havel was uproariously welcomed and real tears were shed.

Imagination

In the introduction to a new edition of *My Sister—Life*, we learn that Pasternak was once asked: "What is Art?" When asked the same question, Verlaine had answered that it was music. Pasternak thought art was greater than music, "for it was concerned with greatness itself." Finally the poet decided that Art was "grandeur." We can see the poet at Peredelkino, his retreat in the last days of his grandeur, considering a question put to him more than once, a tired question, for which he must have been prepared. But no, he decided to speak again and he said to his questioners and friends that "ultimately art derives from human dignity, from charity." Then he became more enthusiastic. Having uttered the expected words, he turned to his interlocutor once again, and we have the feeling that history is now going to enter: "One must live in sovereign freedom like a king, never surrendering to temporal authority or traditions however deeply rooted, but out of one's own acquired perfections, honest with himself." That is, one must live out of oneself.

I want to speak about living out of oneself, as this will bring us to the inner kingdom of the imagination.

Imagination has its orderly zones. It is not always the great tumultuous sea on which we view a small boat. It can lie behind hedges, hide in boxes, even suffer the touch of exile in a world subsisting on invention.

Classical imagination contributes to the beauty of form out of which it grows and which Homer brings to us as he imagines the beauty of Helen or Achilles, the sinew of the arms of oarsmen. Out of myth arose this stupendous imagination and its direct inheritor was the sculpture of Phidias, who molded with his imagination, not from real life only—and here I want to insist that there is no conflict between realism and imagination. The Charioteer is clearly representational and clearly imaginary. The classic form is abstract and concrete at the same time.

In Neoclassicism, to reiterate for my purposes ideas with which you are already familiar, poets borrowed from their reading to subsidize, to endorse their imaginations, which otherwise would have deteriorated into domesticity—given the enclosed world they were now in—as opposed to the seas of Classicism. They turned to libraries to embellish themselves with the ideas of others, just as in early Medievalism clerics had copied from the texts of ancients, and speech and learning were handed down to us.

I bring up this distinction between Classicism and Neoclassicism, because I believe the poetics of today has progressed from Classicism to Neoclassicism and this is an honest removal, although we may regret it.

In appropriation of texts, in subsistence on the words of others, even from the contemporary world, imagination must have its proper position, because only imagination can return the texts to life. One of the implicit properties of imagination is that it resists clear and absolute meaning. If unrestricted, we are welcomed into an activity that guides us into the realm of the self, the oneself where creativity breathes.

There is no substitute for imagination. Words deprived of their stability—that is, if not fed by the imagination—rush around attempting to attach themselves to a surface. They have no stabilized vocation; they become furtive, ready to sell themselves. Wordsworth, not immune to appropriating landscape, wrote:

> Language, if it do not uphold, and feed, and leave in quiet, like the power of gravitation or the air we breathe, is a counter-spirit, unremittingly and noiselessly at work to derange, to subvert, to lay waste, to vitiate, and to dissolve.

It is the counter-spirit we must beware of, even in the presence of despairing academic anxiety that—overwhelmed by the creative spirit, angered by imagination that disrupts its formulaic view of life—would like to convert imagination into a conservative toy.

In such an atmosphere of controlled tedium it is always refreshing to turn to a poet such as Jules Laforgue, who in 1883 wrote:

> In the flashes of identity between subject and object lie the nature of genius. And any attempt to codify such flashes is but an academic pastime.

From these "flashes of identity"—marvelous phrase—and above academic anxiety rises an elite structure, elite not because it is marble, but because it is rock in which Art survives in every era sustained by desire and necessity.

Finally, in case we become discouraged or overwhelmed or even disappointed in our era, in the state of our art, I would like to remind us of the remark Valéry made in 1933, a year that was to initiate the close of an era: "Profound changes are impending in the ancient craft of the Beautiful."

A Talk on "Startling Maneuvers"

I'm so pleased to be here and of course one of my difficulties in life is not just writing poetry; it's collecting my particles and wondering what I'm supposed to do where, so I thought today was going to be a discussion, of what the poem is about, so I brought a poem on Anne-Marie Albiach. About two weeks ago, at home, I was looking through some old diaries that of course weren't completed but still had white pages and I saw at the top of one page—oh this was ten, fifteen years ago—"Wrote a letter to Prynne," "Received book from Anne-Marie Albiach," and, in little brackets, "She inspires me," and now that I know her and know her work more, she inspires me more. So there was a birthday celebration for Anne-Marie in San Francisco and I wrote a poem to her in celebration of this, of her, of her poetry, and after I'd finished it, I realized that what I'd written about, because she is very much on my horizon, that I'd written about the process of writing a poem. So I'm going to read this [poem, "Startling Maneuvers"] and we're going to discuss it—Mei-mei's going to tell you what it means . . . [laughter].

> *Arrived at the terrain of her sensibility / —a stasis and // pull in the composition physical— // remember, a contradictory tug phantom-like— // upon the environs of the poem.*

My interpretation of this is that when you come to the point in a sensibility when you're approaching a poem, that is the preparation, and there is always a stasis, which contains balance and then non-movement. You are prepared to move but you're still balancing yourself. And the pull in the composition, which is physical because it has to announce itself and it announces its frailty, its physical presence, and that's why its tug is phantom-like. And it's beginning to have its phantom-shadow on the poem. And this pull is so extraordinarily important because if you don't feel the pull between the poem and you, then you somehow or other don't manage to produce anything that has much energy.

Darkening of the page and then withdrawal of darkening.

This could be your shadow—

Gradually the page lightens, / the invisible heaviness lifted // Perhaps—cinematic— // this elevation.

Perhaps it's on a screen. I think that I probably, in the screen of distance, projected this figure coming from distance onto the screen, and there is a feeling of a screen, not only to be projected on but between yourself and the poem.

With no warning (from inside the text, // mind attached to the text.) and attacked by dizziness of atmosphere, in the attack of suspense a masterful / development of plot and erasure.

I'm hesitating because I don't know whether I'm going to say that I use Wite-Out a lot . . . [laughter]. I know Anne-Marie does. But that amount of erasure is very necessary to what she has written.

The echo that the words grant us on the page and off

Remember that it's off the page also—

sound of the last few words—, / they will be abolished and this new movement embracing on echo.

And at this point a destructiveness enters the poem. I know that . . . I've been reading the life of Shelley again—fabulous book by Holmes—and the amount of destructiveness that Shelley was capable of was so incredible—everything he touched practically, but this also happens in the poem. It never is the pearl, but it's the pearl with the flaw.

The echo / the words grant us on page and off, / sound of the last few words, / they will be abolished this new movement that embraces an echo / only discovered, here, where, the poem / sustains marginality.

The / timing of this substitution, one idea for another / as we supplant ideas. Count down. / Knuckle of the hand / illustrates itself, tames the sentence covered with a / fist held loftily.

I was very conscious of this in Albiach's work; there's so much physicality and it's all words. And words are physicality. And I always had the sense of a fist that she held over the page.

Muscular control . . . fastidious. / continual restiveness also.

And there is a sense of conversation and you don't know if this conversation (it's not between quotation marks), you don't know whether this conversation is between yourself and some apparition. I believe that I call [my Post-Apollo book] *Quill, Solitary* *APPARITION* because I was conscious all the time of a sense of hauntedness, and I think that it's in many poets, this hauntedness, and either it belongs to you or it doesn't. It's not necessary, but we are haunted by something, those of us who are.

A blissful discontinuity / orders this estrangement of each // available word and the disinclination to advance at / that point in time) or desire to hurry toward an abrupt / ending—.

Don't hurry. This is one of my little problems.

Rushing or spectacular jumps over the hurdles—

That's taking chances, and writing that doesn't take chances isn't worth the old-fashioned—I remember my father's saying, "It's not worth a tinker's damn"—and he said that in North Carolina.

An advanced punctuation bursting from vases // into an arena of sound / the aroma continues as a cloud of invisibility shelters.

The invisible is what else can happen in the poem, in its arena, like

a ghost exiting, there from center right: solid objects, merciless.

That's the phantom of possible ideas, as I would translate it. Now comes the part where the poet is somewhat in charge. I don't believe one's ever in charge; I think that—I always believed that people like Dryden, Pope, were in charge. I don't think Shakespeare was: I think he was too great.

(Maneuvering inside a volume) // the poet employs a force majeur to shred the atmosphere / this fist is imprint almost / observable!

The full meaning becomes clear to the poet.

And all the while movement coalescing / with thought—

There is a strictness that the poet must place, that the writer must place upon the person, the personage that the poet/writer is occupying. It's not to lose sight of the ideas and movements—they must meet. And then comes,

Startling these maneuvers! / of idea and erasure.

And the idea of erasure is also a positive one. It is not negative. It leans to the idea of all the possible choices that there were and are in the poem and some of those that the poet did not make, but it's an idea of leaving everyone slightly hesitant, in the air, behind which are the phantoms and the possibilities of phantoms, so that the poet is never as direct in the idea that is being obtained, and as I've suggested here, the poem does develop and does maneuver itself and its ideas into and past the erasure.

[Turns toward Mei-mei] So that was my essay . . . [laughter, clapping].

Art in America: The Nineteen Fifties and Sixties (Viewed in 1999)

It was an atmosphere of vitality and expectancy in New York in the 1950s and '60s. New York was excited about New York. At last it had an export that was international: Painting. Painting brilliantly dubbed "Abstract Expressionism." Later, in other hands, to be called "Abstract." Who had ever expected Expressionism to return? It was now in modern guise. The word "Modern" was important, it in the air, everything had to be Modern, of the moment. That was the tempo of New York. The work was painted by young people who were beginning to be called masters. So fast was the movement growing. Expressionism was translated into Energy.

The arrogance that once inhabited Europe had arrived in New York. Marvelous arrogance, painters became idolized like movie stars. New York was responsible. New York took painters, sculptors, even poets to its commercial heart.

Madison Avenue, where high-priced stores sold fashion clothes, was not so fashionable as Paris, but more fashionable than anywhere in the US. Here were the art stores where American art was sold. New York galleries were designed by advanced, modern architects. The key word in this new world of galleries was also "Modern."

On Tuesday evenings Madison Avenue was closed to cars. Artists and art dealers and art buyers walked up and down the closed street, going into the galleries, meeting friends for drinks on the Avenue, bars filled for one evening with artists and buyers. The Mayor closed Madison Avenue to commercial and private cars. No one compared this New York to the energy of other cities. The belief was the energy of the world flowed into New York City.

The now-expanded magazine *ARTnews* became the initiator of what is new art. Edited by the brilliant young Thomas Hess, the magazine was responsible for reputations processed each day. Hess was the first to publish art reviews by poets who wrote their reviews in kitchens and downtown studios of the artists. What better reviewers could be found than those living near the painters themselves? In the same block, sharing the same kitchen, the same ideas.

One of those poets, Frank O'Hara, was hired by the Museum of Modern Art to help it build its reputation as upholder of the New. He was sent to Europe to make note of the collections there. Poetry and painting became through O'Hara the official twosome once enjoyed by his marvelous French poets, Apollinaire and Reverdy, who had included painters in their manuscripts. It was the French myth of which the Americans were so aware, of the collusion of poets and painters. Baudelaire, Mallarmé were to be repeated once more. There was also an echo of the collusion of Goethe with painting and sculpture. It was the return of painting to the other arts once lost in the American hinterland. Or so the poets for a brief moment believed. And they believed themselves to be inside the margin, inside the commercial margin also, and heads turned by the amounts paid for the canvas dripping near the shared coffee pot of their painter friends.

Other writers in New York, prose writers, were published in *Partisan Review*, a serious journal whose authors issued mandates about literature and Jean-Paul Sartre. Prose writers did not stroll on Madison Avenue. They were over on the Westside of New York thinking politically while everyone knew poets and painters were thinking about words and brushes that dripped paint onto a canvas placed on the floor.

Poetry was being written about painting, and lo, painting crept into poetry in metaphors and observations. Feelings of great affection were attached to a momentary canvas partaking of the same emotional process as the poem, of the same witchery of the moment.

This l'Air du Temps, this air of being together in celebrating a moment in time, happens rarely, and often its secret is that a great deal of money is being spent on one of the arts, and this leads to a stimulation of the values of art and a stimulation in the arts that leads to production. Attention is being paid to the arts, literally "paid" in dollars. And attention, although momentary, flows out of this art into its companions, poetry and music, and the air is filled with gold and paste celebratory coins. For the time being, poets and musicians are even making a contribution to the economy as they enjoy themselves and are productive. Their contributions are an accessory, now a necessary accessory to art, to explain it with images. They would do this anyways, freely, because the Muses need one another.

Who else, if not a poet, would understand when de Kooning sitting on a sofa in the late evening remarked, "When I was a Classicist," that is, "When I was a Surrealist." And de Kooning spoke of Titian with an awe that leads us to another realm, of the practicality of the artist: "Those old guys had everything in place, the Virgin and God and technique, but they kept it up like they were still looking for something. It's very mysterious." In his blunt manner, always edged with insight, he then said, "You have to keep on the edge of something all the time, or the picture leaves you."

Kant Sees

Kant sees a close similarity between the artist and the dreamers, like fairies in an Irish dream; but these are involuntary dreams, outside the dream of the real artist.

The discussion of the imagination in the *Critique* continues when the *Critique* refers to the imagination as a "productive faculty of cognition." We feel that it (imagination) works in freedom from the law of association. "The productive power of the imagination is animated by spirit and this spirit is no other than the faculty of producing aesthetic ideas."

Preface for *A Portfolio of Poetry: Selected by Barbara Guest*

[Poets in the Portfolio: Ann Lauterbach, Maureen Owen, Rosmarie Waldrop, Fanny Howe, Leslie Scalapino, Bernadette Mayer, Lyn Hejinian, C.D. Wright, Mei-mei Berssenbrugge, Eileen Myles, Kathleen Fraser, Martha Ronk, Norma Cole, Anne Portugal, Daisy Aldan, Anne Waldman, Rena Rosenwasser, Barbara Einzig, Amelia Rosselli, Rachel Blau DuPlessis]

The poets I invited for inclusion here are of a generation of women in that marvelous period when the weaponry of their poetry has been honed. There is a surety in the gesture, a sense of dominance. This is not speculative work. It is fearless and indeed has been tested, not only by male dominance in the Arts, but by the opposition of societal fixtures to the *upstart* experimental.

My poets have not observed the etiquette of the castle, their obedient role of listener. Inside the wimples of these advanced *canzoni*—and I do not use the word "advanced" recklessly—is the voice of the troubadour.

I emphasize the various locales of the poets from which these works emerge. The areas are fairly representative of the United States—Boston, New York City, Santa Fe, Arkansas, San Francisco, Berkeley, Los Angeles, Connecticut, Rhode Island, Colorado, Pennsylvania. From Europe we have France and Italy. The point I choose to make is that although all of these poets live within an imposed geographical position, their poetry connects them in a way that is not latitudinal. Designated as "avant-garde" or "experimental," in that sense they are "in touch" with one another and ignore any boundaries of space. The poetry embraces an intimacy of purpose beyond limitations of spatiality.

Finally, the poets gathered here wish to join me in dedicating this portfolio of their work to the memory of Sonia Raiziss, *Chelsea*'s longtime editor.

Anarchy of the Emotions

Poetry is nothing but the intensely musical

and emotional state of the soul.

Mallarmé

SOMETHING is IN BACK OF everything that
is SAID—A GHOST, OR AN EMERGENCE, BUT DARK.

There is always the something else (with Donne)

(Mannerism) The final effect is of a real figure moving
in an unreal arbitrary space.

Coleridge's concept of *Power* in Poetry based on both
Clarity and Obscurity

Anarchy of the Emotions—both Capitalism and the
Aristocracy have formed a code to prevent this.
Middle-Class poetry is opposed to this anarchy and
pays its poets large sums to 'stay clean.'

(The Baroque yielding to Mannerism which I believe corresponds to our age. Contrast between concrete and abstract, sensual and intellectual elements of the language, often forced ornamental pattern—emphasis on the a-logical the unfathomable and contradictory in life, idea of the theatrical + and dream-like quality, fondness for the complicated.

The Journal of John Wieners: 'What can I write
to set my heart afire' (echoes of the reason for
poetry—echoes down the ages)

Shifting Persona

I

The windows are normally independent of one another, although you may pass back and forth from one view to the other. This absurd interdependence is like a lark at break of day. The altitude is assumed by the upper window. The other window is the lark.

The person inside a literary creation can be both viewer and insider. The window is open and the bird flies in. It closes and a drama between the bird and its environment begins.

When the person who is you is the viewer, you believe an extraordinary strength exists in that position. You are outside the arena of dispute or creativity or blasphemy, dwelling in a private space where emotive speculation is stronger than fact or action, each of which passes before you in an attempt at dissimulation which you are free to dispute. This is called the orchid position, because of the extravagant attention the viewer demands.

Sometimes it is the flap of a tent held back, or a cushion pushed next to a door, or a turban lifted over one eye, even a mountain top is offered where the person who is outside the scene can take up an observation post and gaze closely down into the valley.

Without the person outside there would be no life inside. The scene relies on that exterior person to explain the plangent obsessions with which Art is adorned.

Yet inside the window is the person who is you, who are not looking out, shifted from the observer to the inside person and this shows in your work. When you are the inside person you can be both heavy and delicate, depending upon your mood; you have a sense of responsibility totally different from the you outside. You occupy the lotus position.

You are depending upon yourself to a degree that can cause extreme unease, but this is acute to all species of creativity. You find you cannot always depend upon yourself as absorbedly as when you assumed the orchid positions because you are more vulnerable, dependent upon the psychic phenomena that occupy your mediation. The lotus position is one of exaggerated self-dependency, in which the eye goes inward so frequently that rest stops are required, something like paragraphic encasings.

These rest stops can be seen in the shifts that take place between the persona of the creator and the persona of the observer. In a well-developed persona the shifts take place before our eyes without revealing themselves, as if gauze had been spun especially for the purpose and a curtain falls slyly between the persona of the person and the persona that is now accepted. We travel back to the mountaintop and the valley with the shifting of spatial contacts.

II

The ability to project both windows is a sign of originality and is rare. In writing concealed within a limited physical environment, as in the work of Jane Austen, the threat of claustrophobia hangs over the whole body of the novels. In order to relieve this environmental tension, the writer with her strokes of genius elevates the characters above a physical dimension, so that although their persons appear to inhabit a closed drawing-room they are actually removed from the interior to the exterior as they move beyond their limited space through the projection of the author.

They are persons who are capable in their minds, even in an obtuse mind, of looking outside themselves into another place, of shifting their persons. They are relieved of ordained claustrophobia, as is the reader, who might be stuck in that drawing room, who is lifted by the author's inked quill, her euphemism for time, to project beyond singularity.

She has even trained us to watch for the apparitions of ourselves moving alongside the characters. This is on a grand scale, her knowledge of sequence in time caught in a limited physical dimension. The person of the author travels from afar.

III

There is a book about Picasso that records him during his labors while attempting to create his version of *Las Meninas* of Velázquez. What emerges from this devastating account is his conflict with the person of Velázquez as Picasso attempted to stabilize his own persona. Picasso consistently refused to consider his position as revisionist.

Picasso went into the Velázquez painting very far. Yet his enormous struggle which involved his wife and friends took place far less within the realm of Art than in the psychological struggle of an artist to survive the atmosphere of an originating persona. We are also aware of Picasso's need to endow Velázquez with the Picasso persona.

The painting of Velázquez is even more complicated as several persons compete for the dominating person within *Las Meninas.*

> Picasso said it was a very peculiar affair. Velázquez had painted the King and Queen in the mirror as if they were outside the canvas—which is the fact—but as if it was they who were painting the canvas, since he, Velázquez, was inside it with Las Meninas.
>
> And we said it was an even more peculiar affair for Picasso to paint in that position, while Picasso painted the mirror in which he might have added himself to the King and Queen, who in fact must be on the same side as Velázquez opposite Las Meninas, etc. etc.[1]

Finally out of the hundreds of studies Picasso made of this painting, one in particular succeeds. It is called "The Studio" and there are no persons inside that space.

One of the lessons to be learned from this wildly shortened account of Picasso and Las Meninas is that the deliberate ambiguity of the reigning person produces the Velázquez painting's magnificent climaxes, and prevents revision of the work of the originating person. Las Meninas has added to the mystery of the person in Art.

IV

In *The Uses of Literature*, Italo Calvino writes (I quote from him because he has so rapidly summed up the stunning performance of Flaubert):

> Gustave Flaubert the author of the complete works of Gustave Flaubert projects outside himself the Gustave Flaubert who is the author of Madame Bovary, who in turn projects from himself the character of a middle-class married woman in Rouen, Emma Bovary, who projects from herself that Emma Bovary whom she dreams of being.

. . . It was Flaubert himself who gave us the precise clue to this with his most famous phrase, "Mme. Bovary, c'est moi."[2]

V

The person with the omnipotence of a cloud hovers over a poem pointing to the direction that it should take.

The poem's concealed autobiography. A memoir of itself which is released as it becomes a presence existing in time.

When the person is on its feet, to leave it alone to express its own person. The relief from the intensity of the poem's presence as it heats up.

An astonishment throughout the poem at the vibrations of its ego. "I" becomes the bystander and the poem is propelled by the force of the "person" stripped bare.

Richard Wollheim writes: "The artist is essentially a spectator of his work."[3]

VI

A landscape appears before us, solitary in its incidents of meadow broken by low running water, the sky dour, the earth in twists moving like the water into continuous dark drainage. This landscape appears solitary and yet there in the short grass is the hidden person placed there by the writer who desired a human instrument to bear witness to this attempt to construct with a fictional or real landscape a syllabus of art.

The person is given a place of habitation within the construction and endowed with a knowledge not only of the force of nature, but the aesthetic purpose behind the writer's decision to create this scene.

This witness, positioned inside the work of art, conveys to us the secret intent of the writer so that following the instructions now transmitted we may work our way through to the pitch of the art before us, the center where the writing rocks back and forth before taking its plunge into space.

The person is our conduit. Hidden arms are stretched pointing to the variations, the hollows, the deliberate judgements of time within the work of art.

The person has a voice. It echoes the tone of the writer and it is this echoing voice that assembles what we call the "tone" of poetry or prose.

It is the gathering together of varying instructions by the concealed person that presents us with what we may call a "reliable" landscape.

Notes

1. Helene Parmelini, *Picasso Plain* (New York: St. Martin's Press, 1963).

2. Italo Calvino, *The Uses of Literature*, translated by Patrick Creagh (San Diego: Harcourt, Brace, Jovanovich, 1982).

3. Richard Wollheim, *Painting as an Art: The A. W. Mellon Lectures in the Fine Arts* (Princeton University Press, 1984).

Prague Walking

This beautiful, melancholy, grey city of steeples, clocks, bridges, castles—a city built on a river—a city enclosing its medieval past as the deep layer of a dream—a city of trials, insurrections, executions—where everyone wears the same raincoat and where rain comes from the green mountains, washing color from houses, until the proud city is stripped of her hues and all is grey; everywhere it is grey. Only memory is there resisting, memory presenting itself in a baroque cornice that turns ever so slightly into "art nouveau" or as it is called "le style moderne"; and one is presented with ideas scalloping and in constant movement over the surface of these grey buildings. Prague presents us with the fairy tale made real by ideas; there is the conundrum no politics can erase—Prague is a romantic city created by a vigorous intellect. A native would shrug at this and explain that this "romance" is nonsense, that he comes from the land of *irony*, not Cockaigne.

After the first night's sleep in the hotel where one has discovered in the wardrobe closet an entire set of wine and vodka glasses and exclaimed (much as a Czech would puzzle in the United States over his discovery of the Gideon Bible on the hotel night table), out we go into the city. Amazement. Prague is a city of scaffolding. Over dozens of buildings sits this scaffolding and underneath it workmen are playing their paint brushes. Here at once is the paradox which shall be with us perpetually. What we thought was grey is not so at all; it is Maria Theresa yellow, green, pink, white, for Prague is being painted. She is being returned to her past. After all these years Prague has been handed a mirror in which she can observe her beauty. When other travelers see her, gone will be that first paragraph of melancholy and grey. "A city of delicate and baroque colors with a half-mile on her face and tearless, pale eyes," we shall read. Ah irony, thy name is Praha. And then another native will turn to this traveler and shrug. "Don't you realize," he will say, "Prague is so damp that we can never make the colors last. Eventually these shades you find so charming shall fade into grey."

Yet I wonder if these words are true, if they are not part of a philosophy so natural here which allows for change in all things, and frequently change for the worse, maybe for the better, if one doesn't hope too much. The traveler can never know. If he has a subtle mind he can make himself ridiculous trying to undermine the Czech subtlety. And so for the ironist, and the romantic. The artist is safer for he can be content to observe and allow what is intuitive to all art here in Prague to become attracted to him.

Let us shake off hesitations and preconceptions. Prague is at this moment the center of a movement in the arts that is fresh and creative. The movement has a "newness" about it. So especially it seems to the Westerner exhausted by the fashions of other capitols. These people have "emerged." And with their sophistication intact. Further, there is a *camaraderie* to be found among them which exists in a special degree and which is conducive to collaborative work, to aid to other artists, to the struggle toward a cohesive art form which will be especially Czechoslovak and which will dominate where other forms have failed. This attitude is not nationalistic or programmatic.

There is a verve of a highly trained innocence. And like many innocents these artists have passed through disaster, not scatheless, but intact. The young people are not overwhelmed by a "long memory." For them memory and life are short; there are no great people in their recent past, or even great events whose evidence they might have counted on.

There is a resemblance to the young US avant-garde of the Happening, the new dance, the neon non-music the young America discovering that "that" didn't work and trying to develop new collaborative forms, reaching toward the impersonal as an ultimate comment on the finiteness of all things.

The difference, of course, is politics. The political is a special underground of Czech art. It always has been. The ancient regime was satirized. So is the new. It is natural to wink slightly, or hard, if you wish to remain alive. It is also necessary there to come to terms with political shifts—an area condensed in the US into right and left wing, and of small consequence to the young American artist who takes it for granted that in most cases his politics go leftward and his emotions center around himself and his group. He expects prosecution if he tears up his draft card, or joins a group marching in the South, or is caught in possession of narcotics. He *knows* the limits under which he may act. But not to *know*, never to be relieved of the anxiety of the unexpected which may or may not attack, what extraordinary reticence and slyness may then slip into the work of the gifted artist. It is as if his fears, turning into tears, were caught in paper cups, as mortal as the cups and as precious for their immediacy and their symbolism. And how clever he must be not to allow the message of these paper cups to die with them. That is one reason the artist is so provocative in Prague. He is inventive from necessity.

Now what I have just said may have as much of the quality of sense or relevance as the bottle Alice found which said "drink me." Only here, let me not forget, we are drinking from Bohemian glass. I am positive there is a group in Prague that might even be called decadent, that will shrug off any political connotation. And there are perhaps others waiting until the time when everyone will be decadent and the drifts covering the underground will be painted snow.

Two of the arteries through which the artist's work must pass:

The Writer's Union

This is the clearing and publishing house for all Czech writers. The Czech writer does not lark around. He receives only one acceptance or rejection. Here the manuscript is submitted to a board of five readers. In one year they shall have passed on ten to twenty novels. When published, the new novel will sell from twelve to twenty thousand copies in hard cover at about fifty cents a copy. A well-known writer will, naturally, sell thousands more. In a country where there is little else to buy, culture comes cheaply and a writer can thus live very well. For some time the writer's income was not taxed to the same degree as everyone else, but this exemption has caused an outcry and unfortunately will now be remedied.

The Film School

This is paid for by the state. It has produced a generation of film directors of twenty-five to thirty years old who are making their first films. There are five creative units headed by producers and directors who choose the films and the scenes. Legally there is no censorship; the films must only be accepted by the board. The success of this school is now apparent in the list of prizes Czech films are winning. Everyone knows *The Shop on Main Street* and the season of the fall of 1966 at Lincoln Center in New York City showed us several very superior new films.

These young directors and technicians meet regularly at the Film Club, a nondescript, rather shabby place where they can drink and talk in an atmosphere somewhat that of a college union. A less prepossessing place would be difficult to imagine, or for that matter one less reminiscent of the high scenes of Hollywood filmmaking. What strikes one as so extraordinary, after ridiculous comparisons have been made, is the youthfulness and the urgency of the ideas which have been forced to base themselves on commercial buy and sell.

People

Jiří Brdečka is the animated film designer and director whose cartoons have consistently taken first place in the international film festivals. Brdečka and his assistants work in Prague in a building which resembles a Quonset hut, with no overtones of the Disney compound—no overtones at all. The very modesty of the setting would lead one to expect an element of amateurishness were this not immediately set aside by the cartoons themselves which are professionally competent, both in technique and concept. This modesty is also part of the personality of Brdečka, together with his dedication. Being an historian of the American Wild West (which he has never visited), he has also constructed a permanent Western Village which has been used by American cartoon filmmakers.

Brdečka's cartoons are often taken from children's stories and fables and naturally, as in all fables, have a moral. Like the puppeteer Jiří Trnka, Brdečka has also drawn on the medieval past for his exquisite lyric cartoon, "The Letter L" (for Love). Again the stupidity of war is pointed out in a cartoon called "Look Out!" What is consistent is a rapid movement in the films, an *involvement* with ideas, and in them all the sense of the past-present. The color is also clear and executed, not only from an exterior frame, but likewise an emotional one.

What Brdečka exemplifies in his work is an infinite variety of themes and techniques. How beautiful are his cartoons to watch, and one can only shudder remembering the violence and the utter ordinariness thrust at us from the American screen as one cartoon after another passes on its message of 'ugh' and' 'murder' and 'chase' and 'deceit.'

Josef Nesvadba is one of the four psychiatrists of Prague (a title which indeed suggests a Czech novel). He is one of the most popular authors in the country. Best known for his mystery and science fiction stories, he began by translating English poetry in collaboration with Mr. Edwin Muir. Nesvadba is typical of a popular, bestselling writer, with the usual Prague shade of difference which is that he represents the overtones of an intellectual and sophisticated society with its anxieties and flickering mores.

Jiří Mucha: If there were a permanent Prince of Prague, he would be Mucha. The son of Alphonse Mucha, the creator of Art Nouveau painting and posters of the past century, Jiří Mucha lives under the shadow of Hradčany Castle in his father's former home. Surrounded by objects, bibelots, stuffed owls, sitting in the armchair in which Sarah Bernhardt once sat posing for his father, he writes his novels. Educated abroad (his father lived for twenty-five years in Paris), he continues to travel the continent. Yet one knows immediately that although the roots may be taken up and reassembled elsewhere, the heart is in Prague. There he suffered three years' imprisonment, the dark years of 1951 to 1954. No one is better qualified to ask those questions he does in his novels: "If there are two hospitals—one in the East, one in the West—in which hospital does the patient receive the better treatment?" Or who better able to question the artificiality of such terms as *East* and *West*. Totally interested in the contemporary literature of all countries, he has translated *Two for the Seesaw*, *The Naked and the Dead*, Beckett and Ustinov. On a table near his desk are paperbacks of American poetry.

Places

The Viola Club: It looks like a moderately priced bar-lounge. Rather bourgeois. Comfortable chairs, a bar, people moving about. It is crowded. So crowded that it was necessary to wait outside before a gate—"prison gate," someone said, and everyone laughed—was lifted and we were permitted to enter. It is the avant-garde club of Prague. There poetry readings are given to jazz, there the painters assemble, and there is a small theatre for 'way-out' works. Founded by a young, intense, poetic man named Kusak, it began with a group of actors looking for a stage. ("Not another stage!" one wants to cry.) What gave it its existence? A restaurant chain in Prague. (All restaurants in Prague are run by one chain and the head of this chain recognized the needs and possibilities of these young people.) It was at the Viola Club that Allen Ginsberg was crowned Prince (for a day) of Prague.

A conversation on Czech poetry. Its influences? Apollinaire, Mallarmé, Blok, Mayakovsky, William Carlos Williams, San Francisco, New York. We must remember that Prague was the 'second' center of Surrealism. They will not forget that. There is a national tendency toward surrealism that almost becomes as natural as cabbage soup. Then there are the poets of the 'spiritual' and those of the 'concrete' and of 'lettrism.' And Ladislav Novák has published an *Homage to Jackson Pollock*, a book of poems containing an imaginative portrait of the American painter. A book of poems published by "The Club of the Friends of Poetry" goes into an edition of fifty to eighty thousand. How this is done outside the Writer's Union, one isn't told, except to overhear comments that the poets of the Writer's Union dominate, but are now underrated as "The Establishment."

The Viola Club—it is another club of the ages, as our own New York Cedar Bar of the 1950s, as all the clubs of the world where the young and creative gather to begin their era.

Dobříš Castle: A chateau rather than a castle. An easy drive from Prague through the countryside, past the new apartment house dwellings for factory workers. And handsome they are, modern, decorated by plazas and sculpture, the buildings still visible on an uncluttered landscape. Dobříš has been given by the State to writers. It is the Yaddo, the MacDowell Colony of Czechoslovakia. And it appears to be more casually run than our artists' colonies.

The writer may 'check in' for a few days. He can work, read, pace the long corridors, saunter about the seventeenth-century gardens before deciding to return to Prague. Foreign writers, such as Dylan Thomas, have visited it. There is a handsome drawing room still fitted with the appurtenance of its former owners. There is a billiard room. There are enormous stone staircases. Dobříš has been permitted to retain the atmosphere of leisure and wealth of another regime. And a visitor can go 'below stairs' into a simple dining room where he is offered delicious soup and vodka, as if he had entered a country inn. So large is the chateau that on a June day one may stroll the gardens or corridors seeing no one; the privacy of nobility belongs to him.

Theatre

There has always been a great tradition of the theatre in Prague. And it has always included the avant-garde. Some think the Berliner Ensemble has learned from the Czech theatre of the 1930s, lifted those curious surreal wings perhaps and flown away with them.

Today there are three municipal theatres. Repertoire is found at the Komorní, which is a theatre in the round playing Durrenmatt and musicals. The Comedie Theatre is for conversation plays. The Theatre ABC for detective stories and little musicals.

Then there is the S. K. Neumann theatre named after the popular Czech poet, whose director, Mrs. Luba Pellarová, chooses plays which are currently popular around the world. An example at the moment is Albee's play, here translated as *Who's Afraid of Franz Kafka?* This has had a very successful run, appealing to several layers of society, one is told. It is rather a mad idea to find appeal in those frantic speeches and capers of Americans on a college campus transplanted to Prague. Yet the interest holds and the identity claims its own.

Finally there is the outstanding avant-garde theatre, the Divadlo Na zábradlí, under the superb direction of Jan Grossman. Last June it was playing Kafka's *The Castle.* Toward this theatre are aimed all the aspiring manuscripts.

Laterna Magika (Magic Lantern)

On the stage are real actors. On the film screen flashing behind them are these same actors. As the stage action moves, so does the film which often continues the stage action and lends it a deep perspective. This is riotous, shocking, amusing, and of course extremely ironic. Where else should this style of theatre have been conceived, if not in Prague. A city of shadows. A city whose novelists have written equally of the real man and his shadow. And who is to describe the difference between the two?

Today in Prague, people are complaining that Laterna Magika has run its course. The same actors on the stage are not those portrayed on the screen! Someone has taken a vacation or retired with his shadow. Yet to see this theatre for the first time in its native setting is memorable, it is so natural a part of the dream of the lost who are seeking to piece together their identities.

Doubtless when Laterna Magika becomes a permanent part of the repertoire of the city then a new theatre form will appear. One is certain of this. It will be just as surpriseful, intimate and unique. Behind the scenes the magicians are already at work.

Prague . . . what are its correctives, its disabuses? We are not going to discuss this. We are watching through the slanting rain, through the twilight with its echoes, those shapes that are patterns, that are silhouettes drawn on the screen the artist, the writer, the filmmaker is placing before us. To watch.

Forces of Imagination

The forces of the imagination from which strength is drawn have a disruptive and capricious power. If the imagination is indulged too freely, it may run wild and destroy or be destructive to the artist. "The frenzied addiction to art," wrote Baudelaire, is a canker that devours.

If not used, imagination may shrivel up. Even in old age Goethe wrote that he feared the wild tricks of a lively imagination. "What is the good," he said, "of shaping the intellect, securing the supremacy of reason? Imagination lies in wait."

Plato also suspected imagination. He thought man could be transformed by the imagination and suggested laws that would prohibit the miming of extravagant evil characters. He advised changing from the dramatic to narrative language if writing became overwrought. It is fear of what begins as fiction ending as reality.

Plato said, "If any poet were to come to us and show his art we should kneel down before him as a rare and holy and delightful being, but we should not permit him to stay. We should anoint him with myrrh and set a garland of wool upon his head and send him away to another city."

These words express fear of the possibility of a destructive risk that lurks in poetry. Baudelaire continually reminds us that the magic of art is inseparable from its risks. And this risk is also a necessary component of poetry as it performs its balancing act between reality and the imaginative force at work within the poem. The poet enters the poem with a hood over the poet's eyes. The poet has arrived from a distance from a real world. The poet is conjurer balancing on the barre of risk like a dancer, or acrobat. Have you ever wondered why the painter is prone to painting acrobats, and not only in the famous painting of Picasso. It is because in all the arts, the practitioner—the poet, the artist, even the musician—with a new set of rules, maintains a balancing act between reality or rules, and the imagination. And there is where the risk lies, in that balancing act, so filled with fervor and terror as the little word is placed on its spool of light.

Hegel's language is radical. He believes that art exists in absolute freedom and is allowed to attach itself freely, he says, to any form it chooses that will help it "exercise the imagination." We can view the poem as existing for a time in pure space, exercising imagination, no matter how mundane the exercise may appear, how untidy the bag of words it carries with it. The poem is enjoying a spatial freedom before it settles into images and rhythm and order of its new habitat on the page.

In this state of suspension the art that is created is infinitely susceptible to new shapes because no shape can be regarded as final. No form is safe when the poet is in a state of perpetual self-transformation, or where, as Hegel suggests, the artist is in a condition of "infinite plasticity." This position of "subjectivity" or "openness" the poem desires to obtain, free to be molded by forces that shall condition the imagination of the poet.

In the sixteenth century Ariosto complains that chivalry is being destroyed by the introduction of firearms. This is what *Orlando Furioso* is about, and I borrowed the title in my own mock epic, *Rocks on a Platter.* In *Orlando Furioso* we are given a setting of pure fantasy, and fantasy is written all over the poem. The reader can have no doubt of its unreality.

It is the innovation of Ariosto we admire, an alarming innovation that bespeaks the power of innovation when we are told the poem may have aided in the destruction of the codes of chivalry.

The idea of "infinite plasticity" is a noble one. It causes the poet to breathe more freely. One thinks of *Prometheus Unbound.* And it is the blood of "boundlessness" that enters the poem.

When I was a young poet I was immensely influenced, as you know, by painters with whom I circulated. Their ideas of painting took up my young life. I envied their freedom. I began to use some of their methods. Often titles arrived after the poem was finished, as O'Hara illustrates so humorously in his poem "Sardines."

The idea belonged to Picasso, who said about subject matter: "You have to have an idea of what you are going to do, but it should be a vague idea. It's always something else in the end." This idea of Picasso's also, for some reason, lends an idea of space to the poem.

Painters also gave me a sense of being unconfined to a page. I became experimental without using that word. I wrote "Parachutes, My Love, Could Carry Us Higher" without considering whether my parachutes went up or down.

The Hollywood songwriter Johnny Burke wrote, "Imagination is funny, it makes a cloudy day sunny."

André Breton said, "to imagine is to see."

An Inconsiderate Preface

Someone spoke on the stairway in Spanish, another answered in Italian. There must have been a reasonable communication, as the conversation ended in laughter.

The combined languages as she listened formed a third which may have been, with its rasp, Portuguese. In her former apartment house that language was heard in hallways and near the elevator. It belonged to the super and his relatives who, recently immigrated, spread their language like pieces of broken pottery. The super had an air about him she could not locate. Once she had visited Lisbon which reminded her, with the cold winds and clear air, of San Francisco, the physical prominence of hills. This identification may have interrupted her interest in the local speech. She did not listen to the language, letting it hang beside her, as if in a sling. In New York its flutter teased her. She wrote to a friend that Portuguese was rough, not smooth like jasper or porphyry.

Lately she had concentrated on the work of Tommaso Landolfi and it was while reading a translation of *Words in Communion* that she overheard the landlady and the tenant conversing on the stairway. Made restless by their commotive sounds, she turned to another translation. Literature was bequeathing her a second ear, like factory noise next door. Her ear began to ache with minute figures etched by translation.

In the translator Helen Caldwell's preface to *Helena* by the Brazilian writer Machado de Assis there is an apology for other translations of his work. Several of those books she had read and admired, especially the one with the difficult title combining a dog and a philosopher. A novel of "experiment," or a novel taking experimental exits, was the only way de Assis could explain the reality of literary isolation.

Helena, "not a major novel," was written in 1853 and she was urged to regard it as a "romantic novel" or a "novel of romance." What surprised the translator was how this tag embarrassed the author, who was astonished when by 1873 *Helena* "had reached a vast audience."

"Romantic" words appearing in the text were noted to prove how mistaken de Assis had been in rejecting his title to romance. *Human hearts, love, feelings, soul, anguish, honor, longing*, are strung together like ripe valentines.

Annoyed by the inconsiderate preface, she determined to make her own list of the *themes* of *Helena*, a practice she had discarded when leaving school. She found that outlines or *themes* increased the monumentality of George Eliot or Dostoevsky and spun out their interminable greatness. Besides, these *themes* usually concealed the true temperament of the novel.

1. the restrictions of society on women

She began with this subject because she had found in the translated *Correspondence* of Berthe Morisot similar restrictions suffered by the artist, a victim of her middle-class milieu, that prevented her from attending the brothels of Lautrec, embracing the nude models of Degas, participating in the evenings of Mallarmé, or even entering a café. These severe limitations not only affected her art but, like the fate of Helena, were perhaps responsible for an early death hastened by impotent rage.

2. the Catholic church

Does de Assis imply that the exemplary yet destructive priest was in love with Helena? The activities of the priest belie his sweetened authority.

3. the position of slaves

"Slaves like to go on errands, because it is the only time they can be alone." De Assis, the son of freed slaves, chooses a slave as the innocent catalyst of his "family's" destruction.

4. incest

Friends who wish him to do them a favor sidle up to the brother and whisper, "You know I am terribly fond of your sister." The sister, when accused of being passionately in love with a person other than her fiancé, "blushed furiously." How differently this theme in Thomas Mann's *The*

Blood of the Walsungs, a story of incest between twins, affects us. The colonial story of de Assis breathes less heavily than the German. It is soothing, almost idyllic.

She was distressed by her neglect of the masterful diversions concealing from readers the real purposes of de Assis. She felt foolish for having been taken in by the translator's dubiety that withheld the lash of de Assis, his pretense of writing a sorrowful story of thwarted passion while his attention is placed elsewhere: the exposure of society's appetite.

The list pleased her. She experienced the serenity that comes when one gains control through a discipline. She refreshed herself with a small bottle of grapefruit juice. The juice brought to mind the acrid wind that blows through the novels, relieved by the gentleness with which de Assis attaches himself to the countryside beyond Rio de Janeiro. There, nature in the sensitive embrace of de Assis eludes the modelling of a translator.

The Shadow of Surrealism

I grew up under the shadow of Surrealism. In that creative atmosphere of magical rites there was no recognized separation between the arts. Those of us who shared this atmosphere brightened by Apollinaire, Éluard, Valéry, Breton, considered ourselves part of a hemisphere where all the arts evolved around one another, a central plaza with roads which led from palette to quill to clef. One could never again look at poetry as a locked kingdom. Poetry extended vertically, as well as horizontally. Never was it motionless within a linear structure. Assisting in this poetic mobility would be an associative art within whose eye the poet might gaze for reassurance, and for a glowing impersonal empathy.

We have read of the relation of Gertrude Stein to Picasso. She saw her own work and Cubist painting as engaged in a similar struggle. She even went so far as to write Cubist portraits. What actually she was seeking was an escape from literature, or from "the literary." She saw and envied the freedom shared by Picasso, Braque, and Gris and their breakthrough from formalism to Cubism. Painters are the revolutionaries to whom writers turn in their desire to break from the solemnity of the judicious rules of their craft.

During the explosive era of Abstract-Expressionism we not only admired the work of painters breaking rules of art performing on the canvas the otherwise concealed, emotional state of the painter, we became envious of the activity of their personal lives.

This may be taken by a few as a frivolous remark, but the remark contains a metaphor in which the natural gravity of life is replaced by the gratification of secret desires. Art as reflection becomes more instantaneous, willful, enthusiastic, freed by action. Painters naturally gravitate toward expensive cars, lofts, and chateaux, urged by the prices affixed to their art.

Money, fame pursue painters with a frequency that stuns the poet. Just as the extravagance of painters is admired, so is their ability to leap the boundaries of experiment applauded by their market. In a similar situation of leaping boundaries of experiment, the poet is frowned upon by the academies from which financial reward is infrequently extended.

Some poets even desire to sit under umbrellas at Mougins with Picasso or share a villa.

As a poet who happened to be employed by an art journal, I was exposed to the temperament caused by the explosion of Abstract-Expressionism, and my personal relationships with its painters certainly influenced the way I observed both nature and the book. I have always believed in a direct heritage shared by Frank O'Hara and Apollinaire, perhaps a deliberately decided one. O'Hara was very close in sensibility to the French poets of Cubism. He described the process of Abstract-Expressionism far more closely than any critic or art historian in his poem "Why I Am Not a Painter."

The measure by which one art form works upon another is explained by Rilke in his book *The Art of Cézanne.* I was startled in this book to find a description of my response to painting. Rilke tells us that he was interested in Cézanne because he wanted to find out how the painter worked *so that he might apply Cézanne's discoveries to his own work.*

I confess that often when looking at art I do not ask what it means, or how was the paint applied, the color chosen, but what has led the artist into this particular situation, what permits this particular piece of work, and how is it solved. When I look at certain paintings, they begin to enter my unconscious. I then ask how the metamorphosis took place, and if the process I witness can be used in my own work. An explanation of process is what Rilke asked of Cézanne. He did not question what Cézanne meant to him; he wanted to *borrow his method from the master.*

I admired a Matisse painting of a bowl of goldfish. I put a poster of this painting on my wall and looked at it daily. I began to realize very slowly that this great sensualist was also an intellectual manipulator of space who misled us by his concentration on color. How he created his sensual interiors was a solemn intellectual problem. I was then working on a poem whose ostensible subject was three bodies of water: a pond, a swimming pool, and the sea. Giving the poem a title, "Water Kingdom," I submitted it to a magazine and the poem was rejected.

With a sidelong look at the Matisse goldfish on the wall, I began to reconsider the poem. In the Matisse poster, the goldfish are placed in their bowl on a table. The table appears in another Matisse painting owned by the Museum of Modern Art. It is called *The Rose Marble Table*. I had cherished a fondness for this painting and had attached it to my life. Now I began to consider the table. I became more intimate with the painting and progress of Matisse. The poem is called "The Rose Marble Table."

Once I sublet an apartment overlooking Union Square. I came to dislike the cold north light of the apartment and I admit I was unhappy while I lived there. However, the owner's library included several books on Kandinsky. There was one book that quoted him on the necessity in art for an "inner sound." To me, this is the essential "noise" of poetry. Another book showed photographs of Kandinsky's Moscow apartment. The artist, his ideas, and his dwelling place became a solace to me.

One day looking down on Union Square from the apartment, the sudden realization arrived that Union Square looked remarkably like the Moscow part seen from Kandinsky's apartment.

Several years passed and I moved near the south side of Union Square. I walked over to Union Square one day and looked up at my former apartment. The building now seemed to resemble the old photograph of Kandinsky's apartment. That evening I began to write a poem about the last evening Kandinsky had spent in Moscow before going into exile. I called the poem "The View from Kandinsky's Window."

Poetry the True Fiction

The title I originally gave to this talk is "How I Got Out of Poetry into Prose." This title came to me so quickly because at that time I was encouraging myself to write fiction, and I thought I would discuss the dimensions of fiction with you. However, I was disturbed by this title and rightly so; had I been more intuitive of my own perceptions, and had I listened to the poet William Cowper, who wrote "Poets are seldom good for anything except in rime," I would have entitled this talk more sensitively: "Poetry the True Fiction."

Why has the word fiction become associated with prose? It is poetry that transforms the real world into fiction. Mallarmé understood this. He wrote: "The true fiction is that of the poet."

Mallarmé regarded poetry as an art dedicated to fictionalization, an "*art consacré aux fictions*" where the concrete object is "bathed in a new atmosphere," lifted out of itself to become a fiction. The poet is not there only to share a poetic communication, but to stimulate an imaginative speculation on the nature of reality.

Do you recall the poem of Wallace Stevens "Notes Towards a Supreme Fiction"? And have you considered what the title meant, or what was the underlying meaning of the title? I'm at the point where I take everything he says for granted—the moon being made of ice cream, etc.—so I never questioned his meaning until the other day when I was considering poetry as fiction. In his published correspondence I found a letter from Stevens to his publisher, the Cummington Press. He wrote:

> The title of the book will be Notes Toward a Supreme Fiction. Each of the three groups will develop or at least have some relation to a particular note: as
>
> I
> It must be abstract

II

It must change

III

It must give pleasure

These are three notes by way of defining the characteristics of supreme fiction. By supreme fiction, of course, I mean poetry.

The fiction of the poet is part of restless twentieth-century perception based on the discovery that reality is a variable, and is open-ended in form and matter.

And now that we recognize poetry activates an established world of fiction, I should like to discuss the supremacies or the necessaries of poetry that enable it to transform reality. I would like to speak about Vision and Imagination.

Vision is part of the poet's spiritual life of which the poem, itself, is a résumé. The "spirit" or the "vision" of a poem arises from the contents of the poet's unconscious. Let us say the vision of a poem has above it that "halo" you see in religious paintings when an act of special beneficence is being enacted by one of the persons within the picture and that person is given a halo. The poet is our act of special beneficence and the poet is rewarded this halo. The poet is unaware of the halo, just as in the paintings the persons are unaware of the halo, but it is there as a reward for a particular unconscious state of immanence. Now I am not speaking of a religious state of grace in regard to the poem, the poem let us say is its own religion. I am using the word "halo" because you and I can see it in the painting, and this halo has a value to us; it reflects a state of mind, or a condition that the mind has attained.

The halo has detected the magnetic field into which the energy of the poem is being directed.

I would like you to understand that I am using the words "spirit," "vision," "halo," because I wish to lift us upward away from the desk of a projected poem. I want to emphasize that the poem needs to have a spiritual or metaphysical life if it is going to engage itself with reality.

As closely as possible in the world I am representing here the poet wishes to align the contents of the poem with the vision which directs it. When this occurs we say of the poem that it has "wings."

It is possible that words may occur in a fixed space and sequence so that they are called "words of a poem." We say the poem is made of words. And it is true that many poems are constructed solely of words. These are the words that sit on paper without vision. We all have read these poems and we know that after we have read them we feel curiously bereft. Our expectations of ennoblement by the poem have been disappointed by the lackluster condition of the poem.

We decide that this poem is not very inspired. And what do we mean by this? We desired "inspiration," that the poem contain within it evidences of the spirit of poetry.

We have learned that words are only utensils. They are inorganic unless there is a spirit within the poem to elevate it, to give it "wings," so that the poem may soar above the page and enter our consciousness where we may if we wish give it a long life, a longer life than would occur when the poem lies without elevation on a piece of paper.

There is no reason to signal any decade or era as deficient of vision. Words on a page are deficient of vision and this may occur in any epoch. We are particularly nervous about our own era because we are at the turn of a century which is most usually designated a time of decadence. We see this everywhere, unfortunately in the decay of institutions, but mostly there is a demise of the spirit and that is what should concern us, because poetry will reflect this spiritual absence.

Words without vision are deprived of stability. They cling desperately to a mirrored surface in an effort to attach themselves to a surface, because they have no direction and no stabilized vocation. They become furtive, these words, thirsty for a version of themselves that contains no failure of vision. Words contain their own beauty of face, but they desire an occupation. They cannot exist on beauty or necessity alone.

Words of the poem need dimension. They desire finally—an education in space. The poet needs to understand the auditory and spatial needs of a poem to free it so that the poem can locate its own movement, so that it is freed to find its own voice, its own rhythm or accent or power.

Wordsworth wrote: *Language, if it do not uphold, and feed, and leave in quiet, like the power of gravitation or air we breathe, is a counter-spirit, unremittingly and noiselessly at work to derange, to subvert, to lay waste, to vitiate, and to dissolve.*

It is not the flash of brilliance appropriated in a technique that quenches the pathos of a deprived poem. Although we must not neglect those qualities Leopardi admired in Horace: "courageous metaphors, singular and far-fetched epithets, inversions, placement of words, suppressions"—recognize them? They appear in our own shifting techniques.

Regard the poem as plastic. It is moveable, touchable. It is a viable breathing substance. Nothing is more useless than a poem with a dull sheen that refuses to move, that is inert. This is the essence of dullness and our eyes run quickly past it.

A poem has not only a voice, but a mouth, and the mouth must move just as much as the voice must speak and it must not be careless in its speech. And flesh of a poem. Even as a painting has flesh. The vibrancy of its skin.

The artist de Kooning wrote that in the Renaissance drawing started to tremble because it wanted to go places. He also added that what we call subject matter was then painting itself. There was no subject matter. De Kooning also observed that at this time the artist was too perplexed to be sure of himself. Later, subject matter ruled the arts. And, said de Kooning, when you think of all the life-and-death problems in the art of the Renaissance, who cares if a chevalier is laughing or that a young girl has a red blouse on. De Kooning is telling us to beware of description or "subject matter." In other words, to think of the poem itself.

Vision and plasticity are the two essentials of a poem. The spirit of the poem and its moveable form, not its "adjustable" form. Then we get into posing or chevaliers or red blouses.

I hope you realize that in all these words I have gathered together, or if you wish in the few words I have gathered, I have not come directly to Imagination.

I have first wanted to prepare the ground for Imagination. For us to consider the spirit of the poem, its physicality and its spatial intensity. Now I would like to speak about Imagination because it is really my favorite topic. Without Imagination the red blouse is a piece of description, without Imagination the poem is only words on a page.

This is a very large subject, Imagination. I shall touch upon it only briefly. But I must speak about it, because for me it is the single most important element of poetry and it is my touchstone. When I examine a poem it is not for its form or style or even gravity but I look for its imaginative powers. I find that Imagination comes before style or technique. How empty all the dazzle of style is without the immediacy of the touch of Imagination. And Imagination the changeling can sting you with its fictive barbs.

Coleridge wrote *Biographia Literaria* in his youth when he was trembling with Imaginative power. The book is essential. I believe, for the distinction he makes between Imagination and Fancy. Fancy is delightful, evocative, alas charming, but with fancy you leave those words on the page. A good many poets are endowed with a lively fancy, many more than those who live in the Imagination. Fancy is useful and can shake people up and present itself century after century as the new. But it is not art; it is games.

Imagination lives with the visionary. When you touch its glass there is a ring. The French have a phrase "*clair-obscur*" which translates as obscure light and means the mysterious side of thought. That could well define Imagination.

We tend to think of it as so lively it pierces walls, but that liveliness is fancy. Imagination is *clair-obscur*. It is also "the absent flower" of Mallarmé. A turbulent presence. And we must acknowledge this "turbulent presence" because it is there to save the poem from a disobedient disregard of its own nature.

There will always be poetry, in its search for a language, a desire for the liberation of the Imagination.

André Breton said, "to imagine is to see."

Imagism

> The Image can be of two sorts. It can arise in the mind. It is then 'subjective.' External causes play upon the mind, perhaps emerge, if so they are drawn into the mind, fused, transmitted, and emerge in an Image unlike themselves. Secondly, the Image can be objective. Emotion seizing up some external scene of action carries it intact to the mind; and that vortex purges it of all save the essential or dominant or dramatic qualities, and it emerges like the external original. In either case the Image is more than an idea. It is a vortex or cluster of fused ideas and is endowed with energy. If it does not fulfill these specifications, it is not what I mean by an image.
>
> Ezra Pound, "Affirmations (As for *Imagisme*),"
> *The New Age*, 1915

One day in those early days, Pound himself had looked upon those crossing a bridge over the Seine and written:

> The apparition of these faces in the crowd;
> Petals on a wet, black bough.

Imagism has arrived! Henri Bergson in Paris said: image is a locus between intuition and concept.

In London, Hulme, a friend of Pound, was also exploring the image for a new kind of impressionism. Then Pound was back in Provence writing what could be called, in later days, a form of the *Cantos*. The former impressionism was moved into a new form.

The wind came, and the rain
And the mist gathered about the trees in the valley.

Pound was writing very modern verse. It would be exchanged for *The Cantos*.

In London H.D. was writing Imagist verse.

Modernism presenting itself.

A Reason for Poetics

> For all his purple, the purple bird must have
> Notes for his comfort that he may repeat
> Through the gross tedium of being rare.
> Wallace Stevens

The Infancy of Poetics

The poem begins in silence.

Poetic Codes

A pull in both directions between the physical reality of place and the metaphysics of space. This pull will build up a tension within the poem giving a view of the poem from both the interior and the exterior.

Ideally a poem will be both mysterious (incunabula, driftwood of the unconscious), and organic (secular) at the same time. If the tension becomes irregular, like a heartbeat, then a series of questions enters the poem. What is now happening? What does the poem, itself, consider to be its probabilities? The poem needs to take care not to flounder, or become rigid, or to come to such a halt the reader hangs over a sudden cliff. It is noticeable that a poem has a secret grip of its own, separate from its creator.

The poem is quite willing to forget its begetter and take off in its own direction. It likes to be known as spontaneous. Some poets then become firm and send out admonitory hints. Others become anxious. A few become pleased with the trickster and want to adopt it. There are moments when mistaken imageries can lead in interesting directions. Poets even try to charm the poem. We have all taken these positions.

The conflict between a poet and the poem creates an atmosphere of mystery. When this mystery is penetrated, when the dark reaches of the poem succumb and shine with a clarity projected by the mental lamp of the reader, then an experience called *illumination* takes place. This is the most beautiful experience literature can present us with, and more precious for being extremely rare, arrived at through concentration, through meditation of the poem, through those faculties we often associate with a religious experience, as indeed it is. The reader is converted to the poem. (Invisible magic also passes between poet and reader.)

Mystery, with its elements of surprise and, better word, audacity. At once unexpected dramas have entered the poem. The search for its originating mystery now becomes an adventure. Poet and reader perform together on a highwire strung on a platform between their separated selves. Now an applause for the shared vigilance.

The usefulness of the tension set up in a person is to arrange its dimensions. The poem stretches, looking outwardly and inwardly, thus obtaining a plasticity that the flat, the basic words—what we call the language of a poem—demands and, further, depends upon. This cannot be achieved through language alone, but arrives from tensions placed on the poem's structure, variability of meter, fleeting moods of expression, trebled sound.

Each poet owns a private language. The poet relies on the pitch within the ear. The ear is also a private affair, and so is pitch. Much poetry betrays a tin ear. There is also trouble in possessing perfect pitch, which can lead to an obsessive need to listen to it. Like ravens quothing. But this is not a common trouble. Pitch and ear are the servants of language and cannot make their living anywhere else, even by escapades. Language can lead to trouble when words are selected solely for their sound, and meaning is then forced to hurry along after, trying to catch up. Sometimes it is necessary to dispense with a word, or rather to be cautious, when it intrudes upon form.

The structure of the poem should create an embrasure inside of which language is seated in watchful docility, like the unicorn. Poems develop a terrible possessiveness toward their language because they admire the decoration of their structure.

The Poetics of Survival

Poetry sometimes develops a grayness; the light can never get in. The surface is smudgy. Cézanne was irritated by this murkiness in painting and complained "the contour eludes me."

How splendid when a poem is both prospective and introspective, obeying tensions within itself until a classic plasticity is reached.

I have little regard for poems of mine which have become votives of obsolete reactions. These poems appear to have no conscience, and worse, are passionless.

There is nothing fearsome about the chrome attic. There are more mad poets out on the lawn. And very few wear cloud trousers.

I wish the Emperor's new clothes were less a visual phenomenon and more poetry's plaintive sigh.

And then there is saving laughter. I don't mean by "laughter" what is known as "comic relief." That seems to me to be part of a philosophical argument surrounding questions such as "why did Shakespeare, or Meredith bring in such and such a character?" My laughter is bittersweet and brings us closer to irony, the mole of poetry. Irony is a coagulant of pain when the subject of the poem (the interior meaning) begins to draw blood. Robust poets, it seems to me, too seldom acknowledge this weapon against poetry's sores, the most suppurating of which is sentimentality.

Mandelstam once wrote of "sound spilling into fingers." That could be the noise of a poem when it experiences an ecstasy of recognition.

To keep the poem alive after its many varnishings.

Invisible Architecture

There is an invisible architecture often supporting
the surface of the poem, interrupting the progress of the poem. It
reaches
into the poem
in search of
an identity with the poem;

its object is to possess the poem for a brief time, even as an apparition appears. An invisible architecture upholds the poem while allowing a moment of relaxation for the unconscious. A period of emotional suggestion, of lapse, of reliance on the conscious substitute words pushed toward the bridge of the architecture. An architecture in the period before the poem finds an exact form and vocabulary—,

before the visible appearance of the poem on the page and the invisible approach to its composition. Reaching out to develop the poem there are interruptions, some apparently for no reason—something else is happening, the poet has no control—the poem begins to quiver, to hesitate, to become insubstantial, the desire of poetry to elevate itself, to become stronger . . . The poem is fragile. It needs to reach through the armed vehicle of the poem,

to loosen the armed hand

Losing the arrogance of dominion over the poem to an invisible hand, the poet campaigns for a passage over which the poet has control. Yet the unstableness of the poem is important.

Also the frequent lapses of control of the poem.
The writer only slowly retains power over the poem, physical power, when the poem breaks away from authority of the invisible architecture.

The invisible authority may be the unconscious that swells on the lower level, in a substratum beneath the surface of the poem, and possesses its own reference. A fluidity only enters the poem when it becomes more openly aware of itself.

By whom or by what agency is the behavior of the poem suggested, by what invisible architecture, we ask, is the poem developed? The Surrealists taught us to wander freely on the page, releasing mechanical birds, if we so desire, to nest in the invisible handwriting of composition. There is always something within poetry that desires the invisible.

The desire of the poet to control. This control was earlier destructive to the interior of the poem, to its infrastructure. There is something deliberate about this practice of control by consciousness. It includes the question that is undefined, the behavior of the poem. By whom or by what agency is this decided, by what invisible architecture is the poem developed?

Wounded Joy

The most important act of a poem is to reach further than the page so that we are aware of another aspect of the art. This will introduce us to its spiritual essence. This essence has no limits. What we are setting out to do is to *delimit* the work of art, so that it appears to have *no beginning and no end, so that it overruns the boundaries of the poem on the page.* All of the arts share this need for delimiting.

Coleridge said that a poem must be both *obscure and clear.* This is what we search for in our poem, this beautiful balance between *the hidden and the open.*

What is this poem that appears to be opening within our hands? Mallarmé says that "Poetry is nothing but the intensely musical and emotional state of the Soul."

Do you ever notice as you write that no matter what there is on the written page something appears to be *back of everything that is said, a little ghost*? I judge that this ghost is there to remind us there is always more, an elsewhere, a hiddenness, a secondary form of speech, an eye blink. Not on the print before us. And yet the secret is that this secondary form of writing is what backs up the primary one, it is the *obscure essence that lies within the poem that is not necessary to put into language, but that the poem must hint at, must say "this is not all I can tell you. There is something more I do not say." Leave this little echo to haunt the poem, do not give it form, but let it assume its own ghost-like shape.* It has the shape of your own soul as you write.

John Donne wrote this very modern paragraph describing the state of his mind troubling his prayers, but he might as well be describing, and probably is, the state of his mind as he approaches a poem:

> A memory of yesterday's pleasures, a fear of tomorrow's dangers, a straw under my knee, a noise in mine ear, a light in mine eye, and anything a nothing, a fancy a chimera in my braine troubles me . . .

He can also be saying that these things trouble him as he reaches for his pen to make a poem. The presence of a hidden anxiety about a poem might be a necessary prodding to go intensely into the poem. A poem should tremble a little. Again remember, "Poetry is nothing but the intensely musical and emotional state of the Soul."

Baudelaire tells us that a poem should have within it "a dose of the bizarre." This can be a wake-up call within the poem, to say the poet is nodding, has become too mundane, too involved with a daily recounting. I love this phrase. I suppose it is the basis of Surrealism, but in Surrealism everything is bizarre. I prefer this little dosage. When one is nodding or recapitulating events of daily life and we become mundane, then this little "dose of the bizarre," like *holding a minnow in your hands, or a feather of a riotous color, not too much, or the bizarre will overwhelm the poem and to have nothing but a bizarre account can be very boring.*

To sail off on a ship of delight, a brief, necessary voyage within the poem to encourage pleasure, to escape the mundane, the chain of struggle. If and when necessary, this pleasure will sparkle at the hour of a poem's struggle to endure, the poem's midnight.

Remy de Gourmont suggested that the past must constantly be reinvented. As you take issue with the poetry of the past, remember that it has its usages, its declarations and affirmation, because it has existed so long. Think of the past as the modern poem runs along beside you. As the past darkens the window.

In the youth of my poetry I was fortunate to be surrounded by painters in the art movement of Abstract-Expressionism and I learned from them.

First I noticed these painters appeared to have a lot more joy than did the poets. They were more playful! Their ideas were exploding on the canvas and they had a sense of freedom the poets were only beginning to learn from them. This was perhaps a heritage of Surrealism, but the fact that they were a MOVEMENT and were accepted even by the commercial world, which meant money, lent them this freedom. The entire city of New York liked their art. More importantly the air around them was hesitating as it turned into *the moment*. The idea of a moment with its special apparatus is a good thing for poetry also.

No subject is introduced; the painting is spontaneous. The subject is found as you explore the canvas. And that is a useful idea. I remember when a painter visited and I had a little poem in the typewriter and he looked at it, the little unwritten poem, but with its title already secured. The painter said, "never give a poem a title, let the poem find its subject."

Remember Picasso said, "You may give a painting a title, but it always turns out to be something else." Frank O'Hara's poem "Sardines" plays with this idea. Another thing these painters borrowed from Surrealism was the use of "accident." I know that I have accidentally typed a wrong word and thought, "well that's a better word, anyways."

Behind these sentences is the idea of no pre-planning. I can always tell when I am reading a pre-planned poem; there is no freshness in it. No mysterious element of change, as when the poem lies quivering on its page, its contents wounded, yet the poet is joyful.

An admonishment not to be fearful of tarnishing your wings. To rest in the glow of great poets; they always have something to tell you. To welcome the substance that glitters and rubs off.

I cannot end a discussion of poetics without stressing the power of the Imagination. To lean on it! To trust it! Imagination is the single most important element in poetry. When I examine a poem, it is not for its form or style. There are plenty of "successful" poems. One must look for the vibrating imagination hid under those stones of form and style. How empty is all their dazzle without imagination.

Coleridge wrote that in his youth he was "*trembling with imaginative power.*" *Imagination is the absent flower of Mallarmé, a turbulent presence to be evoked.*

Profiles

"The Work" in *Goodnough*

> The instant you catch sight of a painting by Metzinger, you feel the firm intent of the artist to be serious only about what is serious; and you feel that the occasion, in accordance with a method which I find excellent, furnishes him with the plastic elements of his art. But while he rejects nothing, he does not use anything haphazardly . . . He will delight those who want to know the reasons for things; his reasons are such as to satisfy the mind.
>
> Apollinaire

From Metzinger to Goodnough. Goodnough who has been called, historically, "that Cubist." What *that* term implies is surprise, wonder that a painter brought up on the New York scene which is a corridor stretching from the studio of Hans Hofmann to the Club, whose walls were constructed and decorated by the Action Painters, should so little appear to be one of the group. As if he had discovered within this corridor a separate passage for his private use. Where does it lead? What happens there? Why was it necessary to abandon the historic corridor? Sometimes one believes one has entered a squirrel cage. Or an elevator. Or a room whose dimensions increasingly abstract as we watch the black lines leading us through its surface. The movement in the room is always rapid and the air tends to turn from density to light. We are also aware of silence. The painter isn't there. He has also left out his self portrait. He would rather we looked at animals. He would prefer that the paintings announce themselves.

We begin to understand one of the reasons for his exile. Unlike action painters whose sun rises and sets within the painting, whose moment of joy or grief can be located on the canvas, Goodnough wishes to remove all evidence of his own activity. We thus lose interest in the painter and refer to the picture which has presumably painted itself.

In the early 1950s Goodnough was painting fierce and extraordinary paintings, which he titled by number, because they were not 'of' or 'about' anything at all. They were pure abstractions. He had discovered a moment within time and he was going to paint 'it.' One could guess that he felt a precarious loneliness which he could endure only for a short while. Tony Smith, who was close to Goodnough in this period, has said that only Jackson Pollock was developing so intensely, 'seeing' painting in the most absorbed way possible. Smith believes that Goodnough's talent could have borne the shock, but that Goodnough decided to back away, to explore painting in another manner where the reliance would not have to be so completely on the 'unknown.' It is possible that at this point Goodnough became persuaded by *ideas*, as Cézanne had before him. Believing that the duty of the artist is to permit these ideas to present themselves logically and fulsomely, he decided that the canvas must not be disturbed by any extraneous expression from the artist himself.

Later, as a replacement for a reality which indeed may have become too spacious for him, Goodnough substituted the Myth. He painted Calamity Jane, the Centaur, the Frontiersman. He divided painting into two categories: the Primitive, the Civilized. Concluding that American culture today is a refinement of the covered wagon, Goodnough says: "First you live in a log cabin and then you build a better house. What's important is the house. Then how you fix it up."

For Goodnough *energy* is the most important constant in a painting. He has a Puritan faith which relies not only on good works, but on the amount of energy you expend doing them. This attitude which is shared by many American painters and is certainly significant in the work of Jackson Pollock is perhaps one of the most important factors distinguishing American from European painting. Energy, itself, is a separate totem. The American painter reared in a society which believes labor provides the means, so anti-aristocratic that leisure is suspect, finds himself in the dilemma of recognizing art as the pure white flame, but realizing that he, himself, must burn along with it or no one will suspect him. He must labor. He must also 'feel.' At the same time his painting must show stroke by stroke how much labor has gone into it. This accounts for the type of questions artists ask each other, all of which involve the word "work," which in this context is not ecclesiastical, but physical. Also the emphasis in art circles on productivity which is a reassurance to the collector and dealer. No one is going to put out so many pictures a season, if he contents himself with drawings, or decides to spend his evenings in the Cedar Bar, fateful predictions are made. The American artist is allowed few periods of quiescence. It doesn't matter whether the work is good or bad. Just so the artist is *hard at work*. As Grace Hartigan answered when she was asked to show each successive year: "What do you think I am, a Wampus Bay Star?" This digression has been made easier, because Goodnough, safe in the American tradition, finds that it works for him. The personages of his cosmos who swell in the American past are energetic figures. All concentrated on forcing their form of energy upon the undeveloped country. It was their personal dynamo that intermingled with the dynamics of a land, at once vast, overwhelming (to a lesser figure) and untouched. Goodnough went beyond the White Mountain Boys, beyond the careerists of the gated creatures whose personal energy was to be dissipated, but whose presence we constantly rediscover. One senses also the pathos of an artist who must force creatures back into existence whose destiny was to disappear. We must understand that Goodnough in these paintings and colleagues has sought forms of elemental energy that only the past can equivocate.

More directly, in his painting energy means taking a surface and turning it into areas which have activity. (Calamity Jane in her tavern tableau, marksmen, frontiersmen, a rifle shot on the plains.) Energy for Goodnough is defined in terms of dynamic equilibrium. (Mondrian.) You throw the painting off balance and then bring it back. The energy then surfaces. Goodnough has said: "That's what life is. Take a canvas which is not life and bring it to life. Sometimes it is quieter, more controlled, but always something is going on."

"Rearing Horses" was inspired by a Rubens copy of Leonardo's "Battle of Anghiari." When asked why this picture so interested him, Goodnough explained that he liked its *movement*.

There was an intermediary period when Goodnough vacillated between figure painting and two-dimensional abstraction. These are the counter-clockwise pictures where lines both abbreviate and extenuate.

They are unique paintings, brilliant and sober. At the time he began this series (starting with "11," culminating in 1960 in "Carnival II"), he was concentrating on working from the center outward to reach the edges. He did this, instead of dividing up the surface, in order to attain greater movement. Goodnough was an innovator at that time of the early 1950s. He has subsequently been followed by painters, such as Kenneth Noland, who also progress from the center in order to lift the weight from the bottom of the picture. They desire a weightlessness which will make the image independent of the rectangle. Goodnough laid down his color in short brush strokes, again employing the *expressive* elements of cubism. But he certainly did not construct his painting cubistically. He was very far away from that in his path toward the *edges* of the canvas. He simply saw color, as did the Cubists, as a short exercise in form.

Several painters have influenced Goodnough. Picasso, Matisse, Mondrian. In these counter-clockwise pictures, dependent on line, we recognize Mondrian. Goodnough has said: "After Mondrian we don't see trees. We see wires."

And what about those smudges? Those circles whose shadows are left undeveloped? Unlike Mondrian, Goodnough refuses the Pure. He isn't looking for it. He says, "once you've gotten the idea, why try to polish it up too much. The important thing is to retain the feeling for it."

And that is exactly what happens. What might have been too rigid, exact and ruled, is preserved by these faint tracings, these feelings which begin and are allowed to remain within the idea of the painting, as a tremor, a murmur, the half-sentence that begins, "I am." Because, of course, like many sturdy, profit-and-loss Yankees, Goodnough is a romanticist.

He is an eccentric artist in each of whose paintings can be found elements of previous ones and those to come. He is rather didactic and he certainly has a Yankee stubbornness. He is taciturn and rather inflexible. There is something in his attitude which relates to the Norman painters. Certainly, like Léger, he never gives up.

His style, at one period tightening, at another loosening, has remained unchanged. That is to say, rather abruptly, and Goodnough would prefer to be abrupt, he has four ways of painting a picture:

Shapes with lines outlining them ("centaur," "Calamity Jane"),
Figure images made almost completely with line ("No. 11," "Mediator"),
Shapes with outlines ("Summer," "Movement of Horses"),
Brush strokes ("Ulysses," "Pegasus").

Paintings such as "Figure Group 2" and "Summer 10" are composed mostly of shapes which are indeed areas of color. These "shapes" give the painting its form, but they are at the same time not only schemata, they are color. The conclusion is that Goodnough sees color and form, or as he calls it "shape," as the same thing. It is thus needful to coin the word "color-shape" in order to explain the composition of a Goodnough painting. Beginning with a single color-shape, he adds another until he has areas of these color-shapes, until all combine to a total which is the final painting. Painting is thus a sum of parts each independently important, yet creating a totality. Of course within this whole we have many tonal gradations. When he juxtaposes one *color* against the other, it is to make one *shape* stronger; the smaller shapes then swell into the larger through chromatic values. To avoid too intense a struggle of color-shapes there are relief areas which like clouds and air play between the larger and smaller color-shapes.

These are his means, yet for Goodnough the eyes of the image must be reached. When does the animal appear? Halfway through the painting. Sometimes a little sooner. Then begins the charge, the rush through the undergrowth, the hinting and hunting, foraging and halting. Quick short brush stroke. Fast thin thick line. The painter moves like a huntsman through his picture. Then when this composition of color-shapes works—becomes *agitated* enough—the animal steps through the bush. The hunter takes time off for lunch. The picture paints itself.

This conscious discipline, which is more remarkable today when the advice has been to 'let go,' 'let it happen,' is somewhat released in the brush stroke paintings, such as 4. There the composition, naturally more sensuous and spontaneous, results from the way the brush is moved. In collage Goodnough is a virtuoso. For Goodnough collage is not a thinking-out process as it is for many painters. It is not a means toward an end nor an exercise. Further, he has never been involved in the neo-Dada aspects of collage, or arrangements of the "beautiful."

One would guess he had never seen Schwitters. The Dinosaur series of the 1950s with its intricate layers of small cuts of paper laid on paper from under which emerges the dinosaur figure—or fragments of paper cuts which the dinosaur disturbs as if the great creature were stepping on leaves—are undoubtedly brilliant. Here is movement tightened formally and reduced to the scale exacted by the artist. There is also a Goodnough collage the size of a band-aid of such an intensity it becomes a wound.

He is in the tradition of the formal collagists who regard collage as painting of the highest order.

Above my desk is a Goodnough collage made of paper and adhesive tape glued onto cardboard. It is an act of tenderness to reach out and press down the tape, as the heat from the room causes it to loosen, and as its liveliness ages, one is informed of its youth.

The winter of 1961 at the Tibor de Nagy Gallery, Goodnough permitted himself to reveal all the phases of his painting in their maturity.

Imagine within the graceful de Nagy Gallery—mildly carpeted and walled, its tall fashionable window fronting Seventy-second Street—the rearing running horses, the strokes of paint, the black lines, the flattened color-shapes pitching, a frenzy of movement interrupted by the calm of figures classically bathing, and in the background, "Summer" lavishly anointing one wall. It was Goodnough beginning his middle years, without thought of impoverishment, bestowing ideas. He was both masterful and generous.

Reviewing what he called a "complex exhibition," critic Irving Sandler remarked on the "painterliness, knowledgeability and versatility." He also added "inventiveness." This last word causes concern. It implies thoughtfulness without fancy, or fancy in the Coleridgean sense, without imagination.

In a city of many climates, of many flotsams, where ocean liners are moored and buildings disappear in the night, imagination must find itself more resourceful than ever. Its withdrawal would mean nonexistence for the artist. There are no half-measures such as inventiveness possible here. In New York a painter may have as a necessary fantasy the art scene in Paris, 1920. Why should it be accurate? How could it be? He doesn't care. Imagination erects the ateliers. He will call his next picture "Wanamaker's" and a younger painter who doesn't remember that dear dead building, but who has been to Europe on a fellowship, will accuse him of having painted the Galeries Lafayette in the style of Metzinger.

The solitary path can be dangerous; lacking comrades-at-arms one attacks imaginary dragons. Goodnough has not always successfully avoided these encounters. He has also a tendency to reminisce when the field is embattled. Yet what is positive is his calm during the latest art wave. He has remained immaculate within his single field. No current craze has tempted him. He is immune to new directions. He never appears publicly to regard the art world as in flux nor is he distracted by the new names attacking the crescent. Formidably he adheres to the laws that rule his canvas.

The Vuillard of Us: James Schuyler

To write of a poet entwined in the opaque world of art whom you have known through merging greyness and light, whose own beneficial light has shone on you for so many years . . .

This strains relationships that bear the ripeness of poetry, and solicitude demands an appreciative ear, the rigors of thought, and a personal warmth that settles into the debilitating curves.

The contour of a shared world is invisible. I can only hold it up to a screen where it may be read with words. Even words "fail" or become "wordy," so we proceed into facial description or loose characters "holding hands" or "walking on the street." I once gave them mittens in a poem. You can't really hear what is said, only watch what happens.

When I write: "Jimmy and I met in 1952 in the apartment of John LaTouche," you realize I am telling you of the moment when we entered each other's life. But that is all I reveal. I cannot transcribe the weight of the listening room or wrap you around Jimmy's shadow.

If I continued for several paragraphs I would launch into biography. Chronology would intervene. Someone would begin to skim the multiplying words and deprive them of their fertile source. I would like to begin in another way: to reach into the poet's heart where memory collides with a poet's craft and survives. If not in total amity, if not in complete accord, quick to respond to a particular tone in the voice to understand a boundary has been crossed, or in the peculiar drop of a line recognize a moment is illuminated and set free.

I wish to write about the poet-figure I see in the trees on the lawn of the Porter house in Southampton. As he crosses that lawn he wrote about, the way for me to seek him, as I once dreamed in that very house—running from room to silver room, through the white Southampton clouds that filled the parlor and sliced the piano keys—is through his book I dreamed.

Schuyler translates the vagaries of inhabitancy, of wherever he is, his locale, particularly his into poetry. So that if you are already acquainted with a particular house he has lived in, you come to know it even better. Or if there is a walk you take outside, you'll recognize it from his description and you won't get lost, but you won't exactly be unaccompanied, because his form may block your sight or may prevent you from a private maverick turn.

I can never go to the movie house in Southampton without the shapes of Schuyler and his companion, Fairfield Porter, appearing. And it is always New Year's Eve. I always look up into the sky and wonder if it is going to snow, remembering "Empathy and New Year," where Jimmy quotes Emerson's idea of empathy as "inspiring distrust and connoting irrationalism and mysticism" while together he and Fairfield watch the incautious sky with their separate notions of snow.

Of course the magnetic substance into which Schuyler bites is clarity. And his aura of clarity is without cant. He is like the jack-in-the-box who hides from us this clear vision until out he pops. Or he is the cultivator of seeds who keeps them in the growth box. This clarity is so alive it nearly freezes us.

As an "Intimist," for me Jimmy is the Vuillard of us, he withholds his secret, the secret thing until the moment appears to reveal it. We wait and wait for the name of a flower while we praise the careful cultivation. We wait for someone to speak. And it is Jimmy in an aside. Or from the front of his mouth, letting the words fall out as he wishes, with a small cherishing pat on their sides. I have often watched this way of selection in his speech as he sat beside me on a sofa offering up a well-considered tit-bit on his patten salver. But we always know there is more . . . more . . . more.

As in those deceptive "intimist" pictures—so close—so arranged they cannot manage a secret, yet they can, and do, as Jimmy does in his close perspective on life, pretending to offer the thing, holding back its effect until we are hit bang. And covered with a little tame garment that burns.

He and I share a fondness for the magazine *Country Life*. There is an ineluctable wisdom in that magazine that others cannot place. After the humoring pause, there is the innocent desire to gaze on foreign gardens, yet not too foreign, English, and their houses, especially those photographed "for sale." I think we relish a glimpse into E. M. Forster details or the private Austen manse; it may be the datedness that appeals.

Gardens and houses are essential to Jimmy's domain. And yet one never finds him "lifting" from *Country Life.* It is unnecessary for him to borrow or appropriate, and he never does. He merely owns.

The notion of time is, of course, indelible with the still life painting. And I think often of Jimmy's poems as sharing the still life sequence, the motionless state before it begins to disturb.

His poems invite time; they play with it. The poems touch its forehead and a mood descends. Although Jimmy is fond of sending me a Dutch pastoral postcard, enisled in a flattened landscape with humanized trees, evoking a century of calm, calm, able all calm, I think of the poetry of Schuyler not only in connection with this evocative pastoral, but with Dutch still life.

Those pictures contain the same haunting grasp for perfection contained in one stanza. And a surprise booty often pours from a pitcher or lies on a small table rug, as it does in his poems. In each passage, time exerts a passion. As in the poems of Schuyler where a moment's minutiae becomes aggrandized and we believe its shifting is a permanent whole.

I am always delighted when his poems catch the "unevenness" of the flow of day. Because that is how time flows, so unevenly, above it all, like a glider or plane with air bumping into it. He is so acutely aware of the actual day, much more sensitive to it than poets who write about what happened in their day. They never give shape or authority to day, as Schuyler does. Perhaps there is too much concern with the form of the poem.

The poem's form seems to drop from Schuyler's hand like those drops from a jug in a Dutch still life. It is an effortless shape, that jug, which consistently remains under control; the poet's hand on the jug.

I ask how a poem, if it wanders a little, is going to end up, having imagined Schuyler gave it too much leash, but he always succeeds—there in that tight spot—to talk it back into shape, like the day he writes about that covets a little more time is reminded it has had enough.

The deep recesses of night or time's shadow are in his poems. The pattern of night is certainly there, residual. Yet the intimist pose of the poems is to write about daytimes, the hours hovering over us which contain our momentum, they can usefully be observed from a bed. The bed is an awakening property and when the speed slows down, a place to drowse; to catch memory supine. Embodied, it is also where the eyes are open.

The evidence of his mind. Where it lingers on subjective, on delicate states, observant. Attitudes toward literature. No fudging. No blurs. The unexpected appreciations brought out from memory. The reasonableness. A friend's painting softens his tone. The inward eye now reaching for ecclesiastical celebration.

Why has Louise Bourgeois finally become the Artist of the Moment?

All over the world museums are acquiring her work. She is now considered the "phenomenon" of the decade and will represent us at the Venice Biennale as she did at Documenta IV. And yet, is she truly the "artist of the *moment*?"

The strength of Louise Bourgeois, for me, exists in seeing her art as a *collective statement*. In this essay I believe it is not reliable to select an exclusive work to bear the weight of her strategies.

Louise Bourgeois has never let go of the initial subjects from which she composed in her youth. As she tells us, "for more than fifty years I have been talking about the same subjects so I have a consistency." Obsessively she reviews the stages of her life and their emotional accompaniment as the subject of her art. One after another her sculptures present themselves as figures from her life history or commentary on her emotional life with its secret deposits. She says, "I feel the ambivalence in everything. I try to visualize it and to express the fragile center between extremes."

Today Bourgeois is compared to Marguerite Duras, whose recapitulations of her history in her books and on the screen reflect the injuries and crises of her life. Also directly related to Bourgeois are the Proustian memories, the obsessions of Svevo, the work of Musil, and the labyrinthine Joyce himself. For them, as for Bourgeois, the art form exists in the recapitulation. A writer's past becomes a symbol, a guide, a revelation of experience never separated from an artist's permanent caress.

This caress of the past is not usual to a sculpture. The artist of the surface has created its own sense of time. The sculpture must learn to condense time and permit the work to do its own replay in texture and modeling, the style which is advancing into the future even as the sculptor employs the tools. Yet Bourgeois resolves this necessity through her sense of intimacy, her sense of self, her obsessiveness if one wishes to call it that, which permits her to retire into the timelessness of her own enclosures. She refuses the inherited romantic vision of sculpture as held in the great hand of god; instead she transfers this vision to herself wherein lies her center of absorption.

In an era of fading dependence on modernity we now acclaim work that concentrates less on form within a spatial modality, but rather on forms that propose a speaking body, that "listen" to the body, that hear the body's alarms through new sculptural commands. There is a preference for a "dialogue" to develop between the sculpture and the subject, rather than to witness the loneliness of an art form in the process of creation.

The art of Bourgeois working in an indigenous way has undoubtedly had its influence on younger artists such as Kiki Smith who are resistant to both non-expressionist and modernist art forms. These experimenting artists are drawn to the excitement of Bourgeois's pioneering arrangement of her figures, her throwing pieces of her work into odd corners of the room, piling them up on top of each other—she was stacking bricks of wood, as if reaching for a formula long before conceptualists began to rearrange their tiles. Bourgeois was among the first to experiment with intricate arrangements and odd formations of materials. When she fashioned pieces from wire mesh and wrapped clay, she pointed out that there are uses for any material that comes to your hand; this radical experimentation has influenced sculptors not content with the forging of machine parts, or carving in marble, in search of other forms of expressiveness that afford a more inquisitive examination. Like the radical Frederick Kiesler, architect of the "Endless House" of whom she reminds us, and whose spirit of adventure matches Louise Bourgeois's, she is outside her generation and has remained so, displaced, until her work finds its home in the work of the young.

These experiments took place after she had given up painting. Her *Femme-Maison* (*Woman-House*) paintings, in which women have houses perched on their bodies in place of heads, were taken up later by the feminist cause, and Bourgeois began to attend feminist meetings in the art world. Sculptural ideas began to come into pictures. And then she gave up painting, because she became inhibited by it and she was not "satisfied by its level of reality." She needed an art that was more physical and tangible: "I could express much deeper things in three dimensions."

Bourgeois was among the first to present "performance" art, before the public had even heard of it. She is a natural performer, her work is highly *active*, and, indeed, in a museum or gallery, seems to cry out for more space to move around in. Also, we can suspect that Louise Bourgeois, herself, likes to play dress-up. Photographs show her holding up looping breasts tacked all over her body, sculptural forms she used in her work. Her constructions, such as *Confrontation* of 1978, demanded a participating audience.

She has worked her way through the influence of Surrealism (as did Kiesler) developing other insights, using a surrealism that exists in terms of her own identity. "Identity," she says, "I have too much Identity."

Her art, even on its most trembling and exposed base, is a sophisticated art. When her plaintive personas approach the "lairs" she constructed, this civilized and highly intelligent artist is pretending that their primitivism and her witchcraft indicate a primordial sensibility.

Art Deco as an influence? Born in France and attending the university, only leaving for America upon her marriage to the eminent art historian Robert Goldwater, evidences of this movement would have surrounded her. And in support of her admiration for this form, she has created sculpture in terms of Art Deco. An abrupt surprise for the unsuspecting are the stunning Art Deco gates at the entrance to her Brooklyn studio. The thoughtfully titled *End of Softness* (1967) refers to a period of "soft" sculptural material and is not, as this writer believed, a "poetic title." Under the magic is a literal imagination. This flat sculpture now cast in bronze with waves of movement and molded plateaus, although expressionist in feeling, has the mood of Art Deco. *Fallen Woman* (1981), compared to the puzzled figures clinging to their personalities of the 1940s, is like a shower of Narcisse Noir. Bourgeois has the ability to take us unaware. Those totem-like early figures were followed in the 1950s by leaf-like figures (*Brother & Sister*) that have an Art Deco velvet clinging to them.

The 1960s tell of an intimate struggle to release inhibiting emotions and their history is alarming. Her *Fillette* hangs like the common "file" bag French women use for marketing, and one wonders if this is a word-play. There is the suspicion that this *Fillette* (young girl) is the sculptor encased in the latex over which is poured plaster, and yet that is not the story, because another body may hang in the bag and perhaps the wicked suspect in the sculpture has to do with an incident in the life of the young Louise, etc., etc. In the work of Bourgeois, we learn to search for a hidden story, the sculptural forms in their physical wrapping take on a meaning outside of Art. And always we must watch out for her wit and when the wit, and when it reaches us, it is likely to turn into candor that is startling.

In *Destruction of the Father*, made in 1974 with latex over plaster, Bourgeois first uses the concept of witness or spectator, rather than participant. But this event also celebrates the sculptor's revenge against her father. "I don't like people who aren't angry," she says.

After the death of her husband in 1972, her work was repeatedly "aggressive" as she cut and drilled pieces of wood ("like knitting," she says), but this aggressive work made her doubt her femininity and the materials she used she "dismembered." Plaster, wax, and latex, she says, are friendly materials—bronze is "dead." When bronze is used in her casting, as in *End of Softness*, the aspect of Art Deco is heightened.

Again and again, Bourgeois uses sexual imagery. This is evident especially in *Cumuli I*, a late 1960s piece where she first uses clusters of shapes like penises. *Femme-Maison* (*Woman-House*, 1981), in highly polished marble, is possibly the most challenging. She stacks the penis-like shapes one against the other and the taller ones appear to hold up the smaller ones until the eye begins to follow not the shape but the configuration in its entirety. Bourgeois offers this candid explanation: "The Phallus is the subject of my tenderness. It's about vulnerability and protection. After all, I lived with four men, with my husband and three sons. I was their protector."

(The poet Marianne Moore also protected an obsessive world, that of the animal kingdom. Living beyond her generation, she received the country's attention, then she became a source, like Bourgeois, of ideas for a younger generation. She hid her bushel under a much-photographed tri-cornered hat.)

Today, Bourgeois is frequently photographed in a cap. Not as one might expect, a gamin's cap, but a non-denominational hat that looks as if it belonged to the captain of a freighter in a Jean Gabin film. The eyes under the cap do not, like those of Moore, wear the gaze of a startled faun. They are the eyes of an artist who "does not go through the rites of passage . . . remains a child that is not innocent . . . is not able to [be liberated] from the unconscious. It's a tragic fate."

For Celebration of Allen Ginsberg's 60th Birthday

It was Paris in 1958. Suddenly Allen and Gregory were on the telephone asking if they could come to see me. We had never met in the US, but now here we were together in Paris. I remember their arrival at the very middle-class apartment I had sublet on the Faubourg Saint-Honoré, just before the street becomes a dimmer neighborhood at the Place des Ternes. It was a quarter in which Sidonie-Gabrielle Colette had lived with Willy on the Rue de Courcelles and after her separation from her keeper she had celebrated her freedom nearby in one of the now-demolished villas. Further on was the elegant Parc Monceau, and then around the corner was the church where Picasso had married Olga. For a few blocks it was a Russian neighborhood. But where I lived the rooms were large, gloomy, and filled with faux Louis XVI furniture. Pretentious without pedigree, the sort of place where demitasse and liqueur glasses were handed around. Madame, who was not French, was married to a doctor and this was where he also had his office. A mysterious, dilapidated, and yet gentle-manly person used to arrive once a week. He spoke English after a fashion. For some reason the first time I opened the door to him I understood that his purpose was to receive a donation. Unquestionably and uncomprehending, yet drawn toward him, each week I gave him a small amount of money. The transaction was never mentioned later to my landlord. My landlord had never cautioned me to expect my inherited visitor.

It was into this atmosphere of fidelity to social values of a professional class—I should mention that the good doctor, his wife, and her ever-present mother had sublet the apartment because they were summering in Vichy where his clients could visit him more easily—and the desires of an alien Madame to conform to what she must have viewed from afar as French Society that Allen and Gregory announced themselves. They were in their Left Bank costumes, yet their own manner was proper, alert to whatever echoes this apartment could lend them. They were interested in ferreting me out and in our becoming, even if it were for a short time, friends in Paris. Yet the assumption was there that the friendship would continue outside the bounds of Europe.

I showed them the secrets of my neighborhood. The Russian church first. And then continuing along the Avenue des Ternes to my discovery on a street just off the avenue. I was often lonely, and I found that this loneliness could more easily be dissipated in Paris than anywhere else. One could always walk and besides I was a natural tourist, really a detective. I found all sorts of secrets. Most especially was the chateau I was taking Allen and Gregory to. I had walked along the Rue Pierre-Demours, nose to the ground and the shops. I was surprised by a first-class restaurant in that neighborhood, when I noticed a sudden space and trees between buildings. As in a Cocteau film, I had come upon a hidden, slumbering, seventeenth-century chateau in this rather ordinary and shabby quarter. Naturally I had trespassed and this day I took Allen and Gregory with me into the unkept grounds. The great door was open and there seemed no point in knocking. I led them inside. And there at the foot of a grand stone staircase guarded by a slim wooden railing were trunks lined against the wall. From the distance we heard, yes indeed we did, bars of Tchaikovsky. I pointed to the lettering on the trunks. It was the Imperial Ballet from St. Petersburg. The year was 1919. Resting these many years, the trunks had stood in the hallway. And from in what had once been a grand salon the music drifted out to us.

Alone in the room a woman was playing a piano. All around the empty, unfurnished salon were barres for the dancers. Then we heard steps descending. We went out to the staircase, alarming a young girl who hurried past dressed in black, slender as a dancer or was she under-nourished? We mounted the staircase and found closed doors to what were certainly, as the smell of cooking greeted us, apartments. This once grand chateau housed the families of Russian émigrés. Their children were continuing the tradition of ballet in the bare salon, along the bare corridors and inside the rooms where they must have endured much hardship. I learned later that the Abbé of the Poor had taken over the chateau and installed his flock along with those remnants of imperial Russia.

It was wonderful to share this place, this scene with Allen and Gregory. We were tippety-toe, yet Allen never lost his natural aplomb. Gregory and

I were the enchanted. Allen remained in control, even of this nostalgic world.

Allen next invited me to visit his own world where he would introduce me, he said, to his secret, the man he considered the most important writer in the world, if I would come over to the Left Bank to the Rue Gît-le-Coeur to the hotel he shared with Gregory and his Illuminary. I had showed him the imperial court in exile, so he would introduce me to his own court where the alchemy of literature was practiced. I understood the invitation. It had been extended to repay me for my sleeping beauty chateau.

And so I arrived at his hotel, the Gît-le-Coeur of Henri Magician Michaux in which resided another maître. Up a narrow staircase, not grand this time, yet certainly aged, a brief stop in the Ginsberg establishment and voila! A door opened at Allen's knock and there on the bed reposed, William Burroughs, his dreams interrupted by an eagerness to welcome whatever it was Allen would deposit at his door. Burroughs was interested in me, because I was Allen's find. There was a presence in that narrow room, or at least I felt it, so under the spell was I of Allen's persuasiveness, and later of Burroughs's hypnotic speech. It was less what he said, although as I recall he spoke with an edge of pragmatism, certainly not a cloud Michaux, a deliberate sort of nasal sentence in which he was cocooned purposefully, his speech alternately interrupted by Ginsberg as if it had issued from the source.

It was Allen who truly impressed me. Returned to their meagre quarters he prepared a stew for Gregory and me. There was no cult of cuisine or showmanship of the oil burner. Allen was preparing the food because it was the hospitable thing to do. No trouble. I thought he was exemplary. I never told him that. It would have seemed out of place, because he was only giving what he believed was necessary.

I saw Allen again. He had discovered Arab places to eat in, because his street was becoming partly Arab. Besides he liked to adapt himself to the atmosphere of a neighborhood. It wasn't that Allen really cared much for the food. It was the exoticism he liked, and the way in which he could share the poverty.

Gregory was much petted by the picaresque elements of his environment. Allen seemed to enjoy taking care of this prodigy just as he was proud of his elder mentor, Burroughs. His own system was quite large enough to shelter these two without diminishing his own abilities or energies. This would, although I did not recognize it then, be his conduct throughout his commerce with the world known as professional. It seemed to me that for his own reasons he had resolved to bring reality if not fully, at least partially, to his own terms, whether in his worldly encounters by parodying its manners and dress, or by inscribing his remarkable messages on captured walls. For what was the world to Allen but a place reeking of false judgements, begging to be rescued, a sadly heroic Troy.

Our last meeting in Paris was at a café selected by Allen. Although only a short distance from the fashionable Les Deux Magots, it was a cheap stand-up place with slot machines and cigarette vendors. There were a few chairs outside where we sat. It was on the Rue Apollinaire.

Robert Duncan, As Once I Viewed Him

I saw Robert Duncan as an exotic part of the horizon as he appeared to me, perhaps in the 1960s in New York walking in the distance down Sixth Avenue in a cape, walking along, his cape swinging, dressed like no one else. I had no idea where he was going, but there was determination in his walk.

And then there was another much later time, when I was turning into the Museum of Modern Art. Suddenly there he was in a lovely white suit preparing also to enter the Museum. It was perfectly natural that we should decide to go together to see the de Chiricos. Robert was in a fine mood, anticipating his trip to London few days off, where he was going to be painted by a noted painter, R. B. Kitaj, an American expatriate whose style suited him. I thought of the talk that would go on in London in the studio and how I would like to be there to see Duncan in London, and I ask now where the painting exists. We had an hour together agreeing on de Chirico, each of us looking at the de Chiricos carefully and recalling his surrealist novel. Space was secreted into his novel, *Hebdomeros*, like the handling of space in de Chirico's painting:

> Then one could return? The carriage would drive swiftly away, drawn by five trotting horses and closely followed by a cavalry detachment; all day long under the sun and at night on the great black mountain like a stranded whale that huge man, that hero stretched out on the summit would lie awake watching the stars. Where are you, children? Hebdomeros is in love with Louise . . . he has put on his new suit; the bells are ringing in the steeples of the parish churches and the springtime smiles in the kitchen gardens. Springtime, springtime! Funeral procession, macabre vision.

I had lunch with Robert and Jess during the time I was working on my biography of H.D. in, I believe, 1983, here in the city at their house. I think Robert was eager to know of my progress on the biography of H.D.

I was shown his splendid books, and Jess kindly showed his painting to me, which was an honor I recognized.

The time I spent in their house is positioned carefully in my memory. But I did not notice then the wariness with which Robert viewed a biography of H.D. He then loaned me a book I needed for the work. I believe now I should have consulted with him, should have asked for advice, should have been more generous in my sharing of secrets. But I did not then understand how H.D. was so much a part of his private domain. I did not know of Duncan's H.D. notebooks. Nor did he tell me. It was later that I was to read his correspondence with H.D. Biographers are zealous guards of their secrets.

The last time at Bryn Mawr, H.D.'s college, of course. The large bedrooms looking out onto a real outdoors mist, and late trees. The comfortable Victorian beds—H.D.'s college, Marianne Moore's college, ghosts.

And the reading, one of his fabled readings. Ill,
he brought his concession to how a big poet gave, perhaps a last reading.
Unfailed voice, and ideas, about how poetry reckoned with itself,
ideas about poetry of himself,
within poetry, reading.

The Story of Bryher (A Proposal)

"I have always been in love with freedom," wrote Bryher in her autobiography, *The Days of Mars*, an account of her experiences during World War II. She was the daughter of an industrialist and shipping magnate, Sir John Ellerman, whom she idolized, but against whose autocracy she struggled to create her own life outside the perimeters of her family, among artists and intellectuals. An early step to freedom was to change her name by deed poll to that of her beloved Scilly island, Bryher.

Autocratic in her own right, she was democratic in her ideals. Born to great wealth she was a generous benefactress, supporting not only the talent of the creative, but the domestic struggles of typists, shop owners—those women and men with whom she sympathized. (Salespeople in Harrods, so she relates, always considered her 'one of them' when the authorities stopped her from exiting by the front door.)

Her wartime autobiography, a personalized description of the survival of Britain amid the destruction of the historical settings so beloved by Bryher, modestly conceals the fact that through her efforts over a hundred Jews and non-Jews were smuggled from Nazi Germany, one of whom was the revered Walter Benjamin.

A highly individual novelist who produced eleven historical novels of an unusual kind, she is esteemed by countless historians who in their youth read her fictive accounts of civilizations in crisis. Her earlier autobiography, *The Heart to Artemis*, describes her emergence from Mayfair, boarding school, and introductions into a lifetime of intimate friendships with the literary and intellectual figures of her day. A discerning and amusing chronicler of the early film world which she witnessed first-hand in her visits to Germany during the late 1920s, she published the first screen magazine, the now-classic *Close Up*. During World War II, through a perspicacious salvaging of paper and acquittance with the literary underground of Europe, she published "Life and Letters Today," which among many luminaries contained the first story of Sartre to be translated into English and an early tale of Kafka.

A personage of boundless energy, a feminist all her life, a salvager of the homeless, if a martinet on her own ground, she is a stalwart, uncompromising figure against the background of post World War I and II. The excitement she generated in her time continues among her many admirers who wish to know more about Bryher than her own chronicles have revealed.

In the preface to my recent biography of the poet H.D., *Herself Defined: H.D. the Poet and Her World*, I wrote:

> When I began this book I assumed in my precarious innocence that I would be writing a biography of H.D. After I had reached the first encounter of Bryher and H.D. which was in 1918, I realized that within the chambers of the life I was examining lay another nautilus, Bryher. It was impossible to proceed with my labors without considering on each step of the way a presiding "elf," as H.D. in happier moments called Bryher. I began to think of her as a difficult "genius."

I then went on to describe my visit to Bryher in 1978 at her home, "Kenwin," near Vevy, Switzerland. There was the Bauhaus-style house, the cranky book-filled room with its shabby 1930s furniture, and an illustrious collection of Elizabethiana. Beyond were the Alps, below was Lake Geneva. And Bryher herself, "an aged warrior in her double-breasted wool jacket and tailored skirt, with her short brusquely cut white hair." Those frighteningly blue eyes, "the eyes of a child" as H.D. once said, closed over memories of H.D. Instead Bryher talked about travel; spoke perceptively of war, politics, education. The person who dominated the conversation was her remarkable father, Sir John Ellerman, who had been owner of the world's largest shipping fleet.

When my biography of H.D. was reviewed by *Time* magazine, the reviewer wrote: "Bryher runs away with the book." That sentence both intrigued and annoyed me until I acknowledged just how irrepressible, indeed, was Bryher.

Had she been born a man she would have commanded the enormous shipping fleet of her father, and quite capably. All her long life she subscribed to five financial newspapers and with glee and acuity shifted her inherited sums back and forth from continent to continent. It was a game and she loved it. Not simply for the money; she was frugal as only the rich can be. We delight in reading of the small economies of one of the richest women of the world: saving postage, abbreviating telephone calls, and amid the splendors of a grotesquely expensive house on Lake Geneva, sleeping in a room the size of a ship's cabin with her clothes hung on a coat rack. Yet she was no miser to her friends, and Bryher's many charities provide clues to a character based on acumen and compassion.

Bryher attacked life itself. Freud, one of the recipients of her generosity, remarked that Bryher had too much energy! She attached herself to the gifted and famous—bulling, helping, listening. So long as H.D. lived she was idealized by Bryher as her heroine, yet that same elevation caused H.D. troubled hours. Thornton Wilder drily noted that Bryher not only looked like Napoleon, but acted like Napoleon. She was maddening and she was thoroughly interesting. Finally she also became a writer of note with a devoted following. Yet while she went to extremes to promote the careers of those artists she admired, she viewed her own efforts with unnecessary modesty.

Bryher wrote eleven historical novels. Several historians (and fiction writers) have confessed to me that they grew up on Bryher's books of Hannibal crossing the Alps, of the Norman Conquest of England, of Elizabethan England about which she became such an expert, and those books set in the canton of Vaud, where she lived in Switzerland. She made history vital, immediate, without any heaviness of thought or clumsiness of fact, because when she had been a child she had promised herself to devote her life to the muse, Clio. Not only are the books of historical interest, they make dramatic reading, as pointed out by her consistently favorable reviews. Then came the autobiographies with their candid appraisal of the author.

Let us pause for a moment to look at the preface written by the high priestess of letters, Amy Lowell, to Bryher's first book, *Development*, written in 1919. With startling prescience Amy Lowell grasped the character of Bryher and the prospects of her talent.

> This is a singular book; in many ways a remarkable book . . . This is the record of the growth—not yet of a soul, that may come—but of a mind. Through a series of deft touches we see a small, lonely, imaginative child gradually evolving into an artist . . . A strange contradictory character, supersensitive to a certain set of impressions, quite cold to others; a character overweighed on one side, leaning heavily to a bias, and yet always with the desire to stand upright, to fill the empty places, to tread clearly and evenly to see the world as a whole.
>
> Nancy (Bryher's heroine, obviously a nom de plume) is evidently a writer born. "When I am older I will write a book" is the burden of her childhood years.
>
> Fairy tales delighted her but little, she records; fact is the thing which charms. It is always the actual which stirs her even if the actual be written in the past tense. Always from beginning to end her creative power moves about the real.

Bryher's introduction to the contemporary world of literature and its authors began with her meeting with H.D. in 1918. (The meeting itself had been arranged through contacts of Bryher's father who was a major shareholder in *The London Times* and *The Economist.*) A companionship on that fortuitous meeting was established at once and it never broke off. Bryher had been drawn to H.D.'s poetry because it represented to her the absolutely new, the true avant-garde. She had memorized entirely H.D.'s first book, *Sea Garden*. Bryher, after a childhood passed in wandering with her parents in ancient lands was intrigued by America, for her the New World. And H.D. became her titular American who would travel with her to America in 1923. But first to celebrate their friendship, and under the critical eye of the Ellerman household, H.D. and Bryher went off to Greece, H.D.'s spiritual homeland.

Then, in America, H.D. introduced Bryher to American writers, among whom was William Carlos Williams and his friend, Robert McAlmon. Especially, there was Marianne Moore who became Bryher's greatly beloved friend, and to whose financial welfare she contributed all Moore's life. After travelling to California, Bryher wrote a little book which she called *West*. It is not only a savage commentary upon America (an attitude Bryher was later to modify) but it contains a unique and formidable portrait of Moore and her mother.

Bryher then married McAlmon in New York—a companionate marriage—and brought him back to England. Once there he promptly decided to join the expatriates in Paris. There Bryher met the "Bunch" and gave McAlmon funds to establish Contact Press, which contains the signature work of the expatriates of that golden era of the 1920s—Hemingway, Djuna Barnes, Williams, Gertrude Stein, etc. It was in Paris that Bryher met James Joyce, and McAlmon briefly became Joyce's secretary. Not so briefly did the equally kind Lady Ellerman, Bryher's mother, support the Joyce family, along with the composer George Antheil.

(One day in the life of Bryher in Paris in the 1920s included a visit to Brancusi, a sitting for Berenice Abbott, dinner with James Joyce and Ezra Pound, and a late stop at the Dome!)

The marriage to McAlmon served its purpose in giving Bryher autonomy from her parents, yet its style suited neither partner. Bryher was at the same time travelling to Egypt with H.D. En route they had stopped in Florence, where Bryher found Norman Douglas, whose writing was a major influence on her. Difficult to find a man and woman of such opposite tastes, yet they met on a background of literature. The sophisticated Douglas and the inarticulate, unworldly youthful Bryher. Their friendship lasted until his death and is a reflection of the sympathy Bryher felt for those whose lives were fashioned in far different ways than she had chosen.

Subsequent to her divorce from McAlmon, Bryher remarried Kenneth Macpherson. Youthful, attractive, bisexual, and prepared to live the life of a prince regent, Macpherson was responsible for several changes in Bryher's life. It was he who led the way to the Berlin film world. It was Macpherson sponsored by Bryher who made the film *Borderline*, starring Paul Robeson and H.D. Together Bryher and Macpherson built "Kenwin," a Bauhaus experiment. And it was Macpherson who instigated *Close Up*, although Bryher's managerial gifts kept the magazine going for seven years. Together the Macphersons established Pool Publications, which published their star, H.D., with her finest prose.

Bryher's correspondence with the giants of film of that era, Pabst and Lang, and her descriptions of them are fascinating reading, and more, they constitute an undisclosed record of filmmaking. She also wrote, and Pool published, *Film Problems of Soviet Russia* (1929), in which she discusses five major Russian films that she had seen in Berlin. Her chapter on Eisenstein, with whom she corresponded, is exceptional, not only for her remarks on the Russian master, but for the revealing comments he had made to her, personally.

In 1933 Bryher went to Vienna where H.D. was then being analyzed by Freud. (Her own analysis had been with the eminent Dr. Hanns Sachs.) A brief correspondence with Freud then took place in which Bryher attempted to convince Freud of the danger of a Nazi takeover, interspersed with Freud's eagerness for Bryher to adopt one of his chow dog's puppies. Bryher then gave funds for the continuing publication of *The Psychoanalytic Review*.

From here on Bryher attempted to convince everyone of the Nazi danger. She was bitter the rest of her life about the blindness of those in power to the eventuality of a world war. The only thing she could do, she did. She aided Germans to flee. She remained in Switzerland until it was dangerous for her to do so as her classification would be questionable. She arrived in London in 1940 and thus began the days about which she wrote in her memoir, *Days of Mars*. During the Blitz (what else could one do with the darkened streets and curtains across the windows, except write?) she wrote *Beowulf*, her story of the common man's survival during the war.

The war finally over, Bryher returned to Kenwin. H.D. was established in Swiss hotels and a sanatorium, and Bryher received friends such as Edith Sitwell, Hermann Hesse, Sylvia Beach, and many renowned literary names at Kenwin. It was during the 1950s that many of Bryher's novels were written. She also resumed her travels, and her travel journals show her to be a natural adventurer, noting with humor and detachment both touristic delays and strange sunsets.

Bryher lived for twenty-two more years after the death of H.D. in 1961. She seldom returned to London but went frequently to the US, where she saw Perdita Schaffner, H.D.'s daughter, whom she had adopted. Never a 'homebody,' her visits were brief and her eyes were cast on other horizons. Kenwin when I saw it on my two visits was certainly not a monument to the past, although filled with books written by friends, books that now are in the Bryher Library in East Hampton, a tribute to Bryher from Perdita. Perdita's Traveling Scholarship was continued by Bryher, and more recent benefactors became Dylan Thomas and Margaret Drabble. Bryher was always a listening post for future talent.

Bryher, whose adolescence was pre-World War I and who grew up in the age of Freud (whose defender and disciple she was, as well as Havelock Ellis, with whom she travelled), is an anomaly. As a girl she rebelled against the restrictions of an upper-class Victorian family, embracing sexual and moral codes far in advance of her time, and yet there is something distinctly Victorian about this woman. She wrote that chronologically she might be called Edwardian, but certainly her personal sympathies were not in tune with that age of sophistication and frivolity. She respected the codes of honor and loyalty; she was dependable. She yielded to no one in her belief that mass poverty could be alleviated through mass education, and that what women needed was not so much the vote as education and superior jobs. Her mind was astute, almost without classification. She was interested in economics—she once said she did not enjoy dining with Rebecca West so much as her banker husband. Yet she embraced poets and writers, admiring the most advanced novelists, Joyce, and in particular the pioneer of stream-of-consciousness writing, Dorothy Richardson. Richardson's path-breaking *Pilgrimage* would not have been completed without the moral and financial support of Bryher. She respected the activities of her powerful and self-made father, who had coached her throughout World War I from his position in the ministry of supply never to expect an easy victory, but when it arrived to be prepared to pay its price. A teetotaler herself, each of her husbands was alcoholic; dressed in the primmest of clothing, she adored fancy and exquisite fashion displayed by other women. Socially retiring, she enjoyed the company of actresses. Her nemesis may have been a fear of boredom often experienced by those equipped with exceptional energy. She shared a Victorian pleasure in power along with its indulgencies in plans and strategies, its delight in organization and detail.

Thornton Wilder's characterization of her as "Napoleon" must be set aside. She much more resembles that other shrewd and intelligent woman who lived also outside her country, as she dwelt outside her beloved Paris on the shores of Lake Geneva, Madame de Staël, writer, author, companion of Benjamin Constant, the daughter of Napoleon's great financier, Necker.

Bryher's story, because it is about a woman so different from the subject of my previous biography, the poet H.D., will not share the same framework or method. I should like this book to be shorter, around 250 pages. I want it to convey the savor of Bryher's own writing, as well as her life—a rehearsal of fact not fiction. This places a certain burden on me as a poet, but a welcome one as my evident admiration for Bryher, as well as amusement at her amazing ways, tended to upstage my enthusiasm for the subject of my former biography. In that biography I was writing a dedicated, formal, and also authorized book. Here I would like to conform, if possible, to a demanding and a more straightforward presentation. The title which I have given this proposal will I hope convey both the idea and the manner of writing—The Story of Bryher.

The confidence and permissions which were extended to me throughout the writing of the biography of her mother, H.D., have been assured by Perdita Schaffner in the research of this book.

Private papers and photographs long resting at Kenwin were removed from Switzerland after Bryher's death and are in East Hampton, N.Y., in a specially constructed library. The books, letters, journals, manuscripts are in the process of being catalogued. I am pleased to be able to state that I shall be the first to examine this new material.

The Beinecke Library at Yale with which I am familiar, as it was there my research took place for the H.D. biography, will be most helpful. It was there that Bryher deposited her correspondence when she made her previous deposition of the H.D. papers. Included are letters of Dorothy Richardson, Edith Sitwell, Marianne Moore, Havelock Ellis, Norman Douglas, Compton Mackenzie, Ezra Pound, Richard Aldington, and many others. The Beinecke also contains the complete files of *Close Up* and *Life and Letters Today*.

Fortunately for my immediate plans, I have read at the Beinecke the huge H.D.–Bryher correspondence dating from 1918 to 1961, when they wrote each other every day! This completed task will shorten the time devoted to research considerably. I plan to complete this biography in a halcyon two years. Further research will undoubtedly be needed at the British Library, hopefully the Freud archives and at various localities in Switzerland.

Dorothy Richardson: A Letter from Cornwall

Dorothy Richardson married Alan Odle, a self-employed artist—he never had a gallery and his hopes of an exhibition came to ruin*—or as she might better say, he was a "self-occupied artist," much her junior. Our heroine lied about her years at the registrar's office where they married. This marriage, according to Bryher when we spoke of Richardson several years ago in Switzerland, was the mistake of her life. (It is questionable if Dorothy would have agreed.) All the years of her marriage she was convinced that Alan would die of the consumption that finally killed him. As a result she coddled, nourished, nursed this fine skeleton who wore a wig and was engaged in illustrations for *Candide* much of his indulged life. Grotesque, warped, sexual, these sophisticated images strewed their brilliantly executed presences over the Odle lodgings. And Dorothy was equally obsessed by *Pilgrimage*, the series of books that lent their name to "stream-of-consciousness." Within these pioneer volumes she exhaustively relinquished the fame that was to belong to Joyce. She evidently did not have time, or that sense of urgency which belongs to writers like Joyce, who ceaselessly push their just claims before benefactors and public.

Yet Dorothy had Bryher, a faithful and consistently loyal supporter, without whom it is easily guessed she would never have written her story of Miriam, her remembrance** of a woman which, commenced in 1906, was viewed from the continuing life of the author with its impoverishment and demands to neglect her talent. Dorothy repaid Bryher her loyalty and assistance with the manuscript of *Pointed Roofs*, which Bryher insisted on assessing for the benefit of Dorothy's relatives.

* The work of Alan Odle was finally exhibited in Paris in 1983.

** As in Proust's volumes. Bryher supplied Dorothy with all of Proust in French. After his translator Scott Moncrieff died, Dorothy wished further to exhaust herself by inheriting his job. She never completed *Pilgrimage*.

Here is a glimpse of Dorothy as it found its way to Bryher in a letter. This is Dorothy in situ in Cornwall after she and Alan have returned from Switzerland where they had wintered at Bryher's expense for the first time without worries, tasting also an unexpected and exaltive trip to Paris. Cornwall was surely a summer retreat, yet the Odles are there in blustery winter always, and the rent was cheap, the winds blew, the surf pounded, the cottage shook; they had escaped London for Alan's health. In summer they would return to London to endure the heat, reversing the usual schedule as they went on their enduringly perversely difficult way.

We must also remember that Bryher's subsidy was moderate, consistent with Dorothy's pride. Dorothy added to their funds—Alan's inheritance had long gone and he was by now completely dependent on her—writing innumerable articles, translations from medical treatises to philosophy to Gide—at the cost of the eventual completion of her novel. She labored nearly every minute of her life, it would seem. If not writing articles then there was the housekeeping, real labor as she was an eccentric housekeeper and the Odle menu causes shivers. Bryher, again, subsidized with enormous baskets from Fortnum and Mason each Christmas and holiday, and special orders of Gold Flake cigarettes Dorothy hoarded.

Dorothy must never be viewed as a drudge. She was a willing, an agile and bemused victim of her talent for self-sacrifice, "the windiest corner, the chair in a draught," as H.D. observed. These were doughty rather than obsequious choices.

At last we arrive at the letter addressed from Padstow, Cornwall in 1924:

> I scribble surreptitiously, on my knee, upstairs, getting together something about Paris, about Antheil, about Women & Art for *Vanity Fair*, to work on when I get to town and a table. No room for a table in the tiny bedroom, which I choose because it has two windows . . . Laboring on my last chapter & writing letters, each *very important*, to be posted *at once* & separately, excuse for sending A. to the post office, profiting by his pristine innocence as to the hours of collect & at the same time accounting for the time I spend scribbling. If he thought me at work, he's at work too, but over a table, instead of lounging by an open window blissfully reading,

going cheerfully and importantly up the lane, at frequent intervals to post . . .

It's all there, isn't it? One of the innovators of the century scribbling on her knees in a scarcely heated cottage. And she did not compare herself to Emily Brontë. I don't think she compared her lot to anyone's, or her writing.

An Evening with Charles Olson

Now to the restaurant in Spoleto. Suddenly, without any prior meeting, out of the blue, as it were, Charles came up to me and asked one evening in July 1965 if I would have dinner with him. And immediately I said, yes. We were both attending an international gathering of poets, some famous, indeed, and we were the youngest, from a young country. This might have made it easier for him to wish to dine with someone from his own country. (Ezra Pound would be there and would be greeted, standing up from his chair in an eighteenth-century theatre, mumbling, cheered.)

He took me to a large and beautiful restaurant I had never been near, looking out over the hills. Everything was slightly fancy with heavy red velvet curtains, immaculate tables and waiters. When the Williamsons, who were Icelandic, came up to us outside the restaurant, where they had been examining the building, and asked if they could join us, I introduced them to Charles, who agreed at once. Then began the evening of long conversation, of dancing, and eating, drinking. Charles and I laughed, and danced, and much enthusiasm and laughter. We finally saw dawn had arrived from over the hills without our expecting it when the restless waiters pulled back the curtains.

We had talked little about poetry. This was part of the surprisingness of the evening. There was no argument. No clash of ideas. There were few ideas to be discussed, at all. We told stories and laughed. Williamson was well known in Iceland. I am sure their being from Iceland made it easier. (Who was interested in Iceland or the US among all those major writers from so-called sophisticated countries?) I had met them earlier and liked them, and one of his subjects was the closeness of Scotland to Iceland and the ancient intermarriages. Then came their most curious remark. They said they had believed Charles and I had known each other for a long time. Indeed it was possible we were married! We were very amused by this remark and reminded them we had just met.

The oddest part of all was how Charles and I enjoyed each other, and how simply and easy our conversation was, as if we were old friends. I believe this came from neither of us having read the poetry of the other, as there was nothing to block our enjoyment, open view of each other. I realize now that this attitude was one of his gifts, his ease in the presence of someone whom he may even have decided to trust.

After having left the restaurant the four of us went to the ruins of a Greek theatre and watched dawn come up over the ancient ruined seats. Then the Icelanders and Charles walked me to my hotel. I don't recall any of us being exhausted or troubled. We had experienced an evening lightened by jokes and a sudden, charmed familiarity, the recall of which is not painful, yet regret edges in. It was never to be repeated. Nor did a correspondence between Charles and me ever ensue. Fate had its plan for the evening and for afterwards it had made no plans.

Jeanne Reynal

To know that no other place in the world does there exist another group of these mosaic figures. There they are created out of the myth and reality of Africa. And out of years of apprenticeship. Of studying the mosaics of Sumer, of the Byzantine, of Ravenna. To have traveled to the remote, the exotic, and the unfamiliar, searching for the pure primitive statement. To have been influenced by Surrealism, by Abstract Expressionism. To have created paintings in mosaics, murals in mosaics, freestanding forms in mosaics. To have discovered and introduced into the work the methods of Navajo Indians. And now at this point in her career to create these living, breathing personages with their mosaic skin. To have permitted instinct to lead the artist back to animal form and idea with few visible traces of contemporary influence. To be alone and unique in her field. This then is the position of Jeanne Reynal today.

There they stand, these figures. They might have been standing there in the jungle covered with vines and leaves for centuries. Alone with mud to their haunches. It is easy to imagine coming upon these figures at the end of a long muddy river, a pause in a difficult sweating day in a canoe on that river. Or, we have been searching for a buried temple. Suddenly we come upon these figures guarding the hidden temple entrance. They confront us, and we are wary. Then their magic enters us and we bow to them and depart without transgressing the temple.

Fantasy, yes. But not altogether untrue. These sculptures have emerged out of the life of Jeanne Reynal. Let us listen to her describe one of her journeys.

"Once in the long ago, on a jeep trip from Guatemala City to Copan, the ruined city in Honduras, we veered from our destination to visit the Black Virgin of Esquipulas—just a little side trip.

"After twenty-three hours of side trip, up and down those lovely faraway mountains, we came upon an empty valley. Empty of villages, empty of all signs of life, save for the great white, icy-white Cathedral of Esquipulas, like a giant abandoned cake as rootless as a sombrero in a field."

Or: "We were on our way to Manaus. The Rio Negro, the largest tributary that copulates with the Amazon below Manaus, is truly black . . . I was wading in it one morning. Though a storm was gathering, the strangeness of black water, black water under a deeply purple sky was too tempting. Fully dressed, I was about to dive in when a huge fork of lightning struck nearby . . . Three hours later in steamy sunshine we visited the never-used but very famous opera house in the jungle.

". . . The interior is charming and a surprise, art nouveau, innocent and above all so pretty in an environment of alligators, anacondas, boas, jaguars, and headhunters, and—the giant water lily Victoria Regia, suddenly come upon, a colony in a quiet backwater."

These lines from her journey, although unrelated to the content of her latest work, do convey the *atmosphere* that surrounds that work.

Several years ago Jeanne Reynal and her husband Thomas Sills went to Ethiopia. I almost wrote "visited Africa." But it is impossible for Jeanne Reynal to visit anywhere. She goes there and usually takes something back with her. Not only ideas and memories, but let us say a piece of something useful, such as the obsidian that she picked up in Nevada when she was traveling there with the poet André Breton. That piece of obsidian resides in a female figure in her most recent exhibition.

Which was about Africa. The artist has made mosaic sculptures from her impression of the African scene. Not that an exact explanation of the origin of these sculptures is necessary, or even possible, for they are sculptures existing outside of geography in the region where the creative act occurs.

They are mostly tall figures, from 60 to 120 inches. (When Jeanne Reynal first spoke of her ideas concerning the sculpture to be, the late Barnett Newman said to her, "make them big." And so she did. And it is the height of these figures that adds to their pictorial strength.)

The sculptural forms are covered with glass tesserae, Venetian gold leaf, ordinary tile, cut in half- and quarter-inch sizes, and Japanese pearl shells.

Entering a room filled with these figures, the initial reaction is to their strength, their presence, and their magic. And a realization that you are looking at a scene which has never presented itself before. No ordinary explanations exist for the effect pronounced upon the viewer. The figures are indeed magical and one almost gives up at that point. Searching for derivations or correspondences is useless. The work is that unique product of experience haloed by imagination and a sensitivity strictly disciplined.

A tall figure composed of pearl, red, yellow, green, the pearl jutting out from the sides of the sculpture like a mane. It is called "Emperor's Greys." It is a portrait of the horses of the emperor of Ethiopia. "Africa: King and Queen," a large sculpture with the mosaics of the king and queen leading into one figure, very strong and human, of red, white, black, yellow, and gold. "Bushman." He has pearl along with the other tesserae, but he has also been given a spear, attached from chest to foot. But these are not literal, descriptive figures. They are assimilations, so that in looking at the "Emperor's Greys" one is aware of the landscape outside the horse, as well as the interior of the studio. The king and queen are one person, one piece of sculpture, wedded in a way that makes it unnecessary to trace the male or female outline, yet we are aware of which is masculine and which is feminine—yet not in the Cubism manner of Picasso. And "Woman" in a country where the women are small from the head to the waist, then suddenly bulge with their great hips, has a stunning curve of tesserae, as a Brancusi might curve—yet not quite that. Nothing here is quite that other.

Jeanne Reynal has worked persistently to take herself and the art of mosaic away from the limits of mosaic style which were set in the sixteenth century, after the great period of Byzantine mosaic. It was in the sixteenth century that mosaic lost its own creative rules and became limited to copying painting. The respect accorded Renaissance painting schemed against the mosaic process. It was then that a cartoon was enlarged from the master's sketch and then copied by the students. Thus the mosaic as it finally appeared was a mere translation of a painting. An obsequious, if gifted bow, by minor artisans to great painters.

After a lifetime vocation, Jeanne Reynal has broken away from this tradition. That is not to say that she has gone back to Hagia Sophia, much as she may pay homage to that great mosque. Further, one can detect her dismay as she has pushed away the rubble of twentieth-century commercial ceramics cluttering the walls of apartment houses, hotels, airports.

Mosaic artist Jeanne Reynal was born in 1902 in White Plains, New York. In 1928, she was apprenticed to Boris Anrep, Russian mosaicist, and became one of his assistants in his commission for the Bank of England and the Greek Church in London. She remained in Europe for many years, returning to the US in 1939, living and working in New York City since 1946. She is married to the painter Thomas Sills, has exhibited since 1940, and is represented in many private and museum collections. Her most recent exhibition was at the Betty Parsons Gallery in New York (February 23–March 13).

She has brought back the tactile quality, the firsthand immediacy of mosaic. She has brought back the texture of mosaic. Her figures vibrate. They are spontaneous. Perhaps the magic in her latest exhibition is due to the simple (!) fact that her figures breathe. Her work is bold, unlike the apologetic, careful attitude of the mosaics of the past, wistfully inserting themselves into drawing. Her figures cast their own shadows. There are no notions, there are only declarations.

These are reasons why one can say that these new sculptural mosaics are not only about Africa, mysterious and titillating as that continent may be. Jeanne Reynal has added another dimension to the art of mosaic.

Nell Blaine at Yaddo in the 1950s

I have always believed it was the spirit of Nell Blaine that directed my poem "Parachutes," written when we were at Yaddo at the same time in the late 1950s. What had been before a cautiously growing friendship there grew stronger, held together by the now apparent working ties of our profession. Nell was given a studio on the grounds, while I, inspired by the evidences of her professionalism, wrote "Parachutes" in a tower room facing the Yaddo sweep of real estate.

Nell's rules of residency were to work hard all day and then knock off in the evening. She went in and out of her studio with a sort of useful freedom, and often pure joy would emanate from her. Her real residency lay within the natural world she was offered.

Briefly, while I was there, she regarded the dog cemetery as her special area. I possess a Blaine ink drawing filled with bold usurping lines, and tender at its edges as she appropriates the departing souls of dogs who now are captives of her drawing. Powerful, in part because she catches a slightly sinister aspect of the Yaddo grounds.

In the evenings Nell instituted the poker table over which she presided. Poker brought out that tough side of her, useful in the Art wars. I had noticed that frequently she adopted a special attitude toward me, as if emotionally I were rather delicate, as became a poet, and required sensitive treatment. This attitude vanished at the poker table. (And would vanish in future times when this so called 'delicacy' could no longer be endured by Nell, the warriors.)

I recall the shock of a visiting art critic who arrived at Yaddo in the evening, expected to pass the hours before retiring in an exchange of art theories. He discovered six or seven of us at the nightly poker game, Nell at the head of the table shuffling the cards. I remember her exact words, repeated with her special grin, "Hilton, take a seat." He fled.

Robert de Niro in the 1950s and '60s

Robert de Niro was fiercely engaged with his work. When I knew him at the beginning of the 1960s, his studio was his home in a rundown building in what is now the Soho of New York. He had a few friends, but mostly he was alone in the tremendously cluttered place in which he painted. Sometimes I saw him out walking, and a scene plays across the screen of my mind of the day I saw him standing on the sidewalk talking to a woman friend while he held his mongrel dog on a leash. It was a typical encounter, a repeated scene of his life. There was no social life of dinners, etc. There were many parties he did not attend, or showed up as if out walking his dog.

Yet how many artists in America read Verlaine, Mallarmé, Racine, and also the New York Poets. He loved French painting and modernism, yet it was Matisse whom he studied. Erratic, gloomy, untidy in his studio-home, his mind was elegant.

One day in 1962 he showed up in my village cold water flat, as they were known, with a box containing his volumes of French poetry. He was going to Paris, he said, and asked me to take care of his books. And they lay there in my small room keeping me company, reminding me of him and his devotion to all things French. It had been an act of kindness, perhaps, to ask me to take care of those books I did not possess. They established a presence in the flat. He did return to reclaim them, but not before he painted many pictures in Paris and in the countryside.

Another time he took me to the building where Virginia, his former wife, lived and worked. (New York is a story of buildings.) It was on West 14th Street as I recall. Virginia was working out a system to break the bank at Monte Carlo, or some such scheme with an arithmetic Virginia was so adept with, and helping herself survive by typing manuscripts. She had a real business with assistant typists. Virginia was also a very gifted painter.

As I recall, de Niro's work was thoughtfully defended by Thomas Hess, the editor of the most important art journal, *ARTnews*. It was through Hess and de Niro's dealer Charles Egan, who has now passed into legend, that he sold pictures. It was Hess who wished him to be in the Museum of Modern Art. One day Bob was sitting in my flat and suddenly asked, knowing I needed work, if I would like to write art criticism for *ARTnews*. And the next day Tom called me. He called me also because he wanted poets on his journal. It must be emphasized that Bob was becoming well known among painters and patrons and admired by Clement Greenberg, the Czar of painting in New York.

"Affability" is not a word that applied to Bob, nor is "social." He was given to acid comments about the art scene, with which, I might add, he was thoroughly familiar. He preferred provocative conversations, an exchange of ideas about art with selective people. His attitude toward art trends was speculative. Like most good artists, he had a high opinion of his own work, yet he did not neglect the many-faceted highs and lows of the art scene. In that way, when I knew him, he was not a true recluse. His eye was alert to social and artistic currents, and he listened.

I never thought of him as lonely, although unlike Matisse, his self-selected mentor, he had no domestic life. If he was met on the street walking his dog, instead of socializing, we must remember, his mind was very sophisticated, I must emphasize this.

His painting is selective, like his mind. And this requires a certain respect for time. A thoughtful regard for its wasting. It seems to me that aside from asking it respect his art, Bob made few demands upon society.

I was fortunate in the years of the late fifties and through the sixties that I knew him. He was so intelligent, unusually well read, and as with many sophisticated people, there was a suspicious element within him, and in his outlook. It is in his painting that we encounter him, the person he wished to represent him.

Helen Frankenthaler: The Moment & The Distance

> Surprise laughs savagely in the purity of light . . .
> Apollinaire

Helen Frankenthaler has been active throughout her career in bringing us up to date. When she was a member of the early Tibor de Nagy Gallery in the 1950s, her position was separate from that of her colleagues who had located themselves as "second generation abstract expressionists." In that gallery she was an anomaly. Not that she wasn't absorbing the same atmosphere, going to the same parties, but her eye was focused differently. Eschewing the de Kooning-Kline axis, her influences were to be found closer to Kandinsky, Marin, Pollock. She was an expressionist because she applied the emotional and physical techniques to the canvas that were shared by her colleagues, at first. Later, following the example of Pollock, she painted on the floor, she used drip technique, she became physically involved in the act of painting the canvas: another approach.

Previously, the retrospective of 1969 at the Whitney, organized by E. C. Goosen, offered us paintings from periods in the artist's career beginning with the early paintings and continuing up to 1969. The current exhibition at the Corcoran Gallery, under the supervision of Gene Baro, is concerned with the paintings from 1969 through 1974.

The joy of life is ripe. The experience is more intensive (the maturing eye and mind). The scope is broader, firmer. The artist is at her station, not an overnight arrival, certainly. The productivity, the one-woman shows, the traveling exhibitions, the caravanserai that surrounds the celebrations of the artist are all there in the background. Several critics have suggested the influence of Arthur Dove, which she steadfastly denied. If, as Hilton Kramer has explained, the art of Dove is that of "lyrical meditation," we can agree with Frankenthaler. There is little to parallel their attitudes. One might assume in an exhibition at this point in her career that there would be more meditative aspects—not at all. It is that quality of silence that is rejected in Frankenthaler's work. A product of her own generation and the milieu. Frankenthaler consistently reports the moment or moments which lead to a painting in reflective non-tranquility. At this point she is not going to meditate beside the road. What she sees, feels, thinks, after a necessary period of gestation, goes immediately to the canvas. One does not observe normal quiet thoughts here. Detachment—yes, in the middle of the struggle one senses a detachment, a separation from the canvas, the critical eye.

Action, sophistication, intelligence, the attitude of a city graduate who is called a "landscape artist." A landscape artist? Does she make that transposition? I am not certain she has. Her landscapes exist on the margin of Frankenthaler's universe. She forces nature to copy art. These paintings are interior landscapes. Circe lives on Frankenthaler's island, which furthermore is translated into Manhattan. *Venus Revealed* is Venus observed from a private house.

This exhibition shows that Frankenthaler has forced difficult options upon herself. She is not going to paint from Art History; she is not going to paint "*en plein air*"; she is not going to paint Still Life. These decisions would place heavy burdens on the forte of the artist. In the past some of the weaknesses in her pictures are the result of what may be called a heavy reliance on the dramatization of the Self.

It has been remarked elsewhere that her intelligence is dominant in her paintings. (But how to explain the sensuous appliqué of the paint?) For intelligence one could add sensitive use of the unconscious. This dependence can be traced in part to the influence of Surrealism, which is more apparent in her work than in most of the painters working in a similar genre with whom she is frequently paired. In this splendid Corcoran exhibit we see her intelligence at work, assessing, projecting, criticizing quickly, succinctly, and successfully. It appears to arrive out of a cool and then is metamorphosized into any temperature she chooses.

Correlative to this, unlike the Romanticists and Classicists who made variations on the same subjects, Frankenthaler gives us variations on Mood. At first this would seem to be puzzling, but we all know the many subtleties of which Mood is the victim and charger. Perhaps Mood is not the exact word; perhaps interpretations of Fancy, although obscuring, might be more correct. Fancy implies a modification of the imagination and Mood implies a shifting of the psyche. In all her exhibitions there have existed these variations, which I will not call "themes."

Her methods consist of a series of surprises sprung on us through color and gesture.

Color: A pleasure subsequent to writing about Frankenthaler's painting flows most precipitously around her use of color. Uniquely she is a painter who appears to rely on a loose, apparently extemporaneous structure, whereas in color she is intently formal. Blue, yellow, orange, are they simple or primary? Or are they lavishly Byzantine? One turns from mysterious browns and sad reds, from melancholy greens to solid gold cadillacs; from *Burnt Norton* to *Chairman of the Board*; from Circe's spell to the clever repartee of Rapunzel. Color indicates their moods. The painter has an entire vocabulary of variations on her subjects which she shifts with her color ranges.

Gesture: Inheriting a grandiose concept of space-scale from a generation intent on breaking down the concept of easel painting, Frankenthaler takes it as her natural due that space or scale for her should be inexhaustible. Her manner of flaunting space has the eloquence of a performer who is not only never at a loss for words, but is determined not to bore her audience. The gesture shows itself in a line thrown across the painting as in *Thanksgiving*. *Blue Rail* gives us the flash of a line that shows her manner of suggesting, of surprising, of inventing, of throwing out a clue to the painting. We see this gestural line continuing through the 1970 pictures into 1971 with *Genuine Blue*, *St. John*, and the bucolic, sunny *Mornings*. In *Nature Abhors a Vacuum*, one of the most beautifully realized paintings in this exhibition, this line is less a separate gesture and is more fully integrated into the painting. From then on, we notice that the pictures no longer seem to require this leap, this clue as a point of departure, or declarative sentence. The paintings meld into color.

Throughout the years, the paintings which relied on their color structure, on their flowingness, as we saw in 1969 in the important painting *Flood*, have indicated another attack on the canvas, that from *within*. I would say that by 1974 Frankenthaler slows the momentum and begins to consolidate her terms. From chapter by chapter we are now able to find the continuity of the entire story. This culminates in the aptly titled *Jovian Atmosphere* and the surprising *Mexico*, a statement about geographical borders that does not borrow from a guide to south of the border; as I have indicated, the borders are those of Frankenthaler herself. In these paintings, and in the latest shown here, *The Sound of the Bassoon*, she has decided to treat not only the nature of light, the nature of habitations, of Art; she now sums in her work, de rerum natura, the nature of things.

The picture *Vaporite* is an elegant example of the culmination. This painting bears a separate, almost metaphysical identity and, although painted early in 1971, serves as an indicator of the fine things to come. The picture is also an example of one of her 'surprises,' its serenity contrasting with its daring.

Observing her work over a period of years, progress has taken little toll. Toll? Well, the "coltishness," to use Barbara Rose's word, which showed up in *Eden* (1957) has disappeared (but not the remarkable boldness and wit of that painting). *Mountains and Sea* (1951), a seminal painting, a real breakthrough, has progeny. Certainly its directions have been followed in the large substance of her painting—the lift, the soft vaporish color, the spatial atmosphere. These indicators have settled into the more "classical" structures of 1974, *Nature Abhors a Vacuum* and *The Sound of the Bassoon*. The sudden joke and derring-do are not quite dissipated. The spontaneity leaps forth; probably there are less happy *accidents* in the work and more *decisions*. There may be less humming, but more song. The intelligence has cooled and refined itself, added a sophistication and surety. Then there is maturity with which this exhibition rewards us.

She has rewarded us with the astonishing combination of freedom with restraint, extravagance with discipline, suggestion and definition.

The moment becomes the distance.

Piet Mondrian

The beautiful, spatial Mondrian of 1922, *Composition with Blue, Black, Yellow, and Red* was reproduced in the Art section of the *New York Times* (January 7, 2000). We are grateful to the Harvard Museums who have acquired this masterpiece so pristine and fresh, sheltered in a private collection in Holland. The painting had never left Holland, even for a journey to another collection. Astoundingly it had never been displayed. We learn that "the painting had never been cleaned, restored or damaged, and even retains its original wood strip frame." The spirit of Mondrian, bruised in other paintings, somehow meddled with, impoverished as the "Studio of Mondrian" erected in the Museum of Modern Art, survives in this painting.

It is intact, even in a photograph, "the shiny black lines and fine brushwork, subtle gray tones and sharp primary colors." We see how Mondrian "carefully adjusted the lines and planes as they reached the edge of the canvas."

As they touch the edge of Modernity.

In the 1950s I left Los Angeles where I had lived with my Aunt and Uncle, attending high school and going to college, first at UCLA, later graduating from UC at Berkeley. I had lived in Los Angeles after I graduated, working at several jobs, but I was dissatisfied and friends suggested I go to New York.

A friend let me live in her apartment until her roommate returned which was very soon, I had begun to like living on Eighth Street in the dark apartment with few windows, but it was necessary that I leave. New Yorkers, however, looked after each other. The friend and her roommate did not wish to turn me out of the apartment. They suggested I call another friend who lived on a fifth-floor walk-up, as New Yorkers called those apartments bare of conveniences such as elevators. Bathtubs stood on four legs in the kitchen. "Frieda" let me stay in her apartment, which was also just across the street from the Hans Hofmann School of modern painting.

Frieda Egger was from Austria, and she dedicated herself to her art and to a life of hardship, taking on small jobs when they were offered. The small amount I offered her helped out. As a consequence I did not complain when I was bitten by bedbugs. I learned about painters from her conversation, and about dedication, incidentally, stepping into the spilling-over bathtub, mopping up the water, washing my bites.

One day she suggested we go next door to another studio where an artist was working on a painting. I was not prepared for the cozy cottagey design of the apartment, the maple color of the furniture, the overstuffed chairs. I believed that artists should live like Frieda with bare walls and empty shelves and hard beds. The artist suggested we go into her studio. I was reluctant, believing the studio would be cozy with uninteresting drawings.

A painting, I was told it was by the artist, Mondrian, stood in the corner. It would have been for him perhaps his "middle" period. Several years before *Broadway Boogie Woogie*, yet not the classic Mondrian of this earlier painting in the *New York Times*. Mondrian! The artist had been asked by the Museum of Modern Art to copy his painting.

There it stood in this tenement building, five stories up with snow on the fire escape. So large it took up most of the room. Shiny furniture from a department store in the next room.

The artist was unknown to me. His painting was unappreciated by me. I was afraid of the painting, of its emptiness. The carefully ruled, so I thought, spaces of color. The rigors, the hurdles of the painting, the sense of form from which it derived, the "emptiness," the knowledge and spatiality, were lost on me. The impressiveness of the painting was lost on me.

The Color Green in the Art Work of Richard Tuttle

GREEN IS A NOTORIOUSLY DIFFICULT COLOR IS THE SUPERSTITION. It is a serious color, slightly morose, somewhat intellectual. It is often found among the grays of countryside. It refuses to meddle with charm. Often green seems preoccupied, thoughtful. Green is not the color of heaven. It has a myriad of tasks to perform. Green must take up the burden of other colors on a page or canvas grown heavy with labor. Avoiding purple it sidles up to blue, knowing in the regime of color that blue is thoughtful. Indoors, unless under the panoply of heaven, an aristocratic color, even gay in the eighteenth century. Green has trouble with the heavens, being practical.

Green is will to labor, and often works into the night when other colors dim their lights.

When Richard Tuttle is painting, I examine the surface he works on to see if it is a hilly terrain, requiring the labor of green to maintain the spirit of the artist, to declare it is on earth he labors. Green often comes to the aid of the artist in a difficult situation, when the canvas refuses to speak.

A refusal now provides space for the green comforter of the emotions, reminder of the green provisions.

Courbet, who moved amid a dry country landscape, respected this color and even hid it in the bedclothes of courtesans. On the hunting caps of female riders his green is triumphant.

Manet chose to spread in a green wood a picnic with green resources. Delacroix used the color on his ceilings; green shaded the parks he walked in.

Picasso, in search of invention, hid the green nature of his construction.

Each artist embarks on a personal research, and Tuttle may expect an introspective refreshment from green. And then, again, as if he seized a water sprinkler to hint at rinsed green, so will this tone almost jokingly spread itself among other colors, *noisetone* from a hunting horn when the new color is overtaken. He created intimacy he wants to exist among the primary colors elevating themselves when low-spirited.

Tuttle is consistent in his choice of subject. He likes to surprise the viewer. The surprise is a subsidiary of his technique. We can rely on the setting in which a painting is poised to surprise us. This word 'surprise' may also be a surprise to the artist. Even when clues have been memorized from past artwork. This is the most gala surprise.

The artist gives us an assurance that memory never ceases to flow from the unconscious, an attitude natural to this artist. He cannot abandon the memory of color. If he makes the decision to feature certain colors, the entire spectrum may be linked to the process of recall before the choice is made. Or so it can appear to the viewer, overwhelmed by the glow. If a slice of green rests on yellow, that slice has a territorial claim.

Color initiates form. Part of an instinctive formula in the background of Richard Tuttle, it never exists. A loss of one of the starry patterns, perhaps, but not dispossessed. Color remains this artist's alphabet.

Jean Arp

I like to be in the presence of Arp, the gentle solace of his anarchy:

humor
is water from beyond
mixed with wine from down here . . .

His first known poems were published in 1903 with the first known drawings on the facing page. He had joined together Art and Poetry and forged there a reality, his life would never permit them to be separated.

His need to simplify structure and then permeate it with pure spatial formality of the cube or oval.

He once showed a friend a sculpture on which there was an almost invisible swelling.

"Do you feel the bump?" he asked.

"I am leaving it as it is. If I get rid of the bump the whole thing will become elegant."

This decision relates also to his poetry where we are permitted to read rough passages and parts of speech. He liked to look up words in the dictionary. He discovered the word "Eudemonia," which is the "well-being of genius," and it is man's fateful and personal predisposition for happiness, according to Aristotle. This was a discovery for Arp that worked itself into the language of his poetry where "eudemonia" asserts itself.

His poetry contains happiness. You can hear his sculpture:

If the guides wear wooden aprons
the birds wear ankle boots
the birds are full of echoes
their eggs roll endlessly from their little hearts

slowly I climb the milepole
I put my eggs in the treeholes of the milestones.

Yet his poetry is also filled with *angst.*

Writing about the "inner language," Arp wrote: "The vertical and the horizontal are the extreme signs available to men for touching the beyond and his inwardness." Here he is close to his friend Kandinsky, who in his book *Concerning the Spiritual in Art* wrote of the need for the spiritual in painting that will let artists express their own inner lives in abstract, non-material terms.

When writing of Kandinsky's art, Arp applied the laws of Heraclitus to Kandinsky, who echoes his own belief that "It is always the same substance that is in all things: life and death, waking and sleeping, youth and old age. For, in changing this becomes that, and that, by changing becomes this again."

"Star-in-Boots," written in Alsatian Latin in 1925, was published in the review *de Stijl*, edited by van Doesburg. It begins and ends on a sound poem interspersed with the fully intelligible lines. It is a collage poem. This poem shows Arp in search of an original universal language that would know neither borders nor nationalities, and would need no translation—only we might acknowledge an inner profound acceptance of the needs of language.

He once said, "a word is fresher to me in French. I know German so very well, ever since school, but French, which I have always spoken, feels like a discovery."

Here we are listening to the two Arps—Hans or Jean—the two first names representing the dual nationalities of Arp who was born in Strasbourg in 1887. His father was from Schleswig-Holstein and his mother was Alsatian. And to further confuse his identity he grew up speaking three languages: French, German, and Alsatian. The latter he learned from his cradle, because it is not a written language, and because it existed in such a loose, such a free style, a word-of-mouth language. He incorporated Alsatian into his early poems, phonetically or in Latinese.

naurulam catapult i lem lem
haba haba tapam

his language broke in his mouth
(from "Star-in-Boots," 1927)

Arp longed for a communion of artists who would participate in collective works of art and writing, in which individual personalities submerged while enriching the whole. This is a Bauhaus concept and today it is as if he had described a lost world of idealism. We must remind ourselves that those combined talents were not lost, or swallowed up, but were the incarnation of a group of intensely gifted artists in which the Bauhaus was their collective shrine to the arts.

Arp declared a spiritual dedication to the selflessness which was represented by the Bauhaus and he knew that attitude would enrich art. It is possible that his birth in a "collective place," Alsace, a place where several languages passed on the way to their native tongue, may have contributed to Arp's desire for a collective "one-voiced" art.

Poetry was a continual "work in progress" to Arp, never ended, never completed. Although his poetry appears spontaneous, it went through constant changes and drafts. Even poetry that had been published twenty or thirty years before. Oppositions balance, then contradict one another.

Do you like
the clouds bare
or
covered with plumage?
the night doesn't care about the sky, it saws
the ceiling
in half
the sky doesn't care about the night, it saws the floor
in half.

The *Cloud Pumpe* poems were composed around 1911 and were read at Dada evenings where Hugo Ball performed sound poetry in Cubist costume. When tired of political manifestoes and endless discussions, Dadaists listened to Arp's *Cloud Pumpe* poetry.

The edition of the *Petit Larousse* defines Dada: "One may consider Dada as the most extreme limit of the possible divorce between words and their meanings."

The *Cloud Pumpe* poems tell how Arp was born in five places.

He was born in the cosmos—a Cloud
in nature
in a pumpe (the mechanical world)
in a skirt (the maternal world)

These poems have a navel which is attached to these worlds—here Arp began his almost obsessive preoccupation with the navel, which appears in both his sculpture and his poetry.

There is a relationship between the poems in *Cloud Pumpe* of 1917, and his relationship between the poems in *papier déchirés*, "torn-up paper." In these later compositions he "gave free rein to reality and chance." He said that "if you tear up a piece of paper or a drawing, you let in the very essence of life and death."

Arp made many experiments. He was so visual that he declared he saw poems jump from the page! We have a sense always in reading the poems of Arp that they are going to leave us and enter a spatial world where they belong.

He used every "found object," and what he didn't find on the street or in the newspapers, he invented.

He adored senseless jokes, finding in them what he called "profound reality."

When he settled in Paris in 1925 and met the Surrealists, he began writing directly in French. He mentions this period in a poem: "In those years I wrote my first poems and my genius finally manifested itself regardless of my neighbors." His wife, or companion, as he called her, Sophie Taeuber-Arp, is an artist of talent and originality, whom he met in 1915. Arp said, "it was Sophie Taeuber, who through her clear life showed me the right way, the way of beauty."

The influence is found in many places—his sculpture is copied when a sculptor has need of a brief curve in the axis of the work, and despite the usual product of a craft, desires to reach into the modern. Many times in commercial manufacture, the short-cut is a glance at the sculpture of Arp, this desire for a geometric brevity. In poetry when there is the well hidden, the need for light to finger the open spaces of a poem.

Arp said, if, to suppose the impossible, he had to choose between the visual arts and the poetry of words, if he had to abandon sculpture or poems, he would choose to write poems. In the most difficult hours of his life, he tells us, he turned to poetry.

A year before his death in 1966, he published "The Dream Captain's Logbook," in which he discloses his pessimism about the development of modern man and the modern world.

The dream captain is
at the end of the road.
He wonders who am I?
Where do I come from?

Leatrice Rose

As mysterious as a herd of animals galloping across a moonlit landscape is the interior of a silent room attached to its inescapable voyeur, the artist. Here the stage only appears to be domestic. Upon it a drama of exacting dimensions is waged between the eye and its object. The overexposure of what is considered elsewhere as impassioned painting, with its inclusion of anguished figures who survive in under-delineated space or that use of over-decorated space which attempts to survive without expression, has left these provocateurs unprepared for quiet rooms which impose their own reign of terror on the artist. Craftmanship, sensibility, and above all, experience are at the gallows. Leatrice Rose, in her exhibition at the Armstrong Gallery, has brought a dazzling vocabulary of weapons to prove the impregnability of the silent room.

When she was a student at Washington Irving Art School, her teachers gave her an ultimatum: "You've just got to be a painter." Rose was in delighted agreement and after graduation she went on to study at Cooper Union. Recognizing the new directions that were being revealed to artists of her generation, she enrolled in Hans Hofmann's classes from whence she departed a confirmed Abstract Expressionist, or so it would seem from the painting she then produced and exhibited. Tom Hess, who kept watch over the spawning Hofmann students, recognized her as a gifted exponent of Abstract Expressionism.

In these youthful, rapt days Rose believed that abstract painting (or the form which presented itself under the tutelage of Hofmann) was the only choice through which a breakthrough could be reached into a new concept of form. "Boundlessness" beckoned to her, as to so many of her generation. We see a restless progression of pictures until there begins a subtle entrance of what would be a seated figure, then another; they press their image into expressionist technique. Perhaps the domestic tableaus of her life prompted her abstract, subjective painting into the real-life contours of children and the rooms in which a city life was enacted. A vision of the life-like was riding into abstraction. Slowly it arrived.

There appeared the seemingly meek portraits of a painter's daily motions: the palette, the easel, the window, the chair, the floor line, domestic alterations of landscape. Through abstraction she had arrived at what we choose to call realism (or so it appeared). If we study closely what would be the beginning of this realism, we discover that Rose is not an orthodox representationalist but is very close to Cubism in these realistic paintings. She presents us with ideas of forms, ideas of stationary objects which have an essentially Cubist sense of design that betrays her early, seasoned training. As Willem de Kooning remarked, "When I was a classical painter, that is when I was a Cubist . . ." Rose's realistic paintings are classical in that their underground is Cubist, the mind's eye of contemporary art.

This exhibition marks a progression from 1973 toward a more forceful declarative statement of her arms. That softness which preceded (the blurred edge, the hints, only hints always of the landscape as in time) has disappeared. Inside an earlier tenderness of line, there was often experienced a nudging, sheltered silence. The silence remains, but in back of it, bolstering it up, is a shout.

Like any gifted artist, Rose is a person who has what in opera is known as *temperament*. In the 1970s and before, she used muted colors: grays (she is a master of the use of that difficult Ingres color), soft yellows, fainter ochres. Exhibiting consistently from 1973 to 1985, and likely abetted by her teaching position at the Art Students League, the coolness and detachment gradually have removed themselves. This exhibition is her strongest statement to date. It is a synthesis of the early and late. There is, as always, but now more consistently, a display of technique that is virtuoso. In *Summer Stripes* it would be an error to see the carefully positioned objects, the definitive stripes of the curtains, as an arrangement.

This painting is a study in ideas, an attempt to get behind the arrangement. She is willing both to abstract herself from the picture and to lean upon the personal stratagems arising from her awareness of the depth of painting. All these pictures are painting about the art of painting.

Water Frost is visually the most unproblematic and pleasing of the paintings. This picture has a quality of that sublimeness earlier associated with that "boundlessness" of abstraction. It is a complicated painting rendered easy, a view that doesn't brood, as if one took the mood out of Whistler's views of the lower Thames, the harshness out of the Hoboken waterfront, a way of turning the unnatural into nature.

The most startling picture is *Black Counter.* Here the artist judged her risks. The counter faces a painting of what appears to be a view of city wharves nearly eclipsed by an extraordinary Ryderesque sky. The counter is black; on it is a dark siphon bottle. Placed on a wooden stool which stands shortly below the counter is a vase holding feathery flowers; upon this stool is draped material with stripes. The lower left section of the painting is devoted to the puzzling arabesque of an iron stool. The bare bones of its iron seat would have charmed Max Ernst. Thus several paintings exist here within one painting. *Black Counter* astonishes me.

This is a daring work by an artist whose essential stance toward her paintings led us to believe she would never permit her pragmatism to be outweighed by the mystical. That she is matter-of-fact, dispossessed of any awe, her intensity leashed, surprises us, revealing a sensibility that is not altogether what it had seemed to be.

Today, Leatrice Rose, continuing as always to take matters into her own hands (the picture never runs away from her), may have decided quite objectively to permit her surprises to reveal themselves. There is more than a hint in this exhibition that having proved once again her control over her environment, she will let in strange airs and noises. In *Summer Stripes* we are permitted to look through a screened door upon a suspiciously lighted garden. Nature itself can become wickedly strange, Rose is saying to us. It may elude the grasp of dogmatism and lie beyond our personal projection of the real into the unknown of the surreal.

Observation, concentration, and candor are rarities at any time. In this exhibition Rose decided to wear her coat of many colors (projectile colors and those unabashedly hiding their subtleties), announcing more firmly than ever before their objectives, and leading us further into an unprotected, ambitious future.

June Felter

This retrospective of June Felter's work from the 1960s gave us a privileged view of the painting of an artist whose work came to flower during the heyday of Bay Area figurative painting. The show also understood the tactical error committed by not including her in the exhibition of Bay Area Figuration currently launched on a national museum tour (*Art in America*, Nov. 1990): Felter represents the movements in one of its most lucid, glowing aspects, and she certainly holds her own in the company of Park, Diebenkorn, and Bischoff.

Girl Reading, from Felter's 1963 period (well represented here), shows her painterly sensitivity; in this work, as elsewhere, she maintains an impressive control over detail, lavishing paint upon certain areas, while never permitting them to overwhelm the large composition. Felter possesses an inborn fluency that is particularly evident in the reach of her color. Fluency, of course, may be the distinguishing characteristic of Bay Area painting, but Felter takes it a step further than many of her peers: she never stops to "stage-direct" a given picture. This is not quasi-narrative painterly choreography.

In the smaller acrylic paintings also presented here she uses paint as if it were watercolor—giving it a commensurate speed and luminosity. In fact, it is to be noted how very much at home she is in these quotidian studies, giving their surfaces an authority that transcends their ostensibly mundane subject matter. The faces in the subjects in *Woman in Blue* and *Man with White Hair* are built up in a way we associate with David Park—that is, color glows through successive layers. Felter's work is tactile in a possessive manner; "I have so intimately touched this," she seems to be saying, "that it belongs to me." In this respect *Ironing* is one of the stars of the show. The ironer's simple dress, with its many ranges of color and layered white, suggest a Degas dancer's tutu. The painter does not glamorize her subject to the point of forgetting the concentration demanded by the task depicted. The woman's dress, in its nest of color, is pushed up against the ironing board, and, as she presses down upon her iron, we are aware of the weight brought to bear in the process. This implied identification of the artist with her subject is obviously instinctive; it brings a poignant new dimension to the painting.

These and other strategies of observation consistently concern themselves with a domestic circle—family, friends—pursuing daily life. Not surprisingly, Felter has been criticized (like Berthe Morisot) for being a painter of the "bourgeois" scene. This tarnished attitude has no relevance. This is good painting.

Memorial Service for Tibor de Nagy

I regret very much not being able to be with you, but, poems in briefcase, I am traveling across the same ocean that brought Tibor to us.

For a very long time Tibor has been part of my life in New York. Whole eras of my life have been connected to the Tibor de Nagy Gallery. Poems I have written have been connected to this gallery with the personage of Tibor, sometimes recalled as entering and disappearing, as (not true) overwhelmed by the larger presumptive figure of John Myers. Tibor filling in the background, lending the gallery or the party his elegance, establishing another air, another climate with his dignity and laugh.

In these last few years I often felt summoned by that person behind the large handsome desk who would be sitting inside a separated space in the gallery, a place occupied by his memories. I am so happy he would share those memories with me: Hungary, the villa, the paintings, the books, the sister, the pictures on the walls that needed to be brought here, his wife, his very accurate memories of a place and time foreign to me and which I was eager to enter and which he was pleased to share. He brought to my life his memories and I consumed them. They became part of the myths I gathered.

And when he came to my house in this last year of visiting Southampton, how pleased I was when he settled himself and said how much he liked being in my house. I preened myself on this because, dwelling on his memories of life in a foreign capital, I had appropriated those memories for my house, so it has become more interesting with his memories added to it. Perhaps this is why, glancing around at my rooms, he thanked me with a certain emphasis, for his visit.

It is difficult for me to believe he is not in the gallery that bears his name, sitting at his antique desk.

Mary Abbott

This collaboration on paper was made in the Southampton, Long Island, New York, studio of Mary Abbott in 1971. I had recently returned from Greece, and we were in her huge studio above the little ponds and reeds that led to the sea in Southampton. I was attempting to describe the ar-

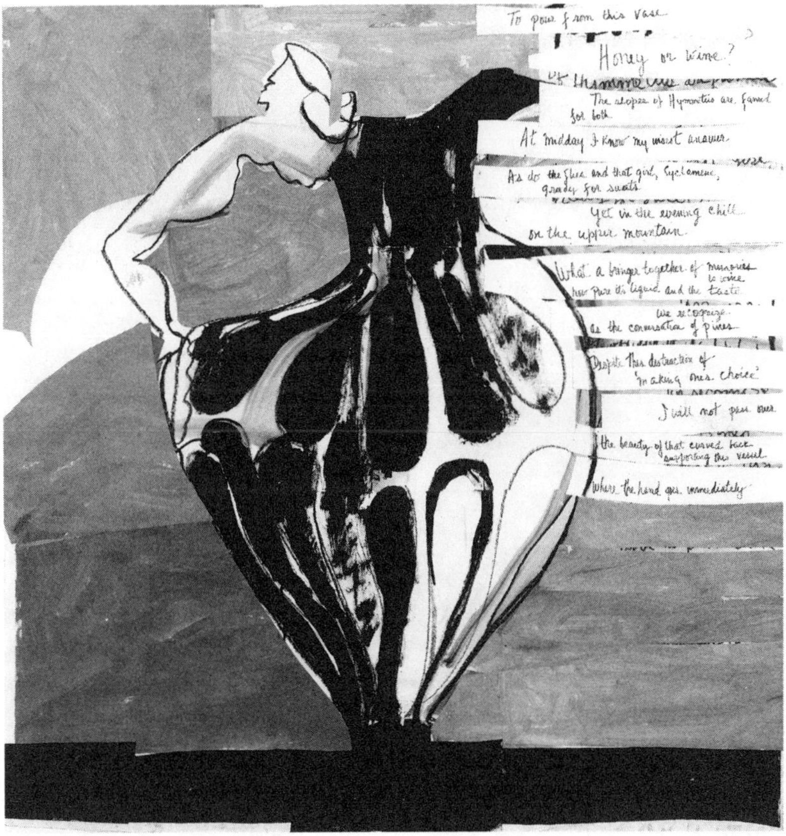

Barbara Guest and Mary Abbott, *Honey or Wine?* (1971), gouache, acrylic, graphite, Conté crayon, collage on paper, 71 × 68 ⅝ in. Smithsonian American Art Museum, Washington, DC.

tifacts I had seen in Greece, and to convey an atmosphere of the Greek Islands I had absorbed.

As Mary's trapeze swung on the rafters above us, she brought out several art books on Greece, in particular one of vases, and the black surface of Greek mirrors. For weeks she drew and I wrote, and together we created our own artifacts.

She drew the vase, and then she asked me to write a poem about the vase. Looking at the vase prompted me to suggest she attach strips of paper, that she "collage" the sides of her drawings, by cutting out strips of paper on which I would write parts of a poem which she could then attach to the drawing. We called our collaboration *Honey or Wine?*

I preferred this invention, rather than writing a lone poem "about" the vase. I wished the poem to look as if it were attached to the vase, as the studio had now become attached to a foreign surface. By now there were several of our personally crafted works, even paintings with poems inscribed on them.

It was a year in the history of American Art when artists and poets responded to, and were encouraged by, the enormous activity in the arts that surrounded them.

H.D.

The Intimacy of Biography

Since the completion and publication of my biography of H.D., I now realize that I have been seeking that special state of grace I had experienced while writing this book, and this has departed with the disappearance of H.D. and her companions from my immediate life. I reach out in search of that powerful light, or that sombre candle that lit the landscape of my own life as I struggled through the successive vales of a heretofore unchartered realm.

In 1971 I was quite innocent of those plans and charts a biographer must consult. To speak plainly I did not know how to write a biography. I had no training as a graduate student or an academic attached to research. One day travelling with the biographer of Margaret Mead on a bus to our country retreats, indeed they were retreats as I shall attempt to explain, Jane Howard and I compared the difficulties of our separate endeavors. "How did you get into this?" asked Jane. My answer was as simple as her blunt question, and we found ourselves in complete agreement with it: "I didn't know any better."

I had commenced with a memory of a conversation in which H.D. had been the subject. That was the root, long neglected. The conversation had taken place many years ago, yet it echoed in my unconscious. This person who had talked so lovingly of H.D. was the only one I had met who had ever known the poet whom I had read while at the university. An intimate detail related to H.D. was the first literary gossip of her past that brushed me. I withheld that memory, stored it for years. And one fine day that memory came alive when for all those reasons so precious and secret to the unconscious the idea of writing a biography of H.D. presented itself to me. The idea had arrived and taken me unawares as if from the shadows of a dream. H.D. would have understood and welcomed this phantom arrival of herself. Even now, more experienced and alert to providence and its mercurial bounty that both gives and takes away, I am convinced that what occurred was "meant to be." From the start I was most fortunate. The private papers of H.D. were placed at my disposal. Events and people suddenly and obligingly presented themselves from out of the vast mystery that was the life of H.D. They beckoned to me and made themselves available. I began as a "shy" researcher. I became a "greedy," a "feasting" one, a voyeur of sights and sounds I had never expected. I was an intruder often exhausted, many times jubilant, and finally after several years I permitted myself to acknowledge that I had become a biographer. I knew too many secrets of the court not to be given that title.

The biographer's path is perilous. Victoria Glendinning, whose progress as a biographer has turned her into one of the wisest and most assured, has written that the biographer is expected to walk between the daily littleness of a subject's life and the inflation of a writer's life into myth. She asks if the task of the biographer is to be the selector of elements significant and fabulous upon which ancestor-worship is based. That is to say that the subject of a biographer for many persons is like a classical god who has left traces on earth. Is the biographer one who leads these people to the sacred shrine? Does the biography provide a role-model for aspiring modern women who believe that a dead but immortal author holds the key to the mystery of life, and is this biographer expected to allow them a closer view of the sources of creativity? I asked myself was I expected to lead the chosen, as Glendinning had termed them, to the pantheon? Is a biographer the sacred keeper of a mythology? A more modest view presented itself. Is not a biography read, as Glendinning proposes, by a person who habitually reads biography rather than fiction because of a hunger for the pattern and texture of lives simply as lives, just as much as from a need to move closer to the flames of creativity?

Virgil Thompson said to me when I questioned him about H.D., whom he had briefly known in Paris in the 1920s: "The important thing is that you must tell the truth." That answer might mean ascribing to the school of "warts and all." Searching among the paraphernalia of what became a biographer's lumber room, it was forced upon me that I was living not exactly with a goddess, or even always a heroine, but with a human being who was rooted also deeply in what is known as "the little life," that of clothes, money, meals, family, love affairs. I recognized then that it was entirely possible that I might write the sort of book which makes some critics cringe and scream (particularly among the male critics) "don't tell me what kind of tea cups H.D. used, I want to know why and how she wrote! I want meaning! The devil with the woman!"

I desired, I say this now somewhat sadly, everything. I wanted meaning, but I also wanted to see my subject plain. All I knew was that I definitely did not subscribe to the mythology school. I knew that I was going to eschew textual criticism. That is not a biographer's job. I was in search of intimacy, not ancestor worship.

Let us leave me and my dilemma and return to the originally described state of grace. I have written a poem I called "Biography" in which I give indications of what the atmosphere of the Beinecke Library at Yale was like during my tenure there among the H.D. papers. It was a region I inhabited for what often seemed an eternity. It is there that the papers, letters, journals of H.D. repose. It is there that the correspondence between H.D. and her companion of a lifetime, Bryher, is deposited. Those precious letters were, before my time, unheard from, unseen, slumbering, unread. They were given into my sole safekeeping. I trembled sometimes as I turned over those intimate pages. I was informed by the strict ruling of the library that my notations from the letters must be in pencil. Then as I graduated into the confidence of the library I was permitted to type my notes. On no occasion was I permitted to xerox these letters.

I lived during the antediluvian state of H.D. scholarship. Today under a more lenient administration, eager students and researchers are permitted to rush in and xerox willfully those once-sacrosanct pages. They may even photograph. Under this more relaxed regime, amid their xeroxed pages, I wonder if they realize they are missing the pungent smell of pen or personal typewriter on the author's page. The lovely, secret wall the researcher and subject begin to build, a wall so intimate, so private, it is made to exclude the outside world. Because time is so important, you must be chary of your notetaking and extremely selective. You must catch the original writer off guard. This would be impossible if another machine interposed. The writer would retreat; an ugly xeroxed blur would send her rushing off, back to her closet. The moment once announced would never return. How could it, lost as it would be amid the jumble of hundreds of unreflected words?

I am of the blasphemous opinion that the word processor, however necessary, can be also a falsifier of memory. I cherish those moments in my cottage, what Perdita dotingly called my "shack," and what I named "the Villa of H.D.," when I would call to the next room to my visiting assistant—and I must add there are too few days when answers come from the next room—"On what page did I write such and such?" And the reassuring voice would answer with the page number. It is the reassurance of another's presence that one needs during the lonely work. Can such warmth and human frailty be returned from a machine? Perhaps so, and perhaps the "frailty" I have mentioned is mine solely. I know, however, I would miss the trappings of an atmosphere I have described.

I have indulged myself in such revelations of research with their scenic backdrops, because I believe these costumes, these trappings, curtains, windows, make the beginnings of what is known as the "identification with the subject." Blanche Wiesen Cook wrote about this identification in "Biographer and Subject: A Critical Connection." According to Dr. Cook, the best biographies come out of an intense identification between biographer and subject.

Dr. Cook and I have discussed this situation. She recently confided to me that, among others, she was also referring to me when she wrote of the intensity of this identification. Near neighbor, she had watched my various psychic crises and compared them with her own experience as a biographer. While writing about Crystal Eastman, who died of nephritis, Blanche suffered a psychic nephritis as intense and painful as if it were not false. In my own absorption with H.D., I too had begun to assume some of her characteristics. A more deliberate association was made when a person quite close to H.D. told me that she was the most selfish person he had ever known. I decided to practice my own brand of selfishness. I knew that selfishness is not necessarily a pejorative term when used in the context of a creative person. A hearty selfishness is needed to complete as much work as H.D. had undertaken. Divine selfishness accompanies the act of divine creativity. Such a wart viewed in a biography can be a sign of distinction. Failure in personal relationships sometimes indicates a growth in a creative relationship between pen and page. Distance can denote concentration, not necessarily always a self-centered retreat into the ephemeral.

H.D. lived constantly as witness to the variability of her mental weather.

She watched the fluctuations of her private barometer. She concentrated so consistently on her hourly weathervane that I came to realize that her biographer must also permit this concentrated observance to enter into the biography. She was exceedingly brave for all this self-imposed suffering. A nosebleed caused her agonies of apprehension, and I believed that in order to chart her course one must also chart her complaints. I suffered along with her. More amusingly, H.D. was a bad speller and a worse punctuater. My punctuation had never been a fine point, but in the process I lost a natural ability to spell.

Now what were the joys of a biographer? I mentioned the state of grace. For me, after the primary research had been completed, I was enriched by an oddly related, if peripheral, reading of books—what some would call unnecessary reading, "plowing through," as one reviewer remarked, "all those tedious books." I never found them tedious. They were the markers lying on a detective's trail. There was the thrill of catching the unexpected scent. As everyone who writes biography learns, part of the work is detection. There is research, detection, introspection, intuition, identification; there is much mulling. One is also a haunted being. I woke up one night and saw H.D. standing at the foot of my bed. I still believe this. Another night in a dream I heard Bryher say, "Beware the Jester." The next morning, like an obedient Freudian, indeed as H.D. had taught me, and remembering her mornings at Küsnacht after her night dreams, I listened to what might have been the association or the play on words of "jester." In this replay I heard "Guest-her." Ever the guardian, Bryher was still up to her tricks of keeping H.D. safe.

There is a passionate absorption, more passionate and more sensitive because one knows—although sometimes in the midst of the welter when indecision and fatigue wave their banners and then the nudging doubts—there awaits the delicacy of the leave-taking. How one fears both its arrival and the suggestion that it might never take place. A physician said to me, "I know what the letters H.D. stand for. They stand for Have Done." Everyone wanted me to make haste to finish my task. You've spent years! they would shout.

And there I remained with all my correspondents. My new pen pals. Few I would ever meet. Some, blessedly, I would come to know. These people, along with such a major literary personage as Ezra Pound, formed a world that was more real to me than my so-called real life. One has to live in isolation, ideally in the country, ideally weather-bound with a good fire in winter, or a shy air-conditioner in summer, then a few considerate friends, to be able to endure the hazards of biography. One needs home comforts to outweigh the physical and emotional constraints. These are ideal circumstances I admit, and they are what I remember as the goodness of life and for which I helplessly seek, now that Persephone has gone underground.

While I was writing this biography I was living with other generations than mine, among memorabilia, furniture, clothes, conversations, affections, even continents that had existed in the past. I was discovering that in a biography everything you find or touch or see out of the corner of your eye is new to you. Because it is new, you must continually be sorting, finding new uses for your discoveries within the pattern which you are weaving. And just as the material was new to me, so did my days have a freshness to them. During my first year of euphoria, and I will confess that this euphoria did not last out my final chapter, the weather had a special sparkle. I looked at nature, birds, the sand on the beach with the eye of rejuvenescence. Wasn't I, after all, in search of a form of rejuvenation? The lost youth, the lost womanhood of the writer, H.D.

Another photograph would arrive, this from a friend of the son of Frances Gregg, the early love of H.D., and as her life remained so fixed in time for H.D., perhaps her only love. And there was Frances who appeared in H.D.'s books and letters. That is what she looked like! The Beinecke Library had no photograph of her. Later I received a revealing and interesting letter from Frances's son bringing his mother back to life. Frances who had been such a mystery. It has been remarked that in my book the photographs of H.D. are eclipsed by those of the people who surrounded her. I displayed her beauty through the successive stages of her life. I may have believed wrongly that it was the turn of others, that those who had reveled in her life should also be given their turn to reveal themselves. I wished to be cinematic rather than schematic. H.D.'s was a face that once seen cannot be forgotten. I can see her reflection today in the visages of her grandchildren, and suddenly a bend of the head, an eye cast downward in that of her daughter, Perdita, and when I listen to her I believe I hear H.D.'s voice.

Frances had showed up circumlocutiously, even as she does in H.D.'s novel *The Usual Star*, where she rings the bell, uninvited, in the late evening. She came via a bookseller in London who put me in touch with Kenneth Hopkins, the biographer of John Cowper Powys (an author now seeing a revival here and in Britain, and a man who had remained close to Frances), who put me in touch with Frances's son, Oliver Wilkinson. That is how it goes. I had originally picked up the scent of Powys when Donald Gallup, then Curator of the American Collection at the Beinecke, in the midst of a conversation in his office suddenly, and with a casualness suggestive of his perspicacity, asked me what I thought of the writing of Powys. I picked up the scent there, but I only acted on it weeks later in a New York library when I began to read the Hopkins biography of Powys, the letters, etc., the so-called "tedious" reading. Detection. Any biographer's tale. Not only was I rewarded with the fresh story of Frances and her portrait, there is now a friendship with her son. And then it continues to the agent, Gerald Pollinger, Lawrence's agent, with whom I had much entertaining correspondence, with whom I shared Lawrence gossip when in London and the ridiculous notion of Lawrence as the father of Perdita. And so it continues. One day at the Beinecke.

A biographer's nights are lonely even in the land of euphoria. I sometimes wrote in the evenings to James Laughlin of New Directions, and he would answer me throughout the writing of the book with his immense knowledge of Pound and his interest in H.D. as her publisher. Then I would follow Perdita back and forth in her large country house with my wispy necessary questionings, days as well as evenings. I was not trained as a journalist. With Perdita, I understood that I should catch a tone of voice, a sudden allusion, I should listen to her laughter and her confessional, shy answers. And always the subtle irony, the bits of gossipy human talk, dressed at times in exceptional sophistication. There was Silvia Dobson, whose name I kept finding at one point in the H.D.–Bryher correspondence and who I finally located outside of Santa Barbara. We met only once, yet we corresponded for the duration of the book and even thereafter. She became an invaluable ally. She posted me much of her collection of H.D. letters. Yet she would never have arrived on my horizon had I not idly wondered while reading the letters, who is Silvia? Such are the mysteries, the suppers and wines enjoyed by a biographer.

Far different from the life of a poet or novelist. All those real people! Life. Not made-up invented life. Real life.

H.D. reflected much on her youth in America when she was an expatriate living in Switzerland and London. The Pennsylvania countryside repeats itself in her letters. And in her poetry. Her early poems, the poems of Imagism and the ones that made her famous as *H.D., Imagiste*, are often located in the Pennsylvania of her youth, even though she lends these poems a classical air.

During World War II, she wrote *The Gift*, a book about her childhood in the Moravian community at Bethlehem and later in Upper Darby where her father was Professor of Astronomy at the University of Pennsylvania. Her novelette *HERmione* is about H.D. and Ezra and Frances, but it is also about Philadelphia and its houses, and it reconstructs Philadelphia before the first World War. Although she lived in a house in which there were brothers and a married brother and wife, a preoccupied father and harried mother, there is still in this house time for thought, for consideration of herself, her dreams, her relationship with the household, and there are always moments to look out the window. Also time for H.D. to be a bit spoiled, the only girl in a household of brothers. And there was the leisurely, if unusual, courtship with Ezra and rides over the countryside, pauses in which she listened to Ezra Pound explain literature and life.

It was Pound who separated her from Bryn Mawr. Those are H.D.'s words, but they are the words a biographer would have chosen. She was grateful to Pound in many ways, but she never forgave herself or, as a consequence, Pound for separating her from Bryn Mawr. She was grateful to Pound for taking her away from what might have become a more ordinary, a more domestic life among friends and kin, for the part he played in her decision to transplant herself to Europe. She was grateful to him for discovering her as a poet, for introducing her to the applause of a public. But she admitted that she paid a heavy price for this. After her abrupt departure from Bryn Mawr—and we have to face it, she did not go on to graduate from that college—H.D. considered herself a failure. She wrote that she became an "outcast" in the eyes of her family, and in her own eyes. I don't believe she ever got over this early sense of having failed family and college, for her upbringing had a puritanical form.

When she was despondent and lonely in London, she realized that she had led a sheltered life in Upper Darby and at a "select," her word, college. A life she had deliberately discarded. When she was triumphant, she congratulated herself for having had the courage to leave home. And in those days it did take courage to cross the ocean to an alien country. The Atlantic was an estranging sea, and in a physical sense it estranged her forever. Yet not in an interior sense. She held onto every scrap of her memory of America.

"The Philadelphia Academy of Music is pure Vienna," she wrote to Bryher. When describing someone rather upper-class, proper, informed, H.D. would abbreviate, "She is very Bryn Mawr." Into her late life she would make this sort of comment, sometimes even in a pejorative sense. And during the early days of their life together, when Bryher would discuss with authority an unknown America, H.D.'s eyes would flash and she would shout to Bryher to remember: "I am the Statue of Liberty. I set you free . . . free." In turn, like the early Ezra, she would succeed in breaking the chains that bound Bryher to her family and would free her to travel to America.

Her friendship with Marianne Moore, which continued throughout H.D.'s lifetime, was based certainly on a regard for Moore's poetry, but I suspect that there was also a need for the Marianne Moore she had first known at Bryn Mawr as a tie to bind H.D. to her native land. In her letters to Moore, H.D. allows much of herself and her girlish self to escape; she is frank, friendly, respectful, sometimes excited in proffering her knowledge of Europe, her familiarity with its magic to be shared with Moore, even advising her to come to Europe to benefit from its culture. Advice Moore wisely refused.

I have written in the introduction to H.D.'s biography that I realized in writing of H.D. I must also take a considered look at her companion. I think that is an accurate word, for each set aside a special part of her life and thought for the other. I think Bryher idolized H.D., came to love her with a loyalty that is rare, and later assumed the role of a guardian, a sort of capable relative who took care of the messy, obligatory details of life. Of course in such a definition, I am restricting myself to a brief explanation of two complicated people. I think H.D. chafed under this regime, depended on it, and respected Bryher with the kind of fury one feels towards a person who interferes continually. An ambivalence arises in an area of mutual dependence until it finally resolves into a willing, not grudging, respect. A biographer cannot consider H.D. without Bryher.

I have also described Bryher's kingdom of "Kenwin" in Vevey, Switzerland, on Lake Geneva where H.D. jointly ruled as the "lady of the lake." I interviewed a reluctant Bryher who refused to come to my assistance in my exploration of H.D.'s life, fending off my questions with extraneous remarks. I hope I conveyed a kind of despotic magnetism I experienced in Bryher's presence. I now remember the "bright blue eyes of a child" H.D. has described. I remember Kenwin's lonely, even desolate majesty. The room so frighteningly empty in which H.D. had written her poetry and fiction. Rooms where H.D. had passed her own difficult hours. Absent, indeed, was Bryher's menagerie of house guests and animals.

Today I look at the photographs, Kenwin, once so bravely new in the Bauhaus style as suited writers and their court who were devoted to what Pound has called "making it new." I see the shadow of Bryher in her staunch tailored suit, viewing me from the doorway where she must have admitted those famous ghosts. The tousled shabby furniture of the house. The many, many books.

I dwell on Bryher, because she had been alive and I attempted to speak to her, even if in a meagre fashion. The details of H.D.'s life were not presented, but there is the minor ear and it was busy. H.D.'s ghost was at Kenwin, if not her vibrating presence.

Today Bryher has departed from Kenwin, and her own ghost, separated so long from England for tax purposes, may for all we know be in the Scilly Isles, or Cornwall. The kingdom is emptied. There is no one there to look down from the terrace onto the lake. F. Scott Fitzgerald had found Switzerland a triste place where "there were few beginnings and many endings." In the eighteenth century, it had been popular and Voltaire and Rousseau and Madame de Staël in their varying decades had lived there. Byron and Shelley. I think H.D., and this may be impertinent of me, with her taste for the bizarre, the lively, with dashes of solitude, might have been happier somewhere other than at Kenwin. She found a form of contentment and tranquility in other Swiss environments—Lugano, Lausanne, finally a sanatorium outside Zurich. She was never too venturesome in her locales, yet once she departed Kenwin, she did not choose to return. I hazard that she may have needed a more robust, or a more ordinary abode; she, herself, was extraordinary enough.

Bryher's books have themselves found a new abode. They are now in East Hampton, New York, on Long Island where Perdita has constructed a house for them. It will be a library containing many of the thousands of books that populated Kenwin, a remarkable library with one of its emphases on the twentieth-century novel, others on travel, on history.

Seeking more "biographical" material about H.D., more presences, oddments which I might add to this evocation of H.D., I went to my own boxes, indexes, letters, material I had collected on the H.D. path. They are in my cellar. Standing there in the early spring light of Long Island, I looked at their crisping pages, realizing that these boxes had been my companions through the days and nights of writing a biography. They once were as real as human voices. Now they appeared to be waiting. What could they now tell me? What aroma would they give off of their subject? What was there about H.D. I had not succeeded in defining? Why had a few critics called her presence in her own books and mine, elusive? I would be the person who should be able to answer that. On this first day of spring, 1985, one year from her hundredth birthday, could I define her more fully?

Searching my conscience, the answer is no. A poet's life, like Fitzgerald's rich, is not like that of any other. It is complex where one least expects it, and takes one unawares by its awesome simplicity. A poet's life is built out of the imagination. H.D. was gifted with a strong imagination. How else could she have constructed her Greece, her Egypt, fabrications of the spirit? She imagined herself in many roles. She was temptress, goddess, mother, artist, she was ripe with personalities. There wasn't one line that might draw with ease the entire profile. She was not, as they say, "of a piece."

She did not possess the kind of "humanness" of say a poet like Louise Bogan. H.D. lived a life of many colors. Her companion, Bryher, was unique, was she not? You would have to go far to find someone like Bryher. And H.D.'s personality was fragmented as an expatriate in a way that resembled the dualities of other expatriates, Djuna Barnes or Ezra Pound. H.D. was never forced into the world to earn her own living. We must remember this. She evaded that sort of reality. She never kept a domestic hearth. She produced a child, but in the usual definition she never raised this child. After the 1920s, she had little personal contact with literary people of her own generation. She never belonged to a coterie. She never joined a literary set. She did not sign petitions, make contracts. With two major exceptions—a wartime "Reading of Famous Poets" in London, attended by royalty; and in 1960, when she was presented the Gold Medal by the American Academy of Arts and Letters—she did not appear on a public platform. She did not attend, in the same year, unable to make two trans-Atlantic trips, the Bryn Mawr presentation of a citation for her contribution to letters. Nor did she engage in literary politics. Her adjunct, Bryher, may have been helpful in that area. Her correspondence, with a few exceptions such as Marianne Moore and Pound, had been with private friends, not literary peers. Horace Gregory, the late noted critic and poet whom I was able fortunately to interview, said that H.D. could never have become a member of an "establishment," literary or otherwise.

And she preferred it that way. She wanted to be left alone to weave her private web, just as she made her tapestries in her own room with their isolated romantic echoes. She wished to live in an imagination peopled mostly with figures of the past, reliving her memories as fiction. She never swigged away at a bottle or got drunk in a pub; she seldom went to little dinner parties or gossiped with literary pals, although she had a willing ear for gossip. She did not write sad letters to vanished lovers. She does not fit into the pattern of a modern literary lady.

As might be expected of her, the people in whom she most closely confided were her psychiatrists, with whom she shared, with the exception of Freud, relationships that bordered on close friendship. In my book, I emphasized her need for psychiatrists, and it is a pity we do not have their files, because they loom so frequently in her life and in her work and in her letters to Bryher. These were the ones whom she may have visited, let us suppose, propelled by a persistent need to talk about herself, and because she could not communicate so privately with others, including the cosmopolitan group with whom from time to time she consorted.

Now to return to my role as a biographer. I decided not to take the usual tack of biography. I would follow the wind where it went or where it lay. As my character practiced an indirection, so would my method. Instead of a privileged narrative, I decided to present material in a form which asked each reader to participate actively by synthesizing the narrative according to the personal determinant of the reader. I was not going to present a formal narrative line. The line would be moving and interchangeable, hopefully, within time. I wanted a chronology to be a viable aid, the way I believed it to be "in real life." I was at risk. I knew that a moveable chronology goes against a consistently taught and expected formula. But life is not linear. It shoots about, takes unexpected turns, goes the other way with its own firmness.

My problem, if one wants to call it a problem, my delight, my challenge, was to write a book about a woman who was not a heroine, a figure of hieratic measure, but a poet. As I have written, early on I made the decision as much as possible to avoid tactical literary criticism. Yet I recognized that my reader would want to know about a writer's life as a writer. I decided to involve this reader in the conditions that prompted the work. Thus I would set a stage. There is the writer up bright and early, at her desk, as was H.D.'s habit (after a thoughtful, lingering breakfast). Robert McAlmon called her a "workhorse." Well, what happens now? Do I say, there is Hilda writing furiously at her new poems? Does she stride around the room? Does she shout at Bryher to be quiet? Do I comment: "Here is the remarkable old workhorse out eating her oats and climbing into harness before that delightful colt has stretched his legs?" You simply do not have in the case of H.D. enough definitive information, such as that supplied by the journals of Woolf in which each working day is related with all its struggles. "The Hirslanden Notebooks," written in later life, are the nearest we come to a journal, and these I employed. I found throughout my writing that, for reconstruction, I needed to rely on invention and intuition.

What I attempted to convey were the mental processes of H.D. Flowing above and underneath, emerging in sudden streams of the unconscious, they set the circumstances of her work. Then I viewed the physical circumstances under which she wrote. This category was alive with people, travel, housing, etc. I even gave the reader a real picture of her little desk, a picture rescued from oblivion in a house in England. I wanted the H.D.

of my book to shiver and exult and celebrate as I believed she did. After which, given the largely hypothetical concept of the unconscious of H.D., together with the factual circumstances of her life, the reader could then synthesize another model conformative to that reader's own conception of H.D. That is what readers do anyway, regardless of my "structuralist" modeling.

Now that I reconsider books about poets, *The Stricken Deer*, a life of William Cowper by Lord David Cecil, the utter charm and poetic investment of that book--what do we see and hear finally: Cowper spitting grapes, his nurse knitting, madness approaching. Or the immense economy with which Dr. Johnson maneuvers his *Lives of the Poets*, his great intelligence letting nothing slip through his fingers, what do we have? A sense of the past, major and minor poets moving against a background in which social and economic attitudes finally emerge stronger than the poetic line.

I have learned through a process of grievous enterprise that although the biography is published, the poet's private chamber remains securely fastened. The muse, the sacred muse is permitted to hover, yet her classic beauty can only be glimpsed; her garments float, they do not rest.

To return to the mundane world of my cellar where rest the H.D. boxes. I was looking for an admirable essay on the art of biography written by James Atlas about 1978 when I began my fledgling writing on H.D. As I recall, I tacked his words to my forehead and convinced myself that I would adhere to his principles. He wrote about the ideal biography. It was so ideal that I don't believe it ever existed. I certainly never achieved this method nor did I punish its vicinity. But I believed at the time in what Mr. Atlas wrote and I do to this day, but I can't find his article and regrettably I have forgotten his words.

The biographer in the intimacy of the study, or on a rushing vehicle, in the middle of anywhere, anything, receives very little help from the outside. I do not mean there are no judicious editors or homeside critics or thoughtful assistants. I mean that despite the vast amount of biographies of the past, or immediate present, no matter how many one had read, admired, and attempted to emulate, alas, one does not succeed in copying or even adapting the style or the content to one's personal method. (I read evening after evening the biographies in my local library and a few made me weep in admiration.) Biography is intimate. It exists between you and your subject. It is an intimate conspiracy, and beware the door to that locked chamber. It is not going to open to a persistent knock. There is no password; there is no final answering voice. You must climb in the window.

"PART FIVE" of *Herself Defined: The Poet H.D. and Her World*

Helen: I never went to Troy. Only a phantom went . . .
Messenger: What's this? Then did we toil in vain there simply
for a cloud?
Euripides, *Helen*

Deep-girdled, the sun in her hair, with that way of standing,
The print of shadows and the print of smiles
On shoulders, thighs and knees,
The lively skin, the eyes and the great eyelids,
She was there, on the banks of a Delta.
And at Troy?

Nothing. At Troy a phantom.
So the gods willed it.
And Paris lay within a shadow as though it were solid flesh:
And we were slaughtered for Helen ten long years.
George Seferis, "Helen" (*Poems*)

Chapter Twenty-Five: Lausanne-Lugano 1947–53

As in 1919 following the Great War, after the Second World War Bryher once again became the preserver of H.D. By the winter of 1946, H.D. felt strong enough to want to strike out on her own. Typically, Bryher set out to help her. She decided that nearby Lausanne was the right-size city. International, with historic associations, it also had the advantage of being a short railway ride from Kenwin. She scouted out what she considered was the most comfortable and suitable hotel for H.D., the Hôtel de la Paix.

In December H.D. moved into this handsome hotel, which is located on the upper slopes of the town, not far from the famed cathedral, in the midst of shops and next to the relaxed and dignified park Mon Repos. H.D. would often go to this park. Mon Repos lives up to its name. It shelters exotic aviaries and quiet paths, one of which leads up to the house in which Voltaire, that hero of Aldington, had lived. Bryher had made a wise choice, as the hotel exactly met H.D.'s needs at the time. She would winter there for the next six years. Bryher was only twenty minutes away, yet she was *away*. H.D. held to the illusion, encouraged by Bryher, that she was on her own and not a dependent. Bryher would make elaborate plans to visit H.D., but only on occasions specified by H.D.

H.D. was sixty. Her beauty was yet more bizarre, the jaw a stricken line, the cheekbones gaunt upon the lean skin. Her eyes, seldom soft, were now Cassandra-like. She looked strange. More than ever she was a woman at whom people would stare on the street. Her wizardry was intact.

Now began the prolific years of H.D.'s life, when she would write her most significant work. She wrote that she agreed with Ellen Glasgow, who has said her life began at sixty. Her productivity would be astounding. She had risen from the grave of the war, from a breakdown so serious as to have required electric shock treatment. An excellent clinic and careful post-treatment care had restored her to the world. From now on there would be no lapses, if she could prevent them, in her schedule. A confidence descended on her—she believed the worst was past; she had survived to live in a place where her work would be nurtured by a conspiring seclusion.

There were no day-to-day domestic problems such as presented themselves at Lowndes Square. H.D. took her meals at the hotel. She also soon found a pleasant café where she could go for her morning coffee while her room was being straightened. She would go down to the port below the town at Ouchy (near the place where once they had made their films) and sit under a marble plaque marking the spot where Byron had sat while composing "The Prisoner of Chillon." In short, she had nothing to occupy herself with except her own writing. All legal and literary details were to be taken care of by Bryher and Pearson. Bryher even busied herself with ordering clothes for H.D. The responsibility of a daughter disappeared with the departure of Perdita for the United States.

A correspondence with Aldington now sprang up. Having left America, he was living in the South of France at Le Lavandou. In 1951 he would move to Montpellier; from there would be a final move to the South of France once more at Sury-en-Vaux. He was just near enough now for H.D. to be aware of his unobtrusive presence; this need became increasingly important to her. Again he was her critic, her friend; the letters began to pass back and forth as if no time or lovers had intervened. Once more they needed one another. Her letters to him illumine her circumstances:

> I am snug enough with old scripts and papers, books, a few friends, the happy sound of tea ships in rain or sun, my eleven o-clock coffee or tea rather a brilliant new Dôme where the music is elegant, candelabra, concealed lighting and masses at present of gladiolus; there were sunflowers and Michaelmas daisies in rotation. There is a really charming shop called Mutrix, with a lively roof, now closed, alas, many bright umbrellas, fish in a pond . . .

Very much a description of a maiden lady's view of paradise, as indeed that section of bourgeois Lausanne still presents.

H.D. was working on "The Sword Went Out to Sea," encouraged by Aldington and Pearson, who believed that it might be the best thing she had written. Aldington suggested that with a few minor changes the book could become a best-seller! He probably based this misjudgment on H.D.'s unreal concept of the book, which shows up in a letter she wrote in January 1947 to Bryher:

> I can not tell you how funny it is, a sort of War and Peace cum the Last Days of Pompeii. It will be one fat Victorian volume, or two or three short or long short novels . . . I am on the second Vol. now I call them WINTERSLEEP AND SUMMERDREAM—sleep and dream and so-called "reality" values contrasted. I did not want to worry you with the war part but later when Cuth [Aldington] sends back the first MSS I will hope that you can find time to read it. It is also the reincarnation but on a rather mosaic of Bulwer L. Pompeii style, scenes with the players at Delhi worked up from my Stratford experiences . . . I just sit down and automatic write. I feel I have a rattling gun in my hands—whatever a rattling gun is. It is a fight to the finish for War and Peace!

H.D.'s wild description is an example of an author's delusion about the written page. "The Sword" was begun on the eve of her breakdown. It is nearly incomprehensible, as Helen Wolff, Bryher's publisher, said (in a conversation with this author) she came to believe when the manuscript was presented to her for possible publication. It is rather like attending one of the London seances. Lord Dowding, here called Lord Howell (although during the war he was Sir Hugh), is one of its heroes, and the story provides a fictional background for his belief in many worlds or "mansions" that presumably dwell beyond our sight. To his credit, Dowding was reluctant to have H.D. publish it, claiming he wished to retain his anonymity.

"The Sword" is a sort of kedgeree of spiritualism that combines H.D.'s concept of Dowding's ideas (based on his book *Many Mansions* and his lectures she had attended in London), in which the dead aviators from World War II continued to remain alive on another plane of existence, together with her own added historical personages, Vikings, Greeks, etc., who enact their fictive lives in worlds heretofore unexplored, outside or beyond the visible. Even Bryher, an opponent of all occult researches, praised it, calling the book not prose, but a series of poems. Honoring the still delicate psychic state of H.D., Bryher may have chosen prudence over criticism. A synopsis of the book is numbing. Those dead Greeks and Vikings are joined by creatures from Oberon's court! So far "The Sword" has remained in its original manuscript form, unpublished. Yet who knows, the world with its rapturous acceptance of extraterrestrial tribunes may now be prepared for H.D.'s earlier servings.

H.D.'s next enthusiasm was for the Pre-Raphaelites. She began to write "The White Rose and the Red." What H.D. really wanted was to concentrate on William Morris, as the Morris table Bryher had bought from Violet Hunt's effects (which had served in the seances) had brought this radiant genius close to her. There was also "the miracle of all that marvelous real Morris period tapestry" that had been purchased. In many ways this Morris period is close to H.D.'s own temperament. Although along with Pound and Eliot she had earlier deserted Dante Gabriel Rossetti as an influence, she had in fact been much influenced by those first purveyors of a contemporary attitude toward art and life, breaking the

Victorian and bourgeois traditions of Edward Burne-Jones and his group. After all, hadn't Rossetti written that "a picture is a painted poem, those who deny it are simply men who have no poetry in their composition"? Rossetti, along with his opium, enjoyed a seance with the spirits. H.D. had probably never read Christina Rossetti's *Goblin Market.* This haunting, even terrifying book of Christina's speaks of hidden worlds without H.D.'s consoling tapestries.

It was the *style* of the Pre-Raphaelites that appealed to H.D., and their Romanticism—she liked their cloudiness, mysticism, concentration of effect. She ignored the Pre-Raphaelite dogmatism, just as rampant as that of the academicians. She was an admirer of Elizabeth Siddal, whom Rossetti had married. Siddal committed suicide; the remorseful poet who helped wreck their marriage had thrown his poems into her grave (although later he retrieved them). The Siddal-Rossetti tragedy appealed to H.D.'s sense of drama.

H.D. while in Lausanne that winter of 1947 asked that two sets of her manuscripts from *Life and Letters Today* be sent her. These would include "Writing on the Wall," her memoir of Freud. She also wanted a pile of notebooks she had written while in Vienna. This request intimated that she wanted to work on some sections of a book she tentatively called "The Professor." H.D. reasoned that she could make use of the material from her private sessions as a patient in a creative way that would keep alive all that Freud had meant to her. Thus began to germinate the "Advent" section of *Tribute to Freud.*

In the spring of 1947 H.D. left Lausanne and moved to the Minerva Hotel in Lugano. This move would initiate a pattern for the next years. So long as she was physically able, she would spend winters in Lausanne and spring and summer in Lugano.

H.D. discovered a Lugano of the imagination. Quoting Petrarch, she wrote to Aldington: "Solitudo transalpina mea jucundissima,"* announcing that she subscribed heartily to these words. She thought Lugano, situated on the lake, was without exception the most beautiful place she had ever lived; she could take long boat trips—more beautiful even than the Nile Valley and the Gulf of Corinth! In praise of Lugano she would cite her

* "The transalpine solitude is most helpful to me."

newly discovered neighbor, Herman Hesse, who loved the place. She now wanted to make translations of his poetry and she needed Schmideberg's help, Bryher's also. It was as if the famous mystic had sent her his blessing for choosing to live in his location. What remains of the translation idea is a poem of Hesse's dedicated to H.D.

Her schedule in Lugano was the same as that in Lausanne: work, posting letters, buying cigarettes and stamps, shopping (she found a "Bloomsbury raffia belt, very V. Woolf"), typing, lunch, then more typing. H.D. was concluding that life was more Greek in Lugano than in Greece. She also had become very India-conscious, and after visiting Campione on the lake was under the illusion that the town of nesting villas was like a Ganges village! Modern Lugano is infested with tourists who, in their haste to reach the gambling casinos, rub off the romance. Yet the site is still beautiful and the hotels retain some of the elegance they once had. Lugano, in a curious way, reflects the Rapallo of Ezra Pound, a combination of provincialism and foreignism, of the rich and the petit bourgeois. H.D. had selected her own place; Lugano was a new "Capri," a Mediterranean town, so she pictured it, yet not too far from the familiar terrain of her earlier Switzerland.

Dorothy Richardson was sent a draft of "The Sword." (Her silence worried and puzzled H.D. Richardson never did comment to her on the book.) Then H.D. completed what she called the "first volume" of "The White Rose and the Red." She had too much material for only one volume and was now considering a second. Although she wouldn't admit it, she had gone too deeply into a subject that would interfere with her other projects, and she soon very sensibly dropped the Pre-Raphaelite book. No matter. She had found as much pleasure in its writing as she did with the needlework of her own tapestry.

Aldington was becoming H.D.'s advisor, just as in their first years together. She had persuaded Bryher to overcome her reluctance to have anything to do with Aldington, and Bryher was now helping him financially. A gift of a secondhand typewriter and much advice went to his daughter, Catha. Bryher, her educational theories still rampant, would have preferred to send Catha to the Sorbonne, inasmuch as Catha had been raised in France. Catha dispensed with this program of Bryher's by marrying a Frenchman in the Camargue, but for some years she was the subject of letters, advice, and money. "Hoping it's enough," H.D. continued to send Aldington cautious sums of money.

In 1949 H.D. was reminiscing about their early days at Mecklenburgh Square, adding that she had always recognized the enormous amount of work Aldington had accomplished. She hadn't minimized it, only she had to do her own work in order to protect herself by keeping "even with Ezra," jostled by her fear of being neglected. Her autobiographical novel had been "on the hob" for thirty years, ever since she had begun to write the story in Cornwall in 1918. She believed, so she told Aldington, that she had written an authentic Lawrence, and it pleased her. The book, which she called "Madrigal," had been rewritten the last summer she was in Vaud (1939).

> I do think I have a very authentic Frederico [Lawrence], and that pleases me as I did not want to let all that go, without a sort of hail and farewell. I did the book the last summer in Vaud, 1939, but I left the Mss there and was about to destroy it with some other old things, but I could not; so I boiled it down and tightened up the last chapters . . .

Aldington in reply mentioned Lawrence, commenting that he was now out of print. It may have been the presences of Lawrence and Aldington that inspired H.D. by 1948 to complete "Madrigal." Yet it was not until 1953 that she got around to sending Aldington her manuscript. His reply was what she wished to hear:

> It is awfully good, Dooley, really good, authentic and concentrated, better than the equivalent chapters in *Aaron's Rod* where Lorenzo was in one of his fits and guying us all.
>
> You bring out splendidly L's mimicry and you were right to do so. It was something much more than monkey tricks, because he could also do it on paper, when it becomes genius. It was that plus his refusal to take people at their own valuation and his seeing through their self-deceptions which made him so hated . . .
>
> I finished reading Madrigal with a temp of about 101 which accounts for the fact that towards the end I found myself rather exhausted, with the intensity of all those self-absorbed emotionalists.

Aldington suggested turning it into a three-act play. He also told her that his secretary, Alister Kershaw, liked it very much. Then with a typical Aldington emphasis, he went on to discuss price and sales.

After considering the manuscript in a cooler fashion, he next wrote her that he thought it far above her other prose. "It seems to me just as well written as Virginia Woolf, much more interesting and 'human' and truly poetical."

Somehow between 1949 and 1951, H.D. found time to write "The Mystery," a story about the early Moravians and their leader, Count Zinzendorf. This story is a lengthy listing of names connected with Moravians, of castles, nuns, sisters, St.-Germain—a story of a religion; yet if read in its natural cadence, it reveals an early development of the form of her later poetry. The story is so personal, involuted, concerned with people unknown who appear as if from out of ancient walls, that there is no way to clarify the tale in a practical way. Yet it has, despite the confusion, H.D.'s distinctive voice. "The Mystery" is a prelude to *Helen in Egypt* and the final *Hermetic Definition*. H.D. had begun to wrap herself in the medium's scarves and veils that would finally assume the visible and craftsmanlike shapes of her last works.

After completing "The Mystery" in 1951, H.D. went to New York to visit her daughter, now Mrs. John Schaffner. When there, her old friend Mary Herr drove her on to Bethlehem. This was a significant return for her, signaling as it did the completion of two books whose tribal center had been Bethlehem. *The Gift* had been her initial confrontation with Moravianism; it had also included an intimate family portrait. "The Mystery" is the echo of another voice, calling ancestors, as later *Helen* would re-create the ghosts of her past and from a foreign city invoke her ancestors.

Perdita had gone to New York City in 1946, where she took out United States citizenship papers. Bryher had urged her to leave Europe, warning Perdita her life could be smothered by herself and H.D. "We would eat you up!" she told Perdita.

In 1950 Perdita married a literary agent, John Schaffner, for whom she had been working. They proceeded to establish the John Schaffner Literary Agency in their home, one of those rare New York City clapboard houses, now a landmark. "Very Olde New York," wrote Bryher to H.D.

The Schaffner household became one of literary enterprise combined with raising a family of four children, born between 1950 and 1960. Children, manuscript reading, and the entertainment of clients were part of Perdita's day. Having assimilated the work habits of her "two mothers," as she would call them, she set aside a period each day for her own writing. Perdita now is called upon to write prefaces to new editions of her mother's books, while she continues with her own writing.

Two of the sons, Valentine and Nicholas, are published authors. The daughter, Elizabeth Bryher, is an artist. Perdita had repeated, remarked H.D. toward the end of her life, the pattern of her own mother, with three boys and a girl. H.D. would now see in the Schaffner household fresh rewards of her own literary creativity. The youngest son, Timothy, wrote on the walls of the third floor shared by the children in their East Hampton, Long Island, country house: "We are the Sitwells of today!"

H.D.'s "solitudo transalpina" in Lugano was sometimes interrupted by visitors from the outer world. Bryher and the Bear, Schmideberg, would visit her, staying at H.D.'s hotel, now the Bristol. They were cautious not to disturb her precious work schedule, but even their presence, though welcome, was an interruption. Around H.D., everyone was inclined to tiptoe. The little maids silently picked up the breakfast tray she had left outside her door. The waiters in the dining room solicitously took her order. Bryher and the Bear mostly kept to themselves, although there were daily invitations to H.D. for walks and meals. Even Perdita's visits tended to throw H.D. off-center. Perdita was solicitous of her mother, almost overly so. Whatever hours or occupations suited H.D., those Perdita would follow. The oracle would speak first; the others would uphold the silence. When beckoned, they scampered; when dismissed, they turned away. What is so astonishing is that H.D. showed no surprise at this obeisance. Her love existed for others but it tended to show its face only when the lady so wished. It was a sublime sort of selfishness, or dedication, to use a gentler word; it brought no alienation from loved ones. The priestess, "sorceress of words," as Isis is called, held within her presence an allure irresistible to mortals.

After the breakfast tray went outside the door, H.D. would go back to bed. Propped up on pillows, she would lie in a half dram for another hour (very like her heroine in "Murex" in the early *Palimpsest*). "I loved this waking dream in the half-stupor of early morning; I was perhaps inclined to over-do this waking-dream state then. I appreciated these little calls, of Bear and Fido but inwardly resented the interruption. I was only half-sorry when they left. I began almost at once, the *Helen* sequence."

In 1948 *The Pisan Cantos* had been sent to her by Ezra Pound's publishers, New Directions. There is no doubt that these cantos were the ferment on both the conscious and the subconscious levels of what would become H.D.'s own book of cantos, *Helen in Egypt*. She wrote to Viola Jordan that she found Ezra's cantos heartbreaking. There were "really more lines of sheer beauty in the Pisan than in any of his work."

The influence of those meetings in the British Museum tea shop would repeat itself in far-off Lugano. The early "Hermes" would change form; *Helen in Egypt* would begin to make herself felt. Ezra's unseen hand would make the corrections on the new page. His genius would challenge her into competition, his evocation of the past would become a lure. If Canto LXXIX refers to H.D. as his "dryad," his "lynx," his attendant at the pools of September (her month), if she was to "guard my vineyard," as she believed the canto indicated, then she must prove herself a worthy inheritor of these duties. (The Pound scholar Wendy Flory does not believe this canto refers to H.D. She accepts the suggestion that Pound is writing about his wife Dorothy Shakespeare.) H.D., although nowhere is there written evidence from her, only innuendoes, must have considered herself the inspiration for this canto. She was Pound's "lovely lynx." Physically, the description suits H.D., to whom such nouns as "lynx" and "dryad" had been attached, much more than the restrained Dorothy Pound. Pound in these cantos referred so frequently to Botticelli's "Primavera" that H.D. thoughtfully mailed a book to his publisher, James Laughlin, containing details of the Botticelli painting so that Pound might have a copy of the original in his room at St. Elizabeth's Hospital, where he was now incarcerated. And H.D. herself was living a second springtime. More frequently in her classical town she consulted her copy of Dante. As the several years of writing and rewriting *Helen in Egypt* passed, Pound would never be out of her thoughts.

There was, nevertheless, another influence that played a primary role in the writing of *Helen*.

In 1949 H.D. was visited by E. M. Butler. Eliza M. Butler, a discovery of Bryher's who had sent Bryher a fan letter, has written a unique autobiography, *Paper Boats*. In this book she tells of her upbringing by a governess, her schooling in Germany, and finally, through her competence, of being made Schroeder Professor of German at Cambridge. On the surface, the career of a balanced, intelligent woman, but Butler confessed she would have preferred to have been an explorer. Throughout her life she took trips to exotic places and, at the same time H.D. knew her, was preparing to go off to a remote part of India. She lived with a woman friend whom she called "Squires," and they kept house in Cambridge. Later, Butler departed Cambridge for the University of Manchester. She wrote biographies of Byron, Goethe (dedicated to H.D.), and Heine. Her underlying interest, however, was psychological in origin and centered on the esoteric. The study of the Faust legend with its attendant rituals of magic and myth was particularly suited to her, and her book *The Fortunes of Faust* is a brilliant consideration of the legend. She also wrote a novel, *Silver Wings*. These two books were to be major influences on *Helen in Egypt*.

When the two women first met in 1949, neither book had been published, but Butler must have discussed with H.D. Goethe's use of the legend of Helen's having fled to Egypt and her double appearing on the walls of Troy. Butler also emphasized the ambiguity of Helen as described by Goethe. In *The Fortunes of Faust* she writes that "the first scene of his Helen-act . . . is one of the most fascinating ghost-stories in all literature; indeed only *The Sense of the Past* by Henry James can be compared with it for subtlety." (Apparently taking her clue from Butler, H.D. decided then to read Henry James.) Butler continues: "The state of mind of Helen is the crux of the situation, a dream-like state of mind, into which doubts of her own reality intrude and bewilder her."

> Can it be memory? Is Illusion seizing me?
> Was I that woman? Am I still the same? Am
> I yet to be
> The dream and terror of city-wrecking men?
>
> Goethe

Then Mephisto in the guise of Phorkyas

> . . . begins to recapitulate her past history, slyly insinuating her essential unreality, since she had been seen in Troy and Egypt at one and the same time. She is distressfully uncertain herself as to which of the two she is: the virtuous wife who (according to some Greek legends) remained hidden in Egypt during the Trojan episode, or the fatal beauty . . .
>
> PHORKYAS: And then they say that from hollow Shades
> Achilles too was joined in passion to thee,
> Who earlier loved thee despite all Fate's decrees.
>
> HELEN: Eidolon I and Eidolon he, yes we were wed;
> It was a dream the works themselves proclaim the truth,
> I vanish hence, a dream now to myself.
>
> [Butler continues] . . . but the tragic irony of her situation remains: feeling and thinking as a real woman, she is but a shade, and one perhaps who has never had a real existence in the minds of men, strange, beautiful, mythological being.

It was Butler who taught H.D. how to *realize* the meaning of the *double*, an idea she had already encountered in the Stesichorus version of the legend, which had Helen living in Egypt, not Troy. Following Butler's lead, in reference to Goethe's Helen, H.D. developed in her own poem the ambiguities that pursued and wearied the "strange, beautiful, mythological being" in her search for her identity.

In his introduction to *Helen in Egypt*, Horace Gregory quotes her as expressing "a wish to make real to myself what is most real." Had not H.D.'s sessions with Freud been a search to establish her mislaid identity?

(Whatever the direction of her research, H.D. has, in fact, re-created the scenes and people from her own life—imaginary, suspended, hallucinated, real, or shelled from the unconscious. Of the characters who appear in *Helen*, Achilles is her war hero, Lord Dowding; Paris is the doctor at the Küsnacht sanatorium, Erich Heydt, who would befriend and captivate H.D.; Theseus, who solved the puzzle of the labyrinth, is Freud; Menelaus is Aldington. In "Winter Love," a poem in her last book, there is an envoi to *Helen*, in which Ezra Pound appears as Odysseus.)

Butler's influence on H.D. extended into her novel *Silver Wings*. This is a second-rate novel; only a creative eye could recognize its possibilities as a model. *Silver Wings* is one of those literary puzzles in which the parts never fit or come together. Events are executed and explained . . . but is the explanation true? Did the events really occur? One person relates these events and gives his explanation, and thus we proceed through several interpretations of what may, or may not, be the real story. Finally an explanation of what has really occurred is given by someone whom we have every reason to believe. This presumably is the final truth. But is it? Are we not finally returned to a realm, which would be seized upon by H.D., where the dead dream their dreams? And who can read them?

In gratitude, H.D. wrote to Butler that she could not have written *Helen in Egypt* had it not been for *Silver Wings*. Finally in 1953, when she mailed the first completed cantos to Bryher—for H.D.'s book, like those of Dante and Pound, is written in cantos—she tells Bryher that at last in *Helen in Egypt* she has set *Silver Wings* to music.

H.D. confessed that Helen was her alter ego, that only through Helen could she remain alive. She could endure anonymity, solitude, so long as she could stay alive to complete the Helen sequence. Her endurance lasted from 1952 to 1956, through several serious illnesses. In 1953 she considered the book complete, but she wisely realized additional prose explanatory introductions needed to be attached to the separate books that comprise the whole. Curiously, she only realized this necessity for prose introductions after she had made a recording of *Helen in Egypt* in a studio in Zurich. This recording now gives us the pleasures of listening to the cultivated transatlantic voice of the poet.

Helen in Egypt is in certain ways a quest for sexual identity. H.D. is asking herself what her sexual feelings were toward the people who appeared in her life, and what her effect was on others. The interior plot of Helen concerns H.D.'s attempt to explain her relationships with other people. This search turns out to lead to another *Silver Wings*. The myth about Helen is the myth about herself. Had she really lived in America, or in Europe? Troy or Egypt? Where had dwelt the real H.D.? All through the war this question troubled her, the loyalty of an exile, perplexity of a lost nativity. During the war she had attempted to relieve this spatial anxiety by writing about her childhood in America. In *Helen* it was the Greece of her early poetry that she wanted to relate to the Egypt of her maturer intellectual interests.

In *Bid Me to Live* H.D. had announced her determinations to tell what had happened to her during the Great War. *Palimpsest* with its separate stories repeats the biographical pattern. She finally summarizes her sexual and emotional difficulties, her wisdom and her loss, in the formidable *Helen*. In each of her former books she had told a different story (as *Silver Wings* does), and yet the plot is the same, but the variations make the difference, and therein lies her talent. *Helen in Egypt*, although difficult, narcissistic, cloudy, obsessive, is high theater. H.D. sets herself up beside Euripides. The book gathers its distinction, apart from the necessary and practical influence of Butler, from the inspired *Pisan Cantos* of Pound.

By instinct, H.D. had found a mature way back stylistically to the "early H.D." Bryher encouraged this return, partly because it was with "the early H.D." that she had fallen in love. (At this time Pound also was searching for his early shadows, letting them fall across his melancholy, late poems.)

That *Helen* is an improvement over the war poetry, *Trilogy*, there is no question. H.D. is returned to the lands that had captured her imagination, and once there she moves with greater surety and control. She is among the scenery and props of her youthful writing—scarves, sheathes, sandals, flowers, islands, sand, and ships. She is on familiar ground, and her writing now shows the rewards of a long apprenticeship. She is an older Helen, wandering in her private haunts, with her sandals securely strapped. When Bryher received the final copy from H.D.'s sanatorium at Küsnacht in 1956 she lovingly wrote: "I think the last poems of the Helen sequence are your major work." H.D. considered that with *Helen* she had repaid her debts—to Freud, Heydt, Pound, Aldington, the men who had helped her create and resolve her own myth.

Chapter Twenty-Six: The Bryher Path

Bryher, never one to remain long in one place, particularly after a war's confinement, had flown off to America in January of 1947. She was divorcing Kenneth [Macpherson] and would receive her decree in February of that year. Bryher adored the flight with all its pleasurable delays. She wrote: "It was almost my ideal life, flipping up and down all over continents."

She found Macpherson "very young, very slim, but has got chubby cheeks and baby blue eyes like an American, or one of the Erotes on a Greek vase." He was living among Peggy Guggenheim's collection of paintings and sharing a house with her. Peggy Guggenheim has written about him in her autobiography, *Out of This Century*—as with others before her, his charm and sympathy had conquered. She ignored his faults, which included an elegant form of opportunism, and instead enjoyed the spectacles he could provide. Bryher never mentions Peggy. As a survivor she was now interested in food, which she decided was more important than culture. She also commented that old "Alexandrine" New York had departed.

Bryher discovered that Kenneth was, underneath the princely window dressing, "very sad, disillusioned and more mature." He didn't want the divorce and wanted once more to be with her. But Bryher was learning to be independent, both of H.D. and Kenneth. This may well have been because at last she had found herself in writing her historical novels. *Beowulf* would soon be published in Paris. *The Fourteenth of October* was nearly finished, and would be accepted by the distinguished editors Kurt and Helen Wolff, of the Pantheon Press. (Sylvia Beach disliked this book. She said she was sure it was beautiful, but she couldn't read historical novels and the characters weren't real.)

Bryher continued to analyze Kenneth, whom she found profoundly disillusioned with the States. She believed that he lived like a hermit, which to her meant that he wasn't attempting to empty his natural talent. She wrote H.D.: "I don't mind if people have a psychological blockage—it can happen to any of us. It is if it's a conscious rejection of responsibility that annoys me." She also mentioned that Kenneth—from whom H.D. had detached herself, because his ideas and prepossessions no longer interested her, in fact bored her—had spoken of her constantly.

Then there was the traditional meeting with Marianne Moore, the person in the United States (besides Perdita) of whom Bryher was fondest:

> She terrified me, she was so very queer about her mother. The mother was thought to be dying of cancer and in such agony Marianne wanted the Dr. to do something, as the mother could neither eat nor speak, and could eat nothing, because she could not eat if Mother could not eat, and thus got rashes and kidney trouble and pains. Now she will only eat her mother's diet—raw vegetable juice. Really I was frightened about Marianne. But she is upset over the worldliness of her niece!

Bryher also saw Harold Doolittle, whom she much respected. She always got along with businessmen. His finances were "immaculate"—the highest praise. At this time (1947) he was beginning to buy cows and wished to retire to the country to raise them. This he eventually did. His family wanted to remain in Pittsburgh, but Harold "lives for his cows!"

No sooner had Bryher returned to London, to the darkened lonely streets, the sad flat, than she was off to the Caribbean with Robert Herring and Schmideberg. This would be the beginning of nearly ten years with Schmideberg as a companion, hostage, and finally a dependent. Before leaving, Bryher secured the address of a dentist in Jamaica from Dorothy Richardson (as the Miriam of her own *Pilgrimage*, Richardson had worked for a dentist now retired there!).

Herring, ultimately lazy, adored the Caribbean; Bryher liked bits of it, but decided the climate wasn't conducive to work and that there were, which was true, a lot of South of France sort of people around, a comment of opprobrium. The Riviera had never been a "serious" resort for the Kenwinites, nor had any of them in their gilded days felt compelled to join the international society described by Maugham and Fitzgerald. Uniquely, Bryher decided that Barbados reminded her of Cornwall—it may have been the combination of wet weather and tropical sun. She also learned that in Barbados Sir Walter Raleigh's son had been buried, and she wrote a very good poem called "Young Rawley," which she sent to H.D. Had Bryher forced herself to remain long in the Caribbean, she might have produced another regional historical novel.

Bryher's next piece of news, which caused no comment from H.D., was that T. S. Eliot had been awarded the Order of Merit and Vita Sackville-West had been a Companion of Honour. Several months later, Edith Sitwell would be made an honorary doctor of literature, and Bryher mentioned that Edith now wished to be addressed as Dr. Sitwell.

During the early 1950s on one of her trips to the United States, Bryher had another of her enjoyable conversations with Harold Doolittle. This time she learned to her surprise that H.D. was a wealthy woman in her own right. Now she chose to speak out to H.D. about money. She had always paid all bills willingly, but the idea of money idling away in a bank was too much for her:

> I am afraid I am rather shocked, and almost a little angry with you. I heard from your brother. I think you don't realize it but you have over £50,000 tucked away with him in good American dollars and he is worried *because you never spend any of it*, and if anything should happen to you, due to death duties, the American government would take about half of it. Now you could buy yourself a car and hire a permanent chauffer or have a maid. And you must try to give people a bit more, and larger tips. Why you've got almost as much as I have. You can't go on asking about cheap pensions and living like thirty years ago as a student. And for heaven's sake, start spending some money, you can't take it with you.

Together with Bryher's 1940 settlement on her, H.D. in today's terms would have been worth several million dollars.

Somehow the idea had been instilled in H.D. that she was impoverished. This dated from the early London days, yet even then an allowance had been given to her by her parents and this continued through her marriage to Aldington. True, most of her friends at that time had little money, and the Lawrences in particular continually needed help. From time to time funds from Amy Lowell were arranged for Lawrence by H.D. The question of money had been raised by H.D. in her sessions with Freud, though she is not detailed about what Freud did say on this subject. Her checkbook had been one of the first of her personal effects H.D. demanded the first time she had been brought to Küsnacht for treatment after the war breakdown. On her own, she would have lived in the cheapest of flats and spent meager amounts of food. Cigarettes she considered to be her extravagance. There was nothing lavish about her—and yet she showed generosity toward her friends. After H.D. met Bryher and realized the extent of her riches, there is no doubt she was impressed. Who could be as rich as the Ellermans? Not even Amy Lowell. After their relationship had been established, it was natural for Bryher to assume the financial obligations. This, in turn, gave Bryher more power over H.D., and such an assumption pleased Bryher's own fondness for handling and dispensing money.

In reality there was this other side to the story. H.D. was in fact extremely well-off. Her brother managed her affairs superbly, and after the sale of family property in New Jersey she was a rich woman. There is the ring of the miser when H.D. writes Aldington that as she cannot get funds through Switzerland and is only living on an income, which she infers is small, that she will be able only to send him one hundred dollars a year. After much hesitation, she continued to do so. Ezra Pound always thought H.D. lived off Bryher and that was the main reason for her remaining with Bryher. In fact, Bryher was constantly sending checks to H.D., which were usually hoarded. At the same time H.D. was very thoughtful about pointing out to Bryher writers who deserved financial aid.

Kenneth had no qualms about spending money. Divorced, by 1949 he had moved to Capri, where he was installed in a villa given him by Bryher. He there attended the aging Norman Douglas, also a Bryher dependent. Perdita visited him on Capri. And she had her brief meeting—the first and last—with Cecil Gray, her father, who would die in a few years. At that time Gray was known as Don Cecilio, the reigning don of music. He lived resourcefully with a former opera singer, dined and drank rather too much.

Later Bryher gave Kenneth another villa outside Rome and an apartment in Rome near the Coliseum, both of which he shared with his friend, the photographer Islay Lyons. Then, tiring of the Roman environment, they moved to the province of Siena to a villa donated by Bryher, where Macpherson died prematurely in 1971. (Islay still lives there today.) Bryher enjoyed her visits with Islay and Kenneth. "Highlanders have the gift of place," she decided. They existed in a graceful atmosphere she was as incapable of providing for herself as much as she was of feeling any jealousy. Whenever on her visits to Islay and Kenneth her letters show her to be blissfully happy.* She even briefly stopped worrying about the upkeep of Kenwin as she admired Kenneth's improvements on the property she had bestowed.

Bryher's letters all through the 1950s are filled with worry about the expenses of Kenwin. Boiler repairs, heat, a gardener asking for higher wages, a maid leaving. She may have lectured H.D. about her miserliness, but in Bryher the anxiety about money took another form. She was perfectly ready to spend money on anyone but herself, and as she thought continually about money (mainly because money became a game for her, an objective around which her active mind could circle), naturally her peculiar monetary worries must have rubbed off on others, causing a permanent uneasiness. With H.D. it took the form of a constant threat of displacement. Like many manipulators, Bryher enjoyed creating a sense of suspense. There was never any question of impoverishment, but she liked to pretend there was.

Bryher was also hostess now for Dr. Schmideberg, who had an extended invitation to Kenwin. Bryher appreciated and respected him and he was a fellow worshipper of psychoanalysis, about which they could make many conjectures. But the sad truth was that like so many she cared for, with the exception of H.D., he drank. Bryher's abstemious self had been curiously dedicated to drunkards. Schmideberg was intelligent, intuitive, amusing, elegant, she admired him enormously. He provided her with treats of conversation and wit. She wasn't lonely at Kenwin when the Bear was in residence.

For a long time the extended visits of the Schmidebergs were anticipated and enjoyed. It is very sad that Schmideberg's wine consumption got out of hand. Bryher began to feel the weight of his problem. She was so concerned about Kenwin and its inhabitants that she finally reached a peak of near hysteria, unusual for her. She threatened to sell the place to Charles Chaplin or Anne Morrow Lindbergh or rich Egyptians, all

* "I like this austere and wolf haunted landscape of the Sabine hills . . . And I had a curious feeling that I knew this place centuries before. Perhaps not." So she wrote to H.D. in 1951.

of whom she learned were looking for property in the vicinity. Then she threatened to cut the place up into flats. Bryher was chasing around her kennel like a maddened Fido. She wanted *out.* After all, H.D. had performed a disappearing act. Bryher was terrified that the responsibilities of Kenwin would prevent her from writing. Pathetically, she wrote to H.D. that she finally had a compliment. "This morning the Protestant-Italian maid from the hills said to me firmly, 'it is Ascension Day, shall you be working?' *No maid has ever asked me if I was working.*"

That little maid, Inez, remained with Bryher until Bryher's death. The nagging problems of the household would soon solve themselves. Bear would become ill and go to Küsnacht. Bryher would find research for her books an acceptable reason for her travels. She began to write steadily. Soon she would accept Kenwin and its winter heating bills as a necessity, and her life would go on, until it ceased at Kenwin. The unnecessary battles and worries were postponed.

Although Bryher returned again and again to England and to Cornwall and the Scillies, it was apparent that H.D. never wished to return to London. The memories of the city must have terrified her. And of those who were close to her, Aldington never returned to London, nor did Kenneth. Ezra Pound, after his release from St. Elizabeth's, visited England only once more to pay his respects to Eliot in Westminster Abbey. Lawrence had never returned.

Meanwhile Bryher continued to keep up with her pets, Marianne Moore and Edith Sitwell. From one of her American trips she reported that Marianne said she had taken more pride in passing the test for a driver's license than she had from her poetry. In 1950 Marianne remarked of Eliot's receiving the Nobel Prize that "the humility of his Noble-ness weighs him down." Marianne had been seeing Ezra, whom she found crazily abusive. In her dress, Marianne was looking "smarter and smarter." She confided to Bryher that she had been interviewed by the "Morgue of Time" (Alden Whitman), who told her that Bryher wasn't as good as she was supposed to be, that is, good in the sense of writing books. Bryher agreed with him.

Edith Sitwell was always material for a story. Bryher reminded H.D. of the honors bestowed on her contemporaries, thus creating in H.D. a natural arrogance mixed with jealousy. But Bryher needled for a reason. She wanted her beloved Kat, "the Queen of Song," to exert herself and obtain the honors she deserved. Bryher unswervingly promoted H.D.'s cause, as did Norman Holmes Pearson, and they were each successful in the pursuit. But at the time of Edith's elevation to Dame Commander, Order of the British Empire, in 1954, H.D. could only be consoled by Bryher's story about a request for a poem coming to Edith from Marya Zaturenska, and Edith's reply that she should have been addressed as Dame Edith because, "The Queen has made me a Lady." Bryher also continued for H.D.'s amusement: "She has got it AT LAST. Her full title on envelopes is now Dame Edith Sitwell, D.B.E., D. Litt. She is out of her mind with joy. She says it is the happiest day of her life." Then Bryher urged a reluctant H.D. to write Edith, congratulating her.

In 1954 Bryher went off to India with Kenneth and Islay Lyons, departing from Kenwin and its responsibilities. As always, her solution to her own problems was a trip. Bryher had a positive mania for making and unmaking travel plans; India required all her resources, and she responded nobly. She again had a marvelous time buying rugs, shawls, looking at sunsets, mountains, admiring Islay's photographs, and disapproving the Victorian remnants that still littered India. She would have made a splendid travel writer. She knew the history of each place she was in, and yet she never permitted her knowledge to overcome her aesthetic reactions. Like any good travel writer, she was alert to the humor of the situation—she could move rapidly from a description of the beauty of the horned moon to comment on how many hours it took to change money.

Bryher's need was for a life that could be built upon and around personages. As H.D. once said, "she had an uncanny ability for vicarious enjoyment." Since H.D. was no longer available, she turned, among others, to Edith Sitwell. She needed a "family" to take care of. All her life she attempted to establish this family with Kenwin as its base. The difficulty had been that she depended on a circle of intense individuals who would not for long permit themselves to be contained within a "family pattern." It is true that Perdita and her husband and children remained faithful through the years, but the others found themselves in various countries, occupied with their own pursuits and pleasures. Bryher could no longer be her father; she could no longer be master of the ship. However, she was not one to be long deprived of her resources.

Besides Edith, there were the faithful Sylvia Beach and Adrienne Monnier. Bryher went to the 1959 exposition in Paris entitled Les Années Vingt, which celebrated youthful days in Paris and was a terrific success. She wrote to H.D.: "It is most beautiful done with everyone we knew and many we did not. Your picture is up between Hymen and Heliodora with Cummings on top of the board." She went on to say that whenever they walked in the street people murmured, "C'est Mademoiselle Beach!" Sylvia Beach came frequently to visit Bryher at Kenwin. They always got along splendidly, despite Beach's inability to read Bryher's novels. Their friendship was based on the mutual admiration they shared for women who had done much to help others.

Shortly after her celebratory trip to Paris, Bryher was once again in London. Here occurred one of those frequent incidents in Bryher's life that resulted from her "sensible," unplumaged dress. "I went to Harrods this morning and as I had a suitcase said I would wait for a receipt after buying some towels, in case they asked me to open it. 'Ah well, you see Madam, you dress and talk like we do and they think you are staff shopping in unauthorized hours . . .'" Ever concerned about H.D.'s career, she went on to advise her to send the poet and protégé of the Sitwells, Alberto Lacerda, her books of *Selected Poems*, as he was going out to Brazil for two months on a lecture tour.

In January 1960 Bryher discovered that Romaine Brooks and Natalie Barney, whom Rémy de Gourmont in 1912 addressed as the "Amazons" in his famous *Letters to the Amazon*, were in Lausanne, having arrived there from Romaine's retreat on the Riviera. They were both getting on to ninety. "But nothing seems to daunt these old ladies," said Bryher, adding that Romaine's great friend was the octogenarian Somerset Maugham.

> Romaine was wonderful, she looks just the same though she must be well over eighty. She only has a little trouble with her eyes and can't manage books, reads Time as it gives her the news in brief. She refused to leave Fiesole (Romaine had been there all during

> the war) as apparently she is very naive about politics and poor Natalie refused to leave her and suffered horribly because Natalie likes people and good food and they did not dare speak to anybody and the food gave out. She has written a description of it all but people were against it as she was a bit muddled over the Mussolini affair . . . I beg her to let me have all her mss.

So much consideration had been given to the work of those whom she admired that a reminder is necessary of the number of books Bryher herself wrote between 1949 and 1972. There are twelve of them. Modest as she always was about her work, she delighted to repeat the bad reviews. She quoted from the London *Times*, which said of *Gate to the Sea* (1958): "Bryher does not display the literary gifts to provide the abstract poetic analogy; her language is jerky and unmelodious; her characterisation too thin." H.D. suspected that Bryher wasn't satisfied with her work, and certainly Bryher had to put up with much criticism from her friends who wanted her to add sex to her themes. They even felt that with a little sex in her writing she could produce a best-seller in the tradition of the more popular historical novels. But Bryher stuck to her guns. She was a historian, not a sex queen. And she was quite right. Young people who were finding themselves interested in history, not fiction, for the first time read her books. They are convincing entertainment for an early age group. Historians have remarked how in their youth they got their first taste of the excitement that could be found in history by reading Bryher's novels.

And it must not be forgotten that Bryher had written not only countless reviews for *Life and Letters Today*, but also earlier books printed for the most part privately, which covered a large range of subjects: poetry, literary criticism, autobiography, geography, Russian film.

Thus writing, travel, friendships, philanthropy, and unceasing, if frequently absent, care of H.D. kept Bryher reasonably occupied. She also enjoyed her visits to the Schaffner household and, although not maternally inclined, would see to a new layette, a handsome present for the new child. She considered the children her own grandchildren.

With her life ordered according to her own pattern, Bryher was still prepared for the demands suddenly created by a crisis in the life of H.D. Bryher might complain about life not being an easy place for little dogs, but she had also written: "There is something to be said for confusion and upheaval sometimes: I don't think I like peaceful surroundings very much." She was not to be threatened by peace so long as H.D. needed to be guided through her imaginary difficulties and helped over what now loomed as a very real hurdle.

H.D. and the Conflict of Imagism

I am going to read from the chapter "H.D. Imagiste" in my biography of H.D. I shall do so because I believe that the scene I describe is well-staged. I use those words carefully. I am not satisfied with this scene, although I have reported it. It plays remarkably like the first act of a drama, as I suppose it is. The figure of Richard Aldington is missing. But we have it here in all its bright clothing, a dramatic meeting between two protagonists who would affect one another for a lifetime and the introduction of a poetics that would for ten years affect the direction of H.D.'s poetry and give permanent luster to her name as an Imagist:

> It is September 1912, a year after Hilda arrived in Europe. She has been at the British Museum studying the Greek friezes and plates of Egyptian figures. She is abstracted, contemplative. And yet there is a purposeful air about her as she hurries down the museum steps to the nearby museum bun shop. Ezra Pound is waiting there for her. He is dressed in his Whistlerian garb, the velvet jacket, the loose tie. Together they are a pictorial couple. She is so tall and lean, beautiful with the squared jaw and the hair falling over her brow. He is certainly no ordinary clerk. His reddish hair is long and tumbled, he has a watchful impudent look about the eyes. Something of that air of inquisitive fantasy Aubrey Beardsley used to catch in his drawings. Neither at this moment is interested in appearances. There is a more direct reason for the meeting. Hilda has consented to show Ezra Pound her new poems.
>
> She puts her books and gloves onto a chair, takes out a notebook, and hands it to him.
>
> He reads "Hermes of the Ways." Hilda's poem had been suggested by an invocation to Hermes by the poetess Anyte that was in the Greek Anthology Pound has introduced her to.

"Why, Dryad, this is good!"

He takes out a sharp red pencil, changes a word here or there, crosses one out. He rereads the poem, and then the next one, "Acon," another poem based on a translation from a Latin Renaissance book he had also given her. Then there is "Orchard." Pound is really pleased. She is a model pupil. More than that, she is a poet; the scornful, exacting teacher is now certain of this. Selecting "Hermes of the Ways," and giving her one of his catlike looks, he again takes up his pencil and signs the poem: "H.D. Imagiste."

That is the story. The attitudes, the gestures, the theatricality are in character. It is a brilliant coup. Pound has created another poet, acolyte. He has added a discipline to the new ism he is about to create and introduce to the market.

Would that today the excised poem with its corrections might rest in the Berg Collection in New York, alongside Pound's similar selective corrections and deletions to "The Waste Land" of Eliot.

And now I will tell you one of the reasons why I am not satisfied with this setting. Aldington, Pound, and H.D. had been in Paris at the same time, in 1912. Paris was the center of Modernism. Of Cubism, Impressionism, Simultaneousism, Symbolism, which would be overtaken by Imagism. The preparation for Pound's doctrine of *Imagisme* must have taken place in Paris and been discussed in his lodgings in London over the previous months.

In the bun shop we have a fairytale setting where the magician waves his wand and anoints the poet. The poems were in her handbag. Did she show them to Pound expecting he would write Imagiste after them?

Perhaps it was the other way around. Pound needed the poetry of H.D. to launch *Imagiste*. Were those poems of H.D. inspired by that remarkable new poem, "The Return," written by Pound, a poem Pound may have considered his first venture into Imagism?

Whatever may be the truth we know that Pound was determined Imagism initiate the poetry of the future. He did not want H.D. or himself to remain unrecognized, "living under the staircase, where all must pass him and no one pays any attention to him . . ." Not Pound the master-magician nor his protégée.

As I wrote in my biography, I wish that the poems she showed Pound that day with his corrections were in a library, as "The Waste Land" is in the Berg Library. We might see for ourselves Pound's editing of "Hermes of the Ways," "Acon," and "Orchard."

In 1915 in "Affirmations," Pound wrote:

> The image can be of two sorts. It can arise within the mind. It is then "subjective." External causes play upon the mind, perhaps; if so they are drawn into the mind, fused, transmitted, and emerge in an Image unlike themselves. Secondly, the Image can be objective. Emotion seizing up some external scene or action carries it intact to the mind; and that vortex purges it of all save the essential or dominant or dramatic qualities, and it emerges like the external original. In either case the Image is more than an idea. It is a vortex or cluster of fused ideas and is endowed with energy. If it does not fulfill these specifications, it is not what I mean by an Image.

This is three years after the meeting in the bun shop. Meanwhile Pound, briefly engaged with the Vorticists, had not abandoned Imagism for Vorticism. Vorticism, he came to realize, was for painters. However, he made clear to Harriet Monroe regarding his own translations that he was determined "to break the surface of convention."

H.D. was beginning her own struggle with what Williams in "Asphodel" calls "the tyranny of the image" (wonderful phrase). Pound had firmly stressed that you did not work up to the image—no reflections, hesitations, equivocations, hints. The image strikes once with its full force—and brilliantly, "it occurs in an instant."

Although her poetry shows that she assimilated in her own way many of Pound's affirmations, I don't believe the program or the vision instinct in Pound's concept of Imagism ever in detail or magnitude penetrated the poetics H.D. evolved for herself.

Essentially she used the movement as a wheel for her own poetry. She was at this time an instinctual poet. She had a small, definite vocabulary of words ("shell," "garden," "flower") into which she fitted a Greek landscape with Greek figures. That is, she narrowed the concept of Imagism. To those today who do not accept the genius of Pound's drive to change, to alter, above all to achieve a modern scheme of poetics that accompanied

Cubism and Joyce's *Ulysses*, that evolved a poetry of Modernism, she is known as the "purest" Imagist of them all.

H.D.'s translations "invent" a method of translation that incorporates her own exceptional ear. In her adaptation of Euripides's *ION* we find a sophisticated use of imagistic poetics. Yet it is a performance. *Hippolytus Temporizes* is an extraordinary example of H.D.'s use of Imagism. The whole mood of the play, based on the Greek myth, completed in 1927 and partly inspired by a play of Euripides, reflects her use of the spatial technique of Imagism. A use which she arrives at in her poetry only when the poetry is fragmented.

The form she has chosen architecturally expands the technique. In this play exist some of her loveliest, most startling effects.

In her poetry, H.D.'s conception of Imagism was of the poem taking place in a much smaller, defined space, a tighter space than Pound conceived. This is why later she wanted to write more "open" poetry. Her later attitude could perhaps be explained by the words of a reviewer of the *Imagist Anthology* who wrote:

> It is always the Imagist's danger that in his statement of facts of form, colour and sensuous impression, he may miss that further vision that may not be confined in exact language which the true poet always suggests to us.

(Note the pronoun "he" throughout. In defense, however, even we can only say "she" regarding the one female Imagist before the Amygist.) I should like to suggest now that we entertain another idea, that is, we consider the situation of Eliot, Pound, and H.D. as exiles or expatriates (to use a more polite word, but one shunned by James Joyce). By choice and selectivity they are isolated from their native country.

Imagism concerns itself with the isolation of the image. The momentum of the poem flows toward the suddenness of the image. This suddenness, this overflowing of an image into space, out of nowhere, is purposeful. All of this energy is employed to give definition to the poem, to gather up the particulars, the threads, the hints of what is being said into a summation or a description, a sudden alarming or beneficent but immediate summation of what the person has been all about. We are dealing with time and with space and movement. There must be nothing, finally, lying around inert. Yet the image despite all its energy and activity has arrived as if it were a foreign substance. It is strangely isolated. This isolation or foreignness of the image from the rest of the poem exerts a fascination to which the poem is willing to submit, but not always the reader. The reader is apt to say, "oh, another image," or "oh, another picture"—remember that Imagism is highly pictorial and visual. If you consider this, you realize the image has a lonely perch.

At the same time we must also recognize that these three Americans in Europe, together with their counterparts in America, Williams, and Stevens, formed the background of the modernist movement as we know it today. (I am going to suggest that Stevens himself, the executive of an insurance company, was just as much isolated in Hartford, Connecticut. That dwelling in the inner sanctum of his home in which he received nobody, sitting in a small garden sipping wine and eating cheese without conversation even with his wife, he maintained the embrace of exile.) I shall not include Williams because, despite Pound's insistence on Williams's Spanish ancestry, he was at home in New Jersey. The embrace of exile and the disease of exile accompanied Eliot, Pound, and H.D. throughout their lives.

In exile there is freedom, also. Freedom to maneuver, freedom to adopt a persona. And freedom, in particular, to use a language in whatever context you wish. Language is private. Language speaks your language. I don't wish to argue that Pound's insistence on Imagism could not have happened in America, although I believe this is true. I conjecture that his exile, his formal isolation into which entered Wyndham Lewis, Ford Madox Ford, and Yeats, minds of such a degree he could not have encountered in the America he knew, assisted him in his concentrations and formulation of Imagism, even the escape from Imagism, briefly, into Vorticism, so that finally in the isolation of Rapallo he was able to refine its principles for his own uses.

D. H. Lawrence rationalized that Imagism "comes from the American psyche, which might, were it not fed the artistry of the poets, have turned into as mindless a poetry as the Futurists produced."

Certainly H.D., who reveled in her new freedom in England, was willing to listen to the dictates of her compatriot. He was explaining the country of the imagination and articulated the power of poetry, and surrounded by such a balustrade she was protected from loneliness, lent strength to cope with the self-questioning that comes to expatriates.

When Pound in 1912 wrote about H.D.'s work to Harriet Monroe seeking publication for H.D.'s poetry, he was not afraid to rely on the civilizing influence of expatriatism.

> This is the sort of American stuff that I can show here and in Paris without its being ridiculed. Objective—no slither: direct—no excessive use of adjectives, no metaphors that won't permit examination. It's straight talk, straight as the Greek!

"Straight as the Greek" is purposeful historicism to Monroe in Chicago.

And it is well to remember that in pre-World War America there was a Victorian America struggling to rid itself of confining ideologies, but still struggling, still gripped in a stronger vise of poetics than was British poetry. British poetry was something to come to grips with. It was a force. An inherited force. One could say the name Swinburne and it had value, it had probity beyond romance; an American could recognize in Swinburne the beginning of a beginning. In America poetry was largely ornament and moralism. The pictorial images contained no shafts of light.

There was no Symbolism to alter and appropriate into Imagism as Poussin was changed into nature, the nature of Cubism.

H.D., once she had become a high-priestess of Imagism, a new struggle began. The struggle with the domination of the image would come later. This other conflict was with the force, the energy, and the persona of Pound himself.

"Toward the Piraeus," published in *Heliodora* in 1924, is directed forbiddingly at Pound, with its beginning line "You would have broken my wings":

> It was not chastity that made me wild, but fear
> that my weapon, tempted in different heat;
> was over-matched by yours, and your hand
> skilled to yield death-blows, might break
>
> With the slightest turn—no ill will meant—
> my own lesser, yet still somewhat fine-wrought,
> fiery-tempered, delicate, over-passionate steel.

This is a very explicit statement and with the high edge of steel she was informing him that her poetry might turn against his rule, his might, that she would indeed find another source. Pound would write "brutally," so H.D. thought, about *Hedylus* which followed *Heliodora*. In *Hedylus* she attempts to evoke the spirit of the woman poet, Hedyle. H.D. later admitted that *Hedylus* is a retelling of her own story in a classical setting. It may be a clumsy attempt to deal with a Greek environment, but we are astounded that Pound warned Circe "to get out of her pig-sty." Pound is no longer interested in, nor did he approve of, her dependence on Greek subject matter.

In her memoir of Pound, *End to Torment* (a title Pound would call "optimistic"), written while Pound was in St. Elizabeth's, and H.D. more pleasantly incarcerated in a clinic at Küsnacht, Switzerland, she wrote: "Ezra would have destroyed me and the Air and Crystal of my poetry."

Pound may at the time have been infuriated by the publisher's blurb on the Jonathan Cape edition of *Heliodora and Other Poems*.

"Her work blends European suavity with a kind of red-Indian terseness, nerve and barbarity of phrase." A more deliberately inaccurate description of one of her most selective books could scarcely have been printed.

Pound would several years later come in for some of that barbarity himself. Max Beerbohm in Rapallo remarked to Phyllis Bottome that Pound "seemed out of place here. I should prefer to watch him in the primeval forests of his native land wielding an axe against some giant tree. Could you not persuade him to return to a country in which there is more room?"

The *Collected Poems* of 1925 summed up H.D.'s Imagist phase. This is a wonderful book. Eighty-eight pages of pure H.D. Imagism. It begins with "Sea Garden," followed by "The Helmsman," "Sea Lily," "The Gift," "Sea Poppies," "Hermes of the Ways"—a powerful, near-perfect poem, "Orchard." The youthful H.D. is here, her poems so carefully formed, delicate with sturdy stems. Of course the theme is minor with too much sand, wind, wave, no wonder she wanted to spread out her wings and she wanted also to celebrate the hermetic world. But here the scene is filled with light. And so is the combination of Imagism and myth of these poems. And the knowledge that the poet is in secure control of her craft.

The doctrine of Imagism gave her this hold on her poetry. "Hard light, clear edges."

The late works of H.D., *Hermetic Definition* and *Helen in Egypt*, are another H.D. She has entered another place; she is reaching for the tools of the unconscious.

Adalaide Morris has called H.D. Imagist, Clairvoyant, Cinemastic, Prophetic. Imagist survives as a subsidiary in the contemplated frame of her work.

Rid of the tyranny of the image, H.D.'s new discovery is the power of narrative form. This is followed by improvisation—actually free association with words and sound: "Marah," "Mar," "Mer," etc. However, her old Imagist training that taught her to avoid the superfluous word would still inhibit her from total submission to the apocalyptic speech she would surrender to in her World War II period.

Imagism provided discipline, even if she wanted to throw out its bathwater.

Then in 1956 H.D. made a celebrated visit to Yale. She was interviewed by the *New Haven Register*, whose lead article was headed "Poet Hilda Doolittle on Yale Visit Assails Imagist Label Used to Describe Her Work." The paper reported that H.D. denounced the label. She emphasized that the term could not be applied to describe her work written since World War II.

H.D. then continued to say, "I don't know that labels matter very much. One writes the kind of poetry one likes. Other people put labels on it." In its own way this is a true statement, if not true to what she specifically refers. Pound had indeed "labeled" the poem she had shyly showed him in the tearoom.

When asked what was meant by Imagism, she answered, "Something that was important for poets learning their craft early in this century. It is still important to any poet learning his craft. But after learning his craft, the poet will find his true direction, as I hope I have."

We, however, know that she was vastly indebted to the Imagist movement. Her renown had come through her association with the movement and her designation as the "purest" Imagist of them all. (Purest if not the greatest. It is my belief that *The Cantos* are the great affirmation of Imagism.) By then Imagism as a literary term had entered literary history. Aldington decried Imagism in a letter to her. Now it was H.D.'s turn to be more gentle in her response toward Imagism. When she answered his letter she wrote: "How sad I am that you so dislike having to do with the Imagist sign. I have been bored with it, too. But at seventy-two it is part of my youth."

At this age she had just completed *Helen in Egypt*. She believed that the early H.D., the poet of the *Collected Poems* of 1925, had matured with this later book and she believed Imagism was too microscopic a term for her later work, which had moved into narrative which she believed was freer, more discursive, more philosophical, more grown-up in dealing with the passions of the world, and which dwelt both in myth and in the immediate contemporary world.

What is noticeable in the late work are the traces of real struggle inside and outside the levels of obedience to form. A move in direct opposition to Pound's "language is made of concrete things."

Her later poetry resorted to a repetitive discursive style whose passages are filled with the esotericism that preoccupied her thoughts. She now used a longer explosive line interrupted by shorter broken lines. The effect is of interior monologue in search of a subject that once found is held up to us like a Medusa head. The poems are instructive, not descriptive as in her Imagistic work.

She came to rely on an emotive reaction to Christian and esoteric orthodoxy in her late poetry. Yet within the form, the shape of her poetry, is a rebellion from the orthodoxy not only of Imagism, but of any formal poetics. She became a law unto herself.

The war trilogy maintains the intensity apparent in her early poems without the control that Imagism demanded. When she abandoned the form of Imagism she abandoned many of its precepts, except Pound's rule against use of "ornament." Her poems are never ornamental and, with all her use of Greek location, there is no archaicism, there are no "quaint devices" of the sort Pound warned about in *Lustra*.

The *Trilogy* poems to me are comparable to the war poems of Edith Sitwell. H.D. speaks in the overtones of Moravianism, of Christianity, although her poetry is more religious than Sitwell's appeal to the pagan. H.D. is both more allusive and more complicated. Yet the sound is similarly alerting, the same effect of high emotion is there. A similar note of authority.

In *The Cantos* of Pound, although the pattern of words on his page seems loose or open, the poems move on many levels of thought; ideas are superimposed above images or images precede ideas. There is order and direction within the multi-dimensional effect of his poetry that derives from Imagism.

"The body is inside the soul," Pound said. We can transpose these words to read: *the body of the work is inside the image.*

When H.D. deliberately turned away from the Imagist principles it can be surmised that she wished her work to expand both poetically and emotionally. Enclosure was what she feared most; being inside a given set of rules was becoming anathema to her. Had she not said early on "I am not a Theorist"? The womb-like claustrophobia of the image both in the poem, and the weight of it on herself as the persona for this invention of Pound, were becoming an affliction.

Her life had taken other turns. "There was an H.D. before the War," as she often said, and there was by 1925 another H.D. It is eighty years since the staged meeting in the tea shop. And today Imagism has entered our literary history, has become an accessory to our skills.

Searching again into the mystery of H.D., her role in literature as an Imagist, and reading the distinctly non-imagistic body of her late work, perhaps we can believe she was in search of the "deep truth" that Shelley in *Prometheus Unbound* declares is "imageless."

On *Richard Aldington & H.D.: The Early Years in Letters*

This modest title conceals Professor Zilboorg's real intention, which is to write a biography. She believes that "neither H.D. nor Aldington have (sic) been served well by biography, and their reputations and their art as a result have been considerably obscured and misconstrued."

She has "avoided" my own biography of H.D., believing that I have "drawn heavily on H.D.'s and Aldington's novels, often confusing autobiographical fiction and primary sources." Zilboorg tells us that she is basing the biography and commentary in her book on "the wealth of previously unpublished correspondence by and concerning both H.D. and Aldington." The correspondence published here, misleadingly entitled "the early years," concerns the years from 1918 to 1919, the war years.

When I began to write a biography of H.D., I worked as did Professor Zilboorg at the Beinecke Library at Yale University. This was in 1978. I discovered that there were World War I letters from Aldington from his training camps and the trenches to H.D. reposing in the Beinecke, but they were forbidden to a reader until a certain date. Recognizing their importance to my biography, I waited a full year, adjusting my research, until that date passed. I remember very clearly the day the packet of letters was placed in my hands by Donald Gallup, then the curator. I regarded the letters with awe mingled with the excitement of an archaeologist.

In those days as Professor Zilboorg may be unaware the biographer worked with a pencil, then a pen, then graduated to a typewriter. There was no easy access such as a photocopy. Letters were sacrosanct and I was the only researcher entitled to look at any of the correspondence in the H.D. papers. Under such circumstances I would indeed be inclined to regard the letters with respect and with an interest heightened by the suspense of a year's wait. I must also add that the correspondence between Bryher and H.D. was restricted to my use and my eyes and I guarded that property and read all of the correspondence and copied as there was no photocopying what I considered necessary onto a typewriter. I emphasize the weight of my duties, because I am somewhat resentful of someone so new in the field reminding me of the adhesiveness of personal correspondence to a biography. However, I will confess to a certain disappointment in the correspondence, not in its fulfillment of biographical material, but the content was far less rewarding than *Death of a Hero*, the remarkable book Aldington later wrote of his war years.

To proceed to Professor Zilboorg's accomplishment. She has succeeded in brightening these letters with her annotations and thereby upgrading their importance. The correspondence between H.D. and Aldington during the years 1916 to mid-February 1919, given this attention, does take on the atmosphere of biographical material. Professor Zilboorg provides us with a Biographical Appendix of the people mentioned in the letters. In addition we are given a Periodical Appendix which illuminates the literary contributions of the era.

She has thoroughly assessed the letters of Aldington. But, and this is a major *but*, of necessity she must point out that this is a one-sided correspondence. *There are no letters from H.D.* This creates a dilemma in what might have been a more vivid excavation. Professor Zilboorg considers that this missingness is "part of the story" of the H.D.–Aldington relationship. Aldington "apparently destroyed them."

Around such a correspondence this book is built. We are alerted to biographical material about Aldington supplied by his executor, Alister Kershaw. The shadow of Aldington hangs heavily. This, it seems to me, is all to the good. I found Aldington a sympathetic character and I believe he has been neglected in subsequent research with its idealization of H.D. He, his women, his divorces, his incomes, his work, and his last years when he leaned heavily on H.D., are all essential to any understanding of her. Although this background may not be secure in a book whose subtitle "The Early Years in Letters" purports to limit itself to correspondence during the Great War. I wish Professor Zilboorg, with her capabilities, and acknowledged help of Alister Kershaw, would present us with a considerate biography of Aldington.

There is much familiar ground worked over once again by Professor Zilboorg, but she has added her own intensity and her own carefulness and respect for the material she deals with. What one is most impressed with is her conscientiousness, which is at times formidable. In particular when she defines her attitude toward biography as a "synthesis of raw material, selection and annotation, commentary and analysis." This somewhat chemical attitude disregards an adherence to the psychological and emotive elements so indistinguishable from life.

However, such a refinement of attitude fulfills a necessity in the biographical field. And it is an attitude which any good worker with a devoted eye can surround with enthusiasm, as does Professor Zilboorg.

She has written a useful, careful book about people whose vividly executed peregrinations are worth the scrutiny and add a dimension to our contemporaneity. These annotated letters tie up loose ends and leave the faces intact. Her tools are honed: letters, annotation, appendices, careful, unceasing footnoting. Diane Johnson once wrote one of the most delightful biographies I ever read using just these tools. It is called *Lesser Lives* and does away with the narrative line of straight biography.

Professor Zilboorg's book does not possess the charm of Diane Johnson's book, but she has a scholar's dedication and she is certainly correct in her desire to reassess material. I wish she had not been so dismissive of my pioneer efforts.

A Review: H.D.'s *Ion, a play after Euripides*; H.D.'s *Nights*

It is difficult to find fault with this new edition of *Ion*, bound as the play is to a thoughtful, distinguished design. Mountains, a ruined temple, broken stones imperishable against the silvery tones of the book jacket, leaves of an olive tree blown against dusted paper, Io and H.D. printed in Grecian blue, the play appears here archaeological, intact. For the reader there are detailed textual notes, H.D.'s preserved "Notes on Euripides," a careful chronology, and reproduction of Man Ray's stylish 1920s photograph of H.D. An impeccable performance.

H.D. worked on *Ion* from 1917 to 1935, beginning with her youthful days in Devon when she was married to Richard Aldington and felt more Greek than the Greeks as her personality and poetry began to assume a Greek guise assisted by her constant referral to the Greek Anthology and her appreciation of Euripides. After her analysis with Freud, she wrote to Bryher in 1934 that *Ion* would "break the backbone of my H.D. repression." With signal messianic fervor she also wrote that if she could "get across the Greek spirit at its highest I am helping the world, and the future." Bryher then was disturbed about the world war preparing in Europe. H.D. admitted that she clung to the Greek translations, because they held her to her "centre"; they were a support upon which she could unresistingly lean. After all Pound had written in 1918 to explain his "pawing over the ancients and the semi-ancients":

> A man feeling the divorce of life and his art may naturally try to resurrect a forgotten mode if he finds in that mode some leaven, or if he thinks he sees in it some element lacking in contemporary art which might unite that art again to its sustenance, life.

Ion is not only an adaptive translation of Euripides, it is a vehicle for H.D.'s poetry. Beginning with "Hermes of the Ways," the early Imagist poem Pound had celebrated, she had dedicated a good part of her life to the Greece of her fantasy, inspired by the lyrics and the drama of Euripides. Not knowing the language, she had relied on Mackail, the Loeb Library, Pausanias for his Baedeker to Ancient Greece, and the Greek Anthology. She was not alone. Her peers were devoting themselves to Greek myth: Pound, Joyce, Eliot. They borrowed from myth space in which to create.

H.D.'s poetry in *Ion* is far less emotive than the best-known translator of her time, Gilbert Murray. It speaks well of H.D. that she was able to strike out from the conventional and praised translations of Murray. Each age appears to project its translator. Dryden, Pope, Shelley. They echo the classical, the baroque, the romantic ethos of their era. Eliot wrote that he preferred H.D.'s selections from "Iphigenia in Aulis" as they appeared in the 1916 Poet's Translation Series to those of Murray. This was a noted heresy.

Ion has the voice of a mature H.D. The language is select, sparse, yet it carries its beat, each word is associated to a clarity our own time still recognizes as Greek. There is none of the speculation of romanticism, and there is no hint of H.D.'s inclination toward forbidden pre-Raphaelitism which occasionally is accented in the earlier *Hippolytus Temporizes*. The play is ideally suited to her, although "we are certainly not reading Euripides," as one classicist commented. Her subtitle is "a play *after* Euripides."

She is working with an ironic story and most of it has to do with ambition. In her own interpolated words, H.D. tells us that she is aware of this suspect "irony" of Euripides, yet she does not "subscribe to it." What she is interested in is youth, beauty, oracles, scenic delight, the role of women and especially the poetic opportunities of the Choros. She concentrates on essence, on picking off verbal arguments until we reach the skeleton of the play. She approaches Euripides through her intensity and her selective vocabulary. *Ion* is vintage H.D.

She also wishes her translation to be not only noble, but the theatrical, and she succeeds. Her training in the 1930s with film, writing for the film magazine *Close Up* and acting in *Borderline* lend a certain glamour to the adaptation that would not have existed in her earlier versions. This glamourizing shows in her interruptions throughout the play as she tells us how a dance should be performed, sets the stage as it might have been for a large, restless, intelligent Athenian audience, lifts a veil, the sun rises, the temple is clothed in shadow. *Ion* in her adaptation now exists within the cinematic boundaries of H.D.'s private theatre.

***Nights* is many-leveled** and it is a surprise to discover that this weave of time, dream, sex, separation, and suicide is dependent on a flimsy structure. *Nights* issues from the mind of a woman who chooses as a nom de plume a man's name. The pseudonym is the successful intimate of her story and it is he who relates it. This action has a quirky urgency that leads us to expect a novel of sexual displacement, contemporarily a fortuitous situation. The narrowness, the privacy of *Nights*, which is restricted to the confessional ambivalence of one person, prohibits this adventure.

H.D. has written about an indulgent household on a lake where men and women do not so much see one another as feel their atmospheres, and this lends a superficial disembodiment to what might have become a haunting pathology.

There are echoes of finery here and sensitivity and beneath is a filigree of a mortal wound. The preface to this new edition of *Nights*, attractively designed to resemble the 1935 privately printed edition, is written by H.D.'s daughter and she recalls the factual details upon which H.D. constructed her novel. Perdita Schaffner's own prose reveals a substance that might well have refurbished the melodrama of her mother's frail story. It is not that the reader prefers naturalism, or a devoted, unpoetic narrative. It is that *Nights* begs for a real fiction. We are given a somewhat seedless autobiography.

When H.D. is not projecting her complex disaffection with life, what exists is the skeletal nonfiction of Kenwin, the chateau where she was living on the shores of Lake Geneva. Hopping in and out of the author's cinematic reel are people who with their historic vitality actually inhabited the dramatic landscape and the house: Bryher, Kenneth Macpherson, and the splendid, unpredictable actress, Elizabeth Bergner. These worthies, although caught by the resuscitating eye of H.D. in her gauzy prose, reduce the claustrophobia. Then *Nights* glows with that starlit pallor of the 1930s.

Letter from Barbara Guest to Susan Gevirtz

Bryher looked upon film as education and entertainment, primarily education. Unlike H.D., who did initiate film into her style, Bryher kept her distance thinking about film in a more or less scientific manner. Although I do believe that film may possibly have given her a sense of background, the necessity for background, and a shortening of the novel form, a physical movement, in her historical novels. I have been re-reading them and some are exceedingly good. I believe she relied on Mary Renault and Henty—for an extraordinary combination. The novels were very post-*Borderline*. 20 years.

Bryher wrote about *montage* in Russian film, and she was aware that for the Russians, even more than for the Germans, *cutting* the film was far more important than actors for a director. And isn't that what you are talking about? Both Eisenstein and especially Pudovkin were intensely preoccupied with *cutting*. Macpherson knew this when he was making *Borderline*, but the irony is that he dropped out of the film after shooting it and left Bryher and H.D. to cut it!

. . . And what video is doing to language-space is another exploration. I admire the ellipses in *Miami Vice* and I wonder if that program has advanced (or is an advance) scientifically (and metaphorically) from film montage.

H.D.:

Margaret Anderson, editor of *The Little Review*, gave out a questionnaire, and in response to the question "What would you most like to do, to know, to be, in case you're not satisfied?" H. D. replied:

Just at the moment I am involved with pictures. We have almost finished a slight lyrical four reel little drama, done in and about the village here with some of the village people and English friends. The work has been enchanting, never anything such fun and I myself have learned to use the small projector and spend literally hours alone in my apartment making the mountains and village streets and my own acquaintances reel past me in the light and light and light. At the moment I want to go on in this medium working with and around pure types, pure artists, pure people, experimenting with faces and shadows and corners. All the light within the light fascinates me, "satisfies" me. I feel like a cat playing with webs and webs of silver. I should like for the moment to be what I am, to know a lot more about camera work, and to have a little more brawn for the lugging of things up hills. Yes, I should like more than anything to have some sort of workable little car that I could work myself and go off and on, on my own, more or less to Italy and wander in and about Italian and Swiss hills making light do what I want. (*The Little Review*, May 1929)

Eisenstein:

In his essay "The Filmic Fourth Dimension," Eisenstein elaborates on his notion of montage:

> The film-frame can never be an inflexible *letter of the alphabet*, but must always remain a multiple-meaning *ideogram*. And it can be read only in juxtaposition, just as an ideogram acquires its specific *significance*, *meaning*, and even *pronunciation* (occasionally in diametric opposition to one another) only when combined with a separately indicated reading or tiny meaning—an indicator for the exact reading—placed alongside the basic hieroglyph. (Sergei Eisenstein, "The Filmic Fourth Dimension," *Film Form*, New York: Harcourt Brace & World, 1949.)

Other Fiction

Seeking Air

to Mary Abbott

It ought to be an exact chronicle of twelve years from the time of spilling the coffee to drinking of coffee. From Dunstable to Dublin with every single passage since . . . two hundred chapters of madness, the chapter of long walks, the Berkshire surprise, fifty chapters of little times.

Dean Swift to Vanessa

Preface

Begin with telling her everything, she had said.

This provoked me into wanting to say less and less.

Yet there was such a marvelous, such an extraordinary circumference around what I might or might not tell. I thought about it. I never thought about it less than an ordinary day. I considered it into the reaches of the night. Even past novel reading or picture seeing. I wondered what it was that I might say to her. These are all parentheses, thoughts also, they go, as one would say, along the routes. They march down the avenues.

There is no point in telling you about the Ecuador or Chinese shops. You have heard about them. You have even visited the squares and sat in front of the flags. You have even entered the buildings. I think you have been just in your remarks. Not always swimming on a bland bright day with the sun at your heels, not always acquiescing to the psalm singing drift of the white lilted bright Asiatic day at your roots. Do you think so?

And now that we are quite away from everyday, now that we have forgotten perhaps to say now and wander correctly groomed, I wonder. Are you like a movie? It began this way.

I am Laffide.

She is Laffida.

We have no nationalities, no borders. We have no wars. We are a couple. One of us likes to travel. One of us fears movement and prefers to stay at home. One of us likes men. One of us likes women; we are objectives. In some way we must make a living. This can be done by changing the verb or noun object. One can also change a record, or perhaps give up a car forgetting the numerals.

I think of myself in a certain age group. And I have been reminiscing. I have been putting myself in the place of—well whoever it is—someone not here. I have been dreaming of a sentimental bookshelf. But you have never read the book that begins with Dark and never in your dearest moments thought you could capture the sequence of that Dark which is what someone once asked of me. Could this be done? Of course I said no. We are living in another generation. We are living.

> *Do you think it will be as if we were unable to find the boat going from shore to shore? I do. I do, indeed. You are the unrecognizable shore and that with the drift of weed about it. It only takes a tunny ship. The big birds go there and we are afraid of them. Someone has defined ship as shore. A quick, lunatic man. I think the gulls know best. One can even describe persons. Why do they draw in sand?*

Why have I sat in a square room in a city describing a plan? Which rooms did I get wrong? How do you spell tobaggan? And words like operetta. Someone said if you think like La Belle Helène, *but I don't. Then it would be another problem. Twinkletoes. I don't believe you think of Fred Astaire, because you never told me so. It well may be. It well may be like the slow lights of a town. The train is going to the city. The workers will go tomorrow to the city. Yet now they are enclosed in their houses. Even they have little stories told about them.*

They have visitors to their town. Criminally assaulting the city with their plans, and their hopes. Yet always withholding like underbrush the rabbit. I don't know. I keep saying I don't know. That is because I am awaiting your answer. Your answer will tell me what I am awaiting. You who are such a foreign person. I don't mean foreign to our shores, yet never have you experienced the dubious joys of sailing forth into this wilderness. Or I don't think you have. Perhaps you have? Perhaps you are a refugee? Perhaps your name is in reality such a foreign cognomen you will explain all this to me.

With you I may place a foot upon the lost way.

1

I began to know you somewhat when you introduced me to your friends. That is, I began to see you outside myself. I was permitted to witness those aspects of your person which were not private. The public view, as a painting seen at an exhibition, is so important. You know how often I have repeated that a painting varies in values when seen in the studio, at a gallery, or in a museum. How often I have been enchanted with the work of a painter when it was showed at the studio, brushes in hand, the cup of cold coffee on the table and here and there the evidence of a struggle in the crumpled sketch paper or the postcard tacked on the wall or the notebook open to the three scrawled lines, written no doubt in the early morning. And the variation at the exhibition of this same painting, its statement lost among the personalities.

And didn't we enjoy that museum in Siena? Despite your cold and runny nose, the missing tissue. Especially keen to us was the landscape outside the window corresponding so exactly to the painting on the wall. We were quite unable to "judge" the value of the paintings themselves. They might have been rather ordinary, as indeed, I remember many of them to have been. Here for an agreeable time was no element of art "triumphing" or "improving" nature. Nature and art were in such similitude due to the exact degree of their presentation; due that is to the light reaching into the room, to the color of the ground and to the distance of the hills, each of which appeared in the painting.

And so it was with you, Miriam, when you said in that voice which is so like the color of your hair: "This is Robert. This is Celestine."

Robert I did not like immediately. I resented his having known of your existence longer than I. Then he is handsome and I am not. An old-fashioned attitude of mine. It seems no longer one makes the choice of deciding if a person is handsome. Like so many disappearing conveniences which have been replaced by other conveniences, the aesthetic of the human face has been withdrawn. Now one says, "He has an interesting face" or more likely, "He looks like his sister," or again, "How virile," or again, "I like a nose slightly out of joint." Note that one never mentions, as ethics also are changing, "a corrupt mouth."

Do you suppose people still say, "He wears his heart on his sleeve"? I know very well that a few romantic exchanges still persist. Just the other day someone said to me, "How Doris has changed. Her eyes are so dark and sunken. She has cried too much." And it was true. The life of Doris was beginning to disintegrate, or rather she was in the middle of that era in her life when a decision needed to be made which she sought to postpone through constant tears, tears that successfully hid what she could not bear to see. I know also that Annette was chastised because her face was becoming too "full."

Actually the plumpness of her cheek line gave it a mature beauty. But it was not the aesthetics of her face which were questioned. No one, I reiterate, cares much about the proportions of beauty. What exactly was meant was the moral comment that Annette had been drinking too much and this incontinence was betrayed by her face. Nearly always our comments are relative to the presence of the superlative. One can permit the comparative, indeed that is what success is based on, but the superlative is disastrous.

There is something a little superlative about Celestine. Can I guess it is because she loves Robert too much? I noticed she was unable to concentrate on our conversation. I wasn't altogether flattered that it seemed a matter of indifference to her whether or not she was introduced to me. Celestine likes you. But I don't think she approves of you. She is given (part of her superlativeness) to conclusions. From a few "chance" remarks, such as, "Miriam you should go out more," I gather she has concluded you live too much the life of a spinster. How ridiculous this is we both know. Celestine really does admire an intense love. You can tell this by the way she dresses. There are so many open spaces in her clothing and then they are flattened out. In order to vary her ensembles she adds a bit too much. It is like her apartment where we went afterwards. I like it when she uses primary colors, but she does not understand dark corners. There is too much eloquence in her window dressing. You see how given one is to criticism of a superlative sort of person? I hope I didn't show my distaste for the way she made our supper.

It wasn't the food, it was the preparation. Those "let's have" and "put in another can" and "one should always use" I objected to. Robert was pleased with the meal and she appeared to enjoy our conversation which might have been about the sunrise for all I know. It was only when he began to tell us of his trip to Asia that I woke up. I was reminded of a trip I had made on the Nile which reminded me of my mother's earrings which reminded me of the garbage which used to collect under her window in our summer house which reminded me of my sister Jennifer's bicycle I used to borrow on a glowing morning which reminded me of you who have always reminded me of Jennifer.

And so I began to relax in the company of your friends, because they were part of you. I knew that after a few hours I should see you alone and then I would see you differently, then you would be part of me, but I did want to postpone your separation from your friends so that I might study you more octagonally; you were still only rectangular to me and I wished to seize the opportunities of our supper party. Now you are more like a pebble. Your sides do not match; you are neither round nor square, yet you are beginning to have a promising shape.

I almost came upon it in the dark. When we were alone at my apartment. You were lying on the sofa and your head fell slightly to the left. Your skin was a dark green. Your eyelids were that natural grey and your hands slightly yellowed, a spot of moisture above your lip. You were speaking of revolutions and the shortening of the span between medieval and modern. Your laughter occasionally broke into black lines, the spaces contravening between thought and speech. Your long upper thigh was stretched tensely toward an object I could not see, but which I understood to be just out of my reach. It was the posture of the lion in the cage whose paw gropes outside the bars for a lump of raw meat. I snapped open the lock and opened the cage. I hoped to discover under that mild manner of yours the ferocity which I had noticed when you bit into a piece of cake that evening in St. Augustine.

Miriam. You have been given the perfect name. There are two vowels and three consonants.

2

The next morning after you had left I was neatening your traces. You do leave behind you an extraordinary disorder. That was what I thought when first I knew you. Now I recognize your assortments. There is a lucidity in your placing of personal objects. On one table the hair pins. On another the powder. Here is a half-eaten pear. In the bathroom the soap has slipped to the floor. A lipstick lies on an ash tray in the middle of the bed. And yet there is "order, clarity, lucidity." And there is a purity in your design, like a Matisse painting of "Studio." It took me a long time to learn this.

As first I was scandalized, as was my mother with my adolescent room. I can see her stooping over a garment, questioning me why I live so differently from her and father. Following her eye to the lawn I would think of the linen closet with those elegant shapes of towels and sheets and wonder, indeed, why my own closet, my bed which I thought of as my splendid tent, should be so messy. Later when I owned my own apartment I became obsessively neat. I missed my mother.

I wanted to tell you about my return to my parents' house. It was last summer when you had gone off on what you call your "assignments." I know they are not assignations, but this business life of yours is so disparate to me; your life in what is known as "outside our world" is so cloudy to me that I cannot fictionalize Miriam meeting a strange person, Miriam asking this person an intimate question, Miriam writing down what is said in her notebook. You have showed me this notebook. To me it is only filled with diagrams of train schedules which explain to me where you will be in one hour when I shall need you.

3

Last summer I went to the country to look at our old house. My parents had always been so unfortunate in business dealings that it had become impossible for them to find a tenant for the house. Going over my objection they still could not find someone to buy the house.

I seldom visit this house, but it was a dry summer, a hot summer. I knew that the house by the sea with its furniture shrouded in sheets would be cool, even chilly. When I opened its windows the sea air would blow through it, pushing out the smell of mothballs and old mattresses. The tap water after the first rush of rusty water would be clear, cold, cold. I could walk to the ocean and bathe each day, returning to that old outside shower under which I used to stand letting the sand and salt water wash off me, the shower water running into the slightly browned grass around the drain. I used to think of myself as a gazelle at a watering spot! Later, many brave animals who had come to the water hole briefly to drink.

In those days I was always changing myself into an animal. When I was a unicorn it was in the parlor near the watercolor picture of Mélisande. I remember that she was looking sadly into a pool where her gold ring had been dropped. I was angry with her because she had betrayed me with King Pélleas. I had confused my centuries; any lady in court dress would hold the head of a unicorn in her lap. For Mélisande the unicorn could only be a myth about which she had read, who had once appeared in another country. You know that I remedied that error in my book which is now translated into several languages.

4

There is a dog who lives near our property. There is always a dog, but this spaniel I could see watching me from across the lawn. As I went from room to room opening the windows I would see him racing back and forth in front of this house. At night when I would climb the stairs, crossing the landing, going from room to room turning on the lights, I would hear him howl. Finally the watchful presence of this animal to whom I had made no overtures, but who so concerned himself with the movements of my life, began to disturb me. I decided that inasmuch as he was the only species of life in that community who was aware of my identity, that is, the peculiarities of my personal habits, I might very well make overtures toward him. Keep in mind I had been staying in the house, talking to no one, going each day to the sea for a swim, and returning to a shrouded house to cook my meal, to reminisce, and go to bed. I was aware that after I had retired he would come to my house, poke into the garbage, roam about the grounds, and sniff at the porch. Yet never in the daytime.

One morning after my swim, when I was showering and recalling my lost animal identities, I saw him sitting halfway up on the lawn. I whistled. How long it had been since I had whistled! It was such a dusty noise, yet he heard it. There he was bounding toward me. To shorten this, Miriam, we became friends. Whereas formerly my tracks had been from the sea to the house, now he began to accompany me about the grounds. He knew those old paths better than I. He took me to the barn, then to the carriage house. It was there I made my discovery, the consequence of which has set me on an entirely new train of metaphysical enquiry. The results of which can only be antithetical to those of my colleagues. Yet what are colleagues? Enemies!

The grass was rougher, tougher in certain clods. These clods stood out against the clean, thin, fresh slips of grass. They were coarse-grained and the clods were in the shape of a horse's hoof. These were the same tracks that had been made by my grandfather's carriage horses. They were the tracks the horses had made when we children rode over the lawn to the fury of our elders. What a cautious hoarder is nature; how sly and penurious, how reproductive, how unforgetful. She likes to hear the same old opera over and over. Nothing new about her. Reflect that I was led to these conclusions, only a fraction of which I have started here, by a dog.

I shall not bore you any longer with these reminders. Long Island is not Balbec, any more than Balbec is Combray. Any more than I would use a bathing machine.

5

Dinner at my apartment. An evening with a New Zealander.

I received a telephone call from young Tom Powell saying he was passing through this city. He was bringing a herd of cattle to New Zealand from Ireland! Tom is the brother of Sheila, a delightful girl who was the governess of the children of friends with whom I had stayed in London. "Gouvernante" was really the term the hotel people liked to bestow upon her, the hotel where she and the child would have dinner. Actually she came from that indispensable British agency, Universal Aunts. Sheila had accompanied a family of Americans when they travelled to France, Italy, and Greece. The good humor and manners of this girl (23) were compelling. If she indulged herself in moods this indulgence certainly took place privately. She was fond of her young wards. She was pleased with the countries she visited. (Liking Italy less, a bit overwhelmed by France, an admirer of Greek ruins.) Her geographical and presumably cultural education completed she wished to return to New Zealand. We had been surprised at her decision, thinking she might marry a Welshman, a farmer, who had grown up near the border, quite near the spot her family had emigrated from. However, such is the pull of her island that Sheila desired to return to it.

I have photographs of her wedding which took place at Waipawa. There stands the wedding party in front of the white wooden church. They are properly arrayed in taffetas and borrowed formal dress. On the wedding group shines that white clean New Zealand light, the envier of shadows. It is an English wedding. An Episcopal style church. Bless Sheila, she will have children named Diana, Rosemary, and Guy.

Arrival of Miriam. Her first New Zealander. She helps with the table. She is in a friendly humor. Arrival of Tom.

He is tall, well formed, blond, and healthy-cheeked. His hair is cut in a bang across his forehead. This once might have signaled the country bumpkin, now it is a modulated version of the current long hair. Fresh from a British barber. Its original cut modified somewhat by his recent stay in Ireland. A ruffling of the locks into authenticity.

Tom delights us. He is simple, direct (as was Sheila), he appears to have none of the traces of inferiority toward more cosmopolitan places as would his contemporary from this country. We were both rather overcome by this person. Later in the evening a wee bit bored.

His most important remark, or so I thought, aside from his description of loading the cattle onto an airplane in Ireland, was made when he told us of visiting Westminster Abbey on Commonwealth Day. The remark was: "You know we used to sing those old Episcopal hymns in our little church. I never quite understood what they meant, although I would sing along. Then we sang the hymns, the same ones in the Abbey. A great throng there was and a large choir. Suddenly I understood about England's fair and green land. I knew about the Lord being a Shepherd, because I had tended sheep, but I hadn't before realized the sheep in the hymns were thousands of people, not just wooly bleating animals."

I think Miriam liked best his telling us of visiting the minister in Shropshire. Miriam was teary-eyed when Tom told us the minister was the last of his branch of the Powells, and further was preaching the last Powellized sermon. Would Tom return to hear another sermon so that another Powell would sit in the congregation? That he wouldn't.

I forgot to say Tom brought flowers. Red and white carnations for Christmas.

A well-articulated man who carried himself well. Large flushed hands.

6

At the movies with Miriam. Another Italian import. I fell to thinking about a review I had read of a book called *The Case for Spelling Reform.* The question was: is there a case for spelling reform? Henry Sweet, "the greatest of all English philologists," thought so. The book was written by Mont Follick. This kept me occupied through three quarters of the film. I then cast a few shadows toward the Shavian alphabet. I finished the last episode of the movie with a Shavian denouement in mind. Follick believed that the adjective "subtile" was derived from "the days when the Roman philosophers used to wander up and down under the lime trees trying to emulate each other with clever arguments and phrases, often splitting hairs over very fine differences, so *subtilis* was born—lime tree being *tilia* in Latin."

7

Things have fallen out and things have fallen in.
HG WELLS

Miriam, we are going to Minna's. Ah, this is when you put your hand in mine. We are going to pass through the corridors of my past. Then stairs. First up to the rooms. We push the bell. Someone nearby says, "They wouldn't let me into the bar of the Seven Seas." We are in a hallway. Miriam. I touch you. You who have never known the years of these rooms. I feel your heavy dress. We go up the stairs. There it is.

This is the water's music. I am walking by the water. I am telling you, my sister, you are syllables. You are the music dropped on leaves. I am saying we are living at the top of the house and there the chords make such a sound the steeple sweeps sideways against the sky. And then we begin.

8

It is six a.m. in Los Angeles. The hour of first light. A beginning of a day which has no changes, remaining all seasons, a boy with his wheel.

Ah, Miriam, we are lying together on such a low bed. Not at all like our old bed. It is really a pallet. The light from the ceiling hurts my eyelids and I think of morning's cool haze. So dark at first then a faint light, then the roses strewn; yet hesitant, somehow careful, as if the roses were floating into day which carried a handful of cards, a bright desk hidden in the palm.

Searching you. The light on your face. The yellow.

Miriam, where are we?

Your skin. Dowsed with light.

Except that, Miriam, we are in New York and you have promised that there will be no deaths. Before I tell you a few extraordinary tales.

It is night. I have told you about the jewel robbery, about the man "who didn't care," and about the bedrooms filled with watches. You have told me how you froze in your black winter coat (like Roman cherries that coat). Even if the fur did rough up the edges and make you fear that "snow will never settle here."

Morgan!

I am listening. My real dreams hurt you. Stabs of joy.

9

It's laudanum time.

A wisp of green sunset falls across the chaise.

The papa of Elizabeth is pacing his study floor.

The dog thumps his tail.

The book of poems quietly turns its leaves.

Robert rounds the corner, his boots chumping in the watery snow.

The heavy eyelids of Elizabeth stoop lower into the smile at the mouth's bend which is slightly plumper with patience.

The Jamaica bananas with their soft round toes.

I like astrakhan sunsets on the rug. And "gaudy melon flowers." And the firm bite of exile.

Robert has arrived. He has brought a present. It is called *The Care of Books in a Tropical Climate.*

It is the last Christmas on Wimpole Street. They are going to the land of Ruddigore.

Miriam exists with a flick of the fingernail. Ta.

10

I have changed to the new typewriter with the large type. Sadly, tenderly I put the old one in the closet. And I confess only to you, Miriam, how near I was to tears. The letters I have written to you on the old typewriter. The hours I have spent in front of it seeking your image, or trying to reclaim your image from the alphabet that settled over your face. The sentence that would describe with its careful punctuation (and its momentous pauses while I lit a cigarette) my exact feeling for you and the tonal area of your solutions.

Now space enlarges in front of me. The proportions are attenuated. There is more prose on the roller. I must maintain my former techniques at the same time as I move stealthily into the new structure whose windows are still dark.

I am only beginning to "touch" it. And I have been seven years "touching" your face.

Foreheads

with Joe Brainard

FOREHEADS
BY BARBARA GUEST
DRAWN BY JOE BRAINARD
START

MY ANTLERS WARM THE COLD NIGHTS OF THE FOREHEAD WHEN THE ATOM STARS BURN MY SCIENTIST PAWS
KRISTA HAS DISAPPEARED DOWN THE SNOW LANES I AM PROMISED A MISSILE FOR CHRISTMAS YET I LONG FOR MY TWIN OF THE POLAR NOSE
THIS ICE BLOCK LIKE A FOREHEAD THESE GLACIAL NIGHTS ARE FOREHEADS FUR COVERS LIKE SNOW FOREHEADS HE HAS GONE SOUTH WITH HIS THIN FOREHEAD
SOUTH TO THE MOUNTAINS WHILE I LIE AWAKE UNDER MY FOREHEAD

SOMEONE HAS STOPPED LEO IN HIS JUNGLE
SOMEONE HAS BLOCKED HIS FOREHEAD
GROWLING LEO
HAS LEFT THE RAIN PATH FOR THE SKIES

THEY GLISTEN WITH MIRRORS
HIS LOST FOREHEAD'S EYES
DISC FOREHEAD
PLANET
OF NO MOISTURE
YOUR FOREHEAD
HAS LAKE CRATERS
I BURY A STAR ON YOU
I WHO AM ROUND
WITH NO FOREHEAD

A SNOUT
ECLIPSED MY BROW
YCLEPT FOREHEAD
"DOWN UNDER"
THE MEDICAL HISTORY
OF THE FOREHEAD CONCLUDED WITH A
SINUS HISTORY. ONLY IN WHAT
TIBETANS TERM "UPPER AIR" IS THE
FOREHEAD FREE OF DRAIN
FURNACES
OXYGEN
RADIOS
ETHER
HYDROPLANE
EVINRUDE
ATMOSPHERIC
DREADNOUGHTS
SUPERTONIC
FLEEING THE EARTH
OF ANXIOUS PALMS
RESTLESS
FOREHEADS
ESCAPING FOREHEADS
PRIMATE
FOREHEAD
NO FUTURE
ZING SINGS A
STAR
TO THE TWO-
SYLLABLED
FOREHEAD

GAUTIER: THE BUTTOCKS OF MARGUERITE RESSEMBLE HER FOREHEAD IN SMOOTHNESS, IF NOT IN...
DUMAS: CAMILLE WAS A NUDE YOUNG GIRL WHOSE FOREHEAD REFLECTED THE WOES OF...
GAUTIER: THE PATRIOTISM OF AN ERA FOUND... IN THE FOREHEAD OF AN ODALISQUE...
DUMAS: COUNT ROBERT DE... WAS ACCUSTOMED TO... AFTER WHICH...
TOGETHER: MON FRONT!
THE END

The Influence of Music on the Work of George Eliot, as recalled by George Henry Lewes

I thought about the day and worried that it had no tone. It wasn't that it was drab; on the contrary, the sun lit the house in various spots, not like the usual conveyance that runs from upstairs to downstairs taking on its own speed. There was a liveliness on the stairs, as witness the housemaid smiling as she carried down the morning tea, her little starched cap jiggling in the light that pierced the hall stairs through the mullioned window.

It had actually gotten off to a fine start with George up early as always in her study where I could hear the pen racing across the page. This sound does not disturb me as my pen scratching the paper annoyed her when we shared a study.

That was long ago when we, in our middle thirties, risking our names and fortunes, had gone off together; I was tired and discouraged, a man of letters who had lost his natural liveliness; someone compared me to a French dancing master, I was so bouncy. (They also injudiciously described George as having the face of a horse.) There was Agnes, my wife, my three babies and the other babes she had precipitously thrust on the household, a result of her liaison with our best friend. His father was the poet who wrote the poem that was like a violin weaving the air, "Jenny Kissed Me."

I did not desert Agnes. I paid dearly for accepting that first child by Hunt and could through the exotic laws of our land never divorce her. It would be George who provided for them later, but we never knew that would happen when we left for the Continent and wandered into our own opera, a many-stringed opera with bassoons and flutes and always the kettle drum.

We departed for Germany. There I planned to begin my Life of Goethe. George, with her finer knowledge of German, was willing to assist me with the translations necessary for this work. I trusted her severe corrections. The clarity she showed in her revisions was like that of a conductor who cautions his orchestra to remain in the right key. Her superiority was everywhere evident in those translations she continued to offer to the "Fortnightly" in her attempt to earn money. Words she took from their native tongue and turned into English reflected an inspired method, similar to that of a passage of music interpreted by a musician of unaccountable sensibility.

When we arrived in Weimar who should be there but Liszt and his Princess flourishing in the illegality of their union. In their atmosphere, the cloud of disapproval hanging over us evaporated. Liszt would strike his baton down firmly on the table, I can see it now, a fine piece of baroque with lacy roses, and declare himself the "cavalier" of love. He looked it, too. The long locks bending over the piano and his music surging around my ankles, sometimes those surges felt like alligators, an indelicate feeling, I admit. George wrote to a friend, "Liszt overwhelming in his attention."

We were fortunate in our musical acquaintances. In Weimar we also met Anton Rubinstein and we saw him years later at his concerts in London. It is he who is Klesmer in *Daniel Deronda*. Wagner we knew also, but we decided he was too modern.

In London we faithfully attended each Saturday the Pop Concerts and I can still see George in her black shawled cap lost in the emotive contemplation that music always stirred in her. At home we usually played on the piano the themes from the compositions we had listened to earlier and George sang beautifully. The room we sat in became more cozy then, more gemütlich than usual and tender at the same time.

One day she confessed that she listened to music so attentively because each composer spoke to her in a separate way and she found she could seize the ideas aroused by musical notes and introduce these into her novels. Absorbed in musical space these ideas would come whirling down upon her out of the music's ether. It was moreover as if a baton crossed her brow releasing the demons of creativity, because she never concealed they were demons and that was perhaps why she suffered those fierce headaches.

Even when she was famous, idolized really, she was still socially not accepted. Men came without their wives to our house paid for by *Silas Marner* and *Middlemarch* and *The Mill on the Floss*. We were always at home on Saturday evenings which were often musical. George played the piano, my son played the violin, and Herbert Spencer and Anthony Trollope and Huxley and Robert Browning hummed along.

It was about this time that she was told how much the Queen admired her books and George found this "extremely agreeable"; she had probably forgotten when she had first seen the Queen at the Opera back in 1852 she found her "deplorable . . . so utterly mean in contour and expression." But George was changed and began now to believe the admiration of royalty to be more conductive than the admiration of other mortals. I wonder if she remembered Liszt. Sometimes at a concert on Saturday I would steal a look at George and she did remind me of the Queen sitting there with that contraption over her head like the Queen's widow cap. She was wise like the Queen in her odd way was, and passionate, each of them restrained yet passionate with something of the full orchestra inside their bosoms competing with the conservative tone of the score.

Although I wasn't aware of it at the time, Charles Eliot Norton on a visit from Boston (a city about which George had never concerned herself) was unfavorably impressed with our house. I am told he wrote home that "all the works of art in the house bore witness to the want of delicate artistic feeling, or good culture on the part of the occupants." He observed in particular "a *common* lithograph of Titian's *Christ of the Tribute Money*." He never encouraged his wife to visit George.

I wish I had mentioned to him that the Queen commissioned her own court artist to portray *Dinah Morris Preaching on Hayslope Green*, a scene from *Adam Bede*, for her private collection.

A note to myself if I am still irritated by that Bostonian, to remember du Maurier's sketch of George done from memory. He used to sing for us his pretty little French song, *Fi de ces vins d'Espagne*.

And what a long way we have come from our first domestic lodging near Kew Gardens and Richmond (an area convenient for our walks) when we read to each other, or sometimes played the piano and sang though fearful of disturbing the clergyman in the rooms below. There were no callers and many an evening I left her for business in London, and on holidays such as Christmas and New Year's Day she was alone when I visited my sons and my mother. These were responsibilities I could not neglect.

She had her music and when not at the piano she read Greek and Latin. She continued her translation of Spinoza's *Ethics.* Much was accomplished in that solitude. The "storm-tried matron" changed into a novelist. The great mind for which she is admired, and an uncompromising frame for her novels, was exercised on those evenings when she wasn't "invited to dine."

I've had an idea, the day turning out to possess a loquacious, a clearly audible tone, to make a list of musical influences upon George Eliot. This could be developed into an article for *The George Eliot Birthday Book of 1878* Blackwood is going to publish.

Motion Pictures

MOTION PICTURES: 10

They were in Alexandria filming *The Vanished Library*. This film was assigned originally to Petaluma, but she was in Minneapolis making The Life of Hiawatha. She kept faxing suggestions to the new director who was already intimidated by her. In a re-run of the first reel of the film there was a curious rush of water "like the Mississippi," someone said.

The film was barely off the ground when the wardrobe head decided to redesign the costumes of Aristotle and Pliny. The film began to act as if it was haunted when the crew was forced to destroy the plywood copy of the Library which an historian told them was incorrect. And there were too many ships in the harbor. Another consultant from MIT recommended an Egyptian director.

They put in an emergency call for an historian from Princeton who happened to be on a dig in Turkey and this historian when he arrived on the set laughed brutishly. He told them the scholarly debate was not over the size of the library. It was whether the Iliad and the Odyssey had both been written by Homer. He reminded them that the library had been burned several times. What they were working with now was a false copy of the second burning of the library.

By this time the crew and the actors had decided Alexandria resembled Los Angeles. Why didn't they take the picture back to the sound studio in Culver City where they could live at home comfortable and mosquitoless. Los Angeles had a burned library, an Art Foundation that could supply them with drawings of historical costumes. The sea of Los Angeles was also poisoned like the waters of Alexandria. It was decided to move back home.

Petaluma had completed her work in Minneapolis and was reassigned to the film. It turned out that midway into *Hiawatha* she had converted to Social Realism. Despite groans from the accountancy department which had approved *The Vanished Library* as a "prestigious" property, she announced she was not going to make another ART FILM.

With her fabulous eye for detail, she now focused on the illiteracy of the populace. "Starving" extras now filled the streets, in rags the locals wept. The Stars weep also for the fragile gowns they cannot wear and the especially cut jewels are forbidden. The actors sigh for the silk and fur of their cloaks and the flagons of wine now missing.

Then begins the actual conflagration when the library like a mighty ship keels, its marble columns felled, the precious literature destroyed. Historical records burn. Petaluma jumps up and down tearing her hair clothes skin throwing volume after volume of books in the fire urging the extras to carry more books: MORE FIRE MORE FIRE BURN MORE books BOOKS BURN MORE BOOKS MOREBOOKS she is all over the set screaming and strangely laughing as one by one the books fall into the flames

MORE MORE FLAMES! MORE! BURN THEM!
GET RID OF BOOKS!

MOTION PICTURES: 11

The film was about nuns shedding their "Habits," it was supposed to be a documentary with a close-up in the cloister of one nun walking in the new dress of a nun. "Something simple in cotton or wool with a cardigan and low shoes" were the orders given to the wardrobe department. The other nun was supposed to be wearing the discarded nun habit with rosary at the waist. Unfortunately the wardrobe department had packed away or sold the original habits and had not ordered any replacements.

The film was about to be canceled when the director had the idea of taking his crew over to a convent and filming his picture there. At this point an argument began about where they would find a convent. A member of the crew told them the nuns lived on church grounds, or so he thought, and why didn't they move their equipment to a neighborhood Catholic Church.

Then an argument broke out about whether they should use the actresses who had already been chosen after much delay and search, or if the nuns in the Church that was yet to be located would permit themselves to be filmed. The nuns, of course, would add more authenticity to what was going to be a documentary and not a motion picture. At this point the actresses said they would sue the company, because their contracts were already signed. It was also mentioned that there might be a clause in the contracts of nuns that did not permit them to be filmed for commercial purposes.

"Commercial purposes" was familiar to the production department and after no more than an hour word came from the head office saying the department would be delighted to make a gift to the "church of choice" if one were selected as soon as possible as the production manager was already annoyed at the delay.

The director, who found himself idle during these conversations, retired to his van to read *The Counterfeiters* while he sipped his afternoon vodka with orange juice. His assistant climbed into the van and they began to discuss André Gide and how seldom in French letters did one find a writer who was a Protestant. The Director remarked it was quite a coincidence that he, the son of a Protestant minister, should be making a documentary about nuns.

They agreed the idea of the picture was stupid. Old films about nuns used "star" material like Ingrid Bergman. It was absurd to make this documentary with third-rate actresses and local churches. They also were agreeing the company should go to Lourdes when the telephone rang. The message that closed down the film was that the church in Beverly Hills wanted too much money and the priest of the Church of the Angels near Olvera St. was in Mexico.

MOTION PICTURES: 12

The more the scenario relies on Corelli, the more fluid it becomes and moves closer to the idea of a master scene whose nuance is fixed in a shadow kingdom which the music of Corelli will underscore. Within the scenario there is built an incredible gaiety that may or may not take place. It is "a strictness within fluidity" which will complicate this film, now experimentally called *Bird on Nude Girl's Hip.*

MOTION PICTURES: 13

A fully dressed man with the exceedingly mobile face of the 1930s, once frequently caught on camera, is standing on an empty beach. He is reading a letter. As the sea gulls screech above him the camera pans in and he looks directly into it repeating again and again, "I refuse to get whipped up by your lonely news."

MOTION PICTURES: 14

She was handed this beautiful opportunity of directing a film she truly believed in. The "truly" had been written into her astonishingly female-oriented contract and for days she had been considering scripts, even books. Now she was in a blue funk.

The color "blue" flew under her lids as did a passing memory of *Erwartung* by Schoenberg. A pink tulip was added with a portrait by Tiepolo. She noticed a bowl of raisins placed near her desk. Did they belong there? All at once she remembered a little girl with a cow, and she believed the little girl once belonged in a nursery rhyme in a book called *Smooth Realities*. The pink dress of the little girl, even the bows on her dress, went with the tulips that went with the room.

Meanwhile the postman delivered a large package wet from the rains that besieged her city. She put the package on a table and a plum rolled out of a grocery bag her daughter carelessly had placed on the table. The cat came downstairs and bit her leg. She remembered the blue cat who had fallen out of the window in Switzerland. There had been a tall old tree under the window and the cat had lain in the tree for days alive and meowing while the people below in the first-floor apartment had told her the cat was dead and had been carted away. She looked at the palm tree outside. She began to weep a little and tears gathered in her eyes just beneath the memory of *Erwartung*.

The door opened and her husband walked into the room. He had been away on a trip. He put his suitcase on the floor and embraced her. His gaze, however, was not on her, but toward the open door of the kitchen from which came the warning smell of burned chicken.

"I am going to get rid of this," she said to herself closing her eyes. When she opened them her husband was gone and so was the odor of burned chicken. "That is real editing," she said out loud, "No one else in the studio does this as well as I do."

Then she began to talk to herself about Montage Montage and how people neglected it, etc. She really began to feel as if she had completed a picture and her husband had come home to celebrate with her. Her daughter, or the cook, she added, as she liked to believe the studio paid her more than it did, had cooked a *coq au vin*, the same kind of chicken they served in the films of Ernst Lubitsch that took place on the Left Bank.

She remembered the champagne they served in Lubitsch films, even when faced with poverty and bitter times. Then another tear formed in her eye with the memory of the chiffon dresses that floated over his shiny floors. She heard the music. The music that lightened the movies' touch. Just enough of it and never moody. The doors that accompanied his motion pictures. Shining like the floors, promising secrets.

You climbed up his handsome stairs to the great doors that swung open to men sitting in chairs and drinking, laughing, lying. People lied in his pictures and you never minded. Only betrayed people opened his doors.

Then the dreamers in Lubitsch films. Gifted people, like herself, determined to exit the web of everyday life. What did Lubitsch know about everyday life! That dream-laden Hungarian. Then she recalled the eyes of a former Baroness who was Hungarian. While she played with a little fan tied to her wrist as the boat sailed along, tears, international tears, of loss and regret, continually nested in her eyes.

Suddenly it occurred to the Director that she no longer needed a script. All day she had been "montaging" bits of stories, putting together placemats for her idle dreams. Her script had already written itself. It was the length of an *Intermezzo*, a breeze in the middle of the day. It would show off her talents which truth-to-tell were not symphonic, were womanly and brief (money-saving). The time of the telling of her story would be an *Intermezzo*, like the name of a restaurant whispered across the table before the half bottle of champagne is served.

MOTION PICTURES: 15

They were on location in the hills above a small California town and before breakfast the Assistant Director and a member of his crew were scouting out possible locations for the movie they were going to make. It was tentatively called "Preparedness" or "He is Prepared" or "Without Preparedness"; the word "Preparedness" or "Prepared" was ordered to be in the film title. This had to do with an idea of the Producer's that all bad things in the world happened because people were unprepared.

"For what?" This was asked all over the set. But no one had found an answer.

The men had climbed to about three thousand feet and were surveying the gentle land that lay about them. There were wildflowers amid the eucalyptus trees and there were chestnut trees with pale rose-colored blossoms at their long fingertips. An azalea or two became part of a disordered group of cultivated flowers blown there by the bay winds. All was serenely natural and even stately with the yellow iris and the browned peony buds a straggling rose and the carpet of wildflowers violet and pink, sometimes yellow. The flowers, the soft breeze laden with scent and trees changing color as the morning passed, and the light filled with yellow charmed these Hollywood men and their talk became less indignant.

They could see the water of the Bay below them with small boats anchored at its shores. A cloud rolled over from a mountain above the Bay. The light changed on their mountain to a dark grey. The sun slowly entered the cloud and the cloud was mottled with a yellow glow from the sun forcing its way through the grey cloud. On top of the far mountain there was a contest between the color of the sun forcing its way through the cloud and the dark cloud coming from behind the mountain forcing itself into the yellowed light.

The movie men noticed that the ground below them and beside them was mottled with this color coming from across the bay and the leaves on the ground began to pick up a little wind. The flowers began a slow nodding and what had been simple now began to turn into a darker more complicated color; the breeze was picking up and this caused the leaves of the tree near them to flatten and show their dull greyish green sides. The odor of the flowers began to penetrate this slow changing of the guard on the mountain. The odor began to enter the new stillness and halt there.

One of the men who was sensitive to attacks of heat and cold began to shiver. Another took out a package of cigarettes and was going to light up when a hand reached across and closed the package. He was reminded that smoking was forbidden. The land had been too dry, too crisp and eager for fire, and they began to discuss the terrible fire that had ravaged a mountain nearby.

A bird flew across the horizon. He was large and the swoop that his wing made was slightly disturbing. Yet the dipping of his wings as he sailed across the canyon created no disorder in their vision, but indicated a calmness, as always in an elegant finesse of nature, it was noted. This brought the men to a conversation about elegance and how sometimes it was needed in a film. Just enough of it might save a picture from the tawdriness it was willing to fall into. Elegance, as in the length of the swoop of the hawk's wing. One of the men looked at his watch wishing to time the swooping, if possible. The hawk obligingly flew over them again even as the first drops of rain fell. With the beginning of the rain the hawk began to fly higher like an airplane, seeking another altitude. So they were unable to time the hawk and its elegance became a memory. But memory is useful they remarked. They were talking about the memory necessary to a film, of course, because none of them had much use for anything outside their work.

The rain had by now muddied the hill path and the color of the flowers became more brilliant against the ground before their soft heads were utterly destroyed. Across the bay a streak of lightning hit a mountain peak and they watched the rain pour from a cloud and into the bay. The men had brought no umbrella or raincoats, they were unprepared for this natural seizure of land and color. They were unprepared for the sudden swirl of water around their ankles as a torrent got in their way going down. But they were laughing. Their teeth outside their mouth in the widening of the mouth for laughter getting wetter and wetter until each of them was swallowing the rain water. They had been unprepared for this torrent of water but now they knew how the scene would play out.

Chinese Ghost Restaurant

SCENE: CHINESE GHOST RESTAURANT

[*Four or five (number determinant upon actors) people are seated at a table in a Chinese Restaurant*

Enter Waiter: Bamboo Shoots?

All: Bamboo Shoots!

(1) [*questions*] Bamboo Shoots?

(2) [*agrees*] Bamboo Shoots.

(3) [*serious*] Bamboo Shoots.

(4) [*leans back considering*] Bamboo Shoots . . .

(1) [*eagerly*] Bamboo Shoots!

(2) [*sadly*] Bamboo Shoots.

(3) [*wryly, then laughs*] Bam boo Shoo its

(4) [*hungrily*] Bammmmmboooo shooots

(1) [*gourmet*] Bamboo shoots

[*However, before they can lift their chopsticks the food is lifted from the table by three or four silent figures costumed in red—the Chinese color for death—so these are our ghosts.*]

Waiter: [*enters, bringing in snow peas*] Snow Peas?

All: Snow Peas!

(1) Snow mountain peas

(2) Snow valley peas

(3) Snow country peas

(4) Snow landscape peas

(1) Snow

(2) Mountain

(3) valley

(4) Country

(all) Landscape

peas

(1) Green

(2) Pear green

(3) Nature green

(4) Bean green

(5) Sky green

(6) Throat green

(3) Stomach green

(4) Cough green

(1) Sneeze green

(2) Hurt green

(3) Well green

(4) Kiss green

(1) Everything green

(2) All green

(3) Green snow

(4) Green mountain

(1) Green valley

(2) Green country

(3) Green picture

(4) Green peas!

[*The figures enter and take away the snow peas.*]

Waiter: [*enters*] Plain mushrooms?

(1) Wavy

(2) browny

(3) Musky

(4) Not musky

(1) Little dish of mushrooms

(2) Mushy

(3) Wavy

(4) Roomy

(1) Small Chow

(2) Small talk

(3) Eat fast

(4) Try bite

[*The figures have again entered and the mushrooms taken away.*]

Waiter: [*enters, this time he does not ask a question, he simply states*] Rice wine.

(1) Ahm

(2) Oooh

(3) ummh

(4) swallows in dry throat

(1) Licks lip

(2) heh heh heh heh heh heh heh heh heh

(3) We make small Chinese sounds

[*All look at each other and lift cups.*]

(4) Much wine here

(1) Small cups

(2) Disappear

[*And so they do, carried out by figures.*]

Waiter: [*enters*] Irresistible Duck?

[*Now we have what may be called an 'international conversation.'*]

(1) I do recall in 1933—Hankow—Such food!

(2) Number 3 houseboy

(3) Number 2 houseboy

(4) Number 1 houseboy

(1) Ah polo!

(2) Ah tennis

(3) Ah houseboats

(4) Ah Pekin Caucasian Club

(1) Ah Pekin Picnics

(2) Ah Pekin pony rides

(3) Ah Pekin young consulate men

(4) Ah afternoon on shady verandah

(1) Ah pink gins!

(2) Ah Singapore slings!

(3) Ah Far Eastern tummies!

(4) Ah last glowing Empire embers of evenings

(1) Ah Imperial days!

(2) Ah Duck!

(3) Ah Emperor's Duck!

[*As before, food is removed by figures.*]

Waiter: [*enters*] Thousand year eggs.

(1) I remember old Guston-Wheasy, great collector.

[*Now they all look carefully at their eggs which are set in front of each person—each to an egg.*]

[*They speak as historians and connoisseurs.*]

(2) Exquisite

(3) Turn of the century

(4) Turn of what century?

(1) At least Ming

(2) At least Tang

(3) Much too early for Ch'iang

(4) Sung?

(1) Definitely before the Boxer Rebellion

(2) I say

(3) Museum?

(4) Terribly Great Wall

(1) A little Tartar Horde?

(2) No Genghis Khan

(3) Advent of Taoism?

(4) Slightly Buddhistic

(1) Some Tibetan influence

(2) I know! Late Empress!

(3) Definitely sack of the Winter Palace

(4) Then you would say—a museum piece?

(1) Frightfully antique

(2) Worthy of?

(3) Opium War!

(4) In in in [*he stutters*] deed!

[*As before, Thousand Year Eggs are lifted.*]

Waiter: [*enters*] Sweet and Sour?

(1) I wish I had eaten.

(2) Then I could say, "I simply can't eat anymore."

(3) Why do these ordinary dishes come in when you're usually so stuffed?

(4) I'll never say "no" to "sweet and sour" again.

(1) Nor will I. I'm so hungry I could eat those ridiculous, common little morsels of pork.

(2) With that glutinous sauce.

(3) So fattening.

(4) Made of starch.

(1) Why do the Chinese use so much starch in their sauces . . . when starch can't be indigenous to the native diet? (This begins to look as if we're going to have a customary boring dinner conversation.)

(2) I don't suppose they ever heard of starch before the 10th century.

(3) And those floating tomatoes.

(4) And green peppers.

(1) I simply can't see coolies growing green peppers.

(2) For real green peppers it takes the peons.

(3) I suppose peppers are contraband. Like everything else.

(4) Peppers, or tomatoes, or whatever, I am very hungry. I shall never go to a Chinese restaurant again.

(1) I think that what is occurring now is part of the phenomena they have classified under the title: The Mysterious East.

(2) It certainly is mysterious.

(3) I only wish we could call in the Fifth Hussars Scottish Guard Royal Irish Welsh Fusiliers Kensington Barracks!

(4) Um. Um. So do I.

(1) Do you suppose we could go to a Korean Restaurant and get fed?

(2) Not before the bird's nest soup.

(3) Why?

(4) It's the dessert.

[*And now they resignedly hand their uneaten plates to figures.*]

Waiter: [*enters*] Bird's nest soup?

[*Record plays bird sounds.*]

[*All pick up their spoons.*]

All: Chirrup Chirrup Chirrup

[*End with record playing bird sounds.*] [*Diners rise from table and solemnly bow to red figures who bow in return.*]

SCENE: DIFFICULT MOUNTAIN

Young Man: [*trudging up difficult mountain*] I promised Mike and Sam and Jim and Joe I would make it. Also Sandra and Linda and Gloria and Jill. And Adam and Roman and Marlow and Allen and Laird and Dean and Dick and Bess and Lana and Charlotte and Jacqueline and Pat. I musn't forget Pat. Or David. I musn't forget him. I told all the kids I would make it. And Lawrence and Louis and John and Teddy and Tony and . . . I've got so many commitments. Julie, too. And Dodd. And Houston. And Austin. Such good friends. Dallas, darling, I almost forgot you. I've just got to keep up my strength. [*sings a song like "Tennessee Jail Break," or one of the Johnny Cash specials*]

Old Man: [*leaping along mt. path*] Hi young fellah!

Young Man: Where do you get your energy, man?

Old Man: From the source, man.

Young Man: [*eagerly*] I'm lookin' for the source, man. Can you put me on it? I hear it's really high in Nepal, man. Lots of yum yum yum yum.

Old Man: Chinese say, Yum yum Amelican.

Young Man: Come on, you know what I mean. Big high. Yum yum.

Old Man: Mountain here called "Big High."

Young Man: I don't mean this silly mountain. You know, like they say in Tibetan, man, "lots of smoke." Sleep—talk—hash? many bags.

Old Man: Ah ah see.

Young Man: You see. I see. You tell me. I on right road?

Old Man: Yes, you go road?

Young Man: Very high road?

Old Man: You look for high?

Young Man: How difficult it is to communicate with the backward nations.

Old Man: You ask me direction?

Young Man: [*pats him on the back*] Now you're with it man. You're really starting to send. I want to know if I'm on the road to Kubla Khan?

Old Man: You wish to see dream palace?

Young Man: I wish to see.

Old Man: You not on right road to Xanadu.

Young Man: How could I have missed it?

Old Man: You not on right road.

Young Man: Well, if I've missed Xanadu, is there some sort of minor place, not on the usual tourist list—but, you know, man, a small palace, a few erotic—[*sways suggestively back and forth*] engraved stones—like sculptures, man—making it—Like West call "Pornography"????

Old Man: You're beginning to bore me.

Young Man: I'm boring you! All I really want to know is how to get to the top of the mountain. They told me down there that there were some fabulous gardens that grow . . .

Old Man: You missing Xanadu.

Young Man: But there's a minor Xanadu. Still untouched. One of those out-of-the-way places. With gardens growing—

[*It is getting darker on the mountain.*]

Old Man: We really get high here now.

Young Man: [*panting*] We must be 20,000 feet above sea level.

Old Man: You already see the sea?

Young Man: I began there, man. You picture it. Boat. Cross water.

Old Man: You see the sea?

Young Man: Yeah.

Old Man: What it look like?

Young Man: Blue-green-grey. Heh, why we talk about the sea? I want to go to the top of this mountain!

Old Man: Sea once on top this mountain. I never see the sea.

Young Man: So—you've missed a lot. It's getting darker. [*looking around him*]

Old Man: Dark like middle of sea.

Young Man: No high there. [*trying to laugh*]

Old Man: New high here. Old high sea. You look for high, follow me.

Young Man: You're running! I can't run up this mountain. I'm out of breath.

Old Man: Mountain once low. You run on it like sea shore. You run. Follow me.

Young Man: I'm out of breath. [*grasping*]

Old Man: You by sea shore.

Young Man: You're going too fast!

Old Man: I find mountain by sea shore. Seek very high. You follow me!

Young Man: I follow you. You show me. I tried. [*collapses*] [*breathing short and heavy, then notices that he is alone*] Where is the old man? [*he's scared*] There must be 3,000 feet ahead of me. Now it's foggy. And I've missed Xanadu. Where where where?

[*And fog swirls*]

SCENE: THE BRITISH EMBASSY. PEKING. TIME: PRESENT, OR RATHER, 1968.

English Consul: I am an Officer of Her Majesty's Government. You cannot arrest me.

1st Guard: Heh heh

2nd Guard: Ho Ho

1st Guard: You resist arrest?

Consul: I don't resist anything about which I have not previously been informed.

1st Guard: I bet.

2nd Guard: Heh heh. Moral immoral English gentleman. [*in English accents*] I sweah.

Consul: See here, what do you think you are doing?

1st Guard: We no think.

2nd Guard: Somebody do that for us. [*lifts eyes*] Somebody way up top.

Consul: Will you please put me in touch with your governors?

1st Guard: Governors? That's a good one. What does he think this is, "The Dream of Red Chamber"?

2nd Guard: What's that?

1st Guard: Forget I said it. [*aside to guard*] A book on the black list. Old China governing class.

2nd Guard: Look, I've got this warrant to read out to him.

1st Guard: Go ahead.

2nd Guard: Inasmuch as you, a representative of Her Majesty's Government have been found guilty by—what do we call ourselves now? I can't read the fine print—Anyway, Mao says you're a foreign ugly despicable smelly big-nosed guy and we don't want you dirtying up our streets anymore. So we're telling you. We're telling you—Buddy—Stay home. Don't leave your digs. Sit tight. Don't try to get out until we tell you to. You're on first base until the pitcher lets go with a homer.

1st Guard: That means you, baby.

Consul: I take it you are attempting to tell me that I am now under "house arrest."

2nd Guard: Yeah. Live it up.

[*Now the lights go down. A few days have passed. We are inside the British Embassy with Her Majesty's Representative and his wife.*]

Consul: I say, Jean. I hope it's not too rough on you.

Jean: Darling, when we married I said I would follow you . . . somewhere East of Suez . . .

Consul: By the old Moulmein Pagoda . . .

Jean: Looking eastward toward the sea . . .

Consul: I never told you this, Jean. But one of the reasons I married you was . . . your real comprehension . . . and almost total . . . recall . . . of . . . Kipling.

Jean: So many times I've thought of what Kipling wrote about The East . . . "Where the best is like the Worst."

Consul: We're certainly experiencing the worst.

Jean: Darling. I'm so happy just being with you. Alone. It wasn't always so easy for me to have those pretty—young—Chinese—servants hovering about. But now they're gone. And we're alone.

Consul: I rather miss those servants. [*uneasily*]

Jean: They were such—such competent servants. [*looking directly and meaningfully at him*]

Consul: Now we are alone. I say, Jean, can you cook?

Jean: Oh rather. I mean, well it's been such years—what with the native servants and all. [*swallows*] But I am able to prepare . . . I am able to prepare. Remember, Mummy's recipes? The ones she so carefully tucked into my suitcase I packed for the P and O boat coming out? I think I have lost them. How dreadful. How simply dreadful. Darling—do you like [*triumphantly*] pigeon pie?

Consul: Jean . . . [*he is not aggravated, he is just sad*]

[*Late night. Jean enters her husband's bedroom, carrying a lighted candle.*]

Jean: [*then carrying quilt*] Darling. I know it's been such a long while since we've shared a room. I won't trouble you. I promise. Oh Timothy. I'm so frightened. If you would just permit me to lie on a quilt here near your bed. I hear such strange noises.

Consul: [*from bed*] I have heard them also. By all means, Jean, take your quilt and lie there on the floor. If I can be of any comfort to you.

Jean: Oh you can. Just your presence—

Consul: What was that!

Jean: Just a cool breeze. Nothing to disturb us.

Consul: I thought I saw something.

Jean: So did I. One's imagination does run away with one.

Consul: Why don't you move your quilt nearer my bed?

Jean: Only me, darling.

Consul: If this house arrest goes on much longer, I shall be a wreck. I do hope they have received my telegram at Whitehall.

Jean: White . . . did you say white? I thought I saw something white . . .

Consul: Jean, do ignore your Scottish ancestry. I have never approved of that Celtic—what was that?

Jean: Just my hand, darling. I was trying to pull the quilt over me. It's quite chilly here on the floor.

Consul: Forgive me, Jean. One of the qualities I most admire in the Scots is their ability to endure hardship. Quite the only people in the world who can put up so well with draughts.

Jean: I saw something yellow.

Consul: Probably the dawn. We really must get down to sleep. [*yawns*] I must be alert tomorrow when those guards question me . . . I say, Jean . . . there is yellow light in this room . . . Jean! Do please come here on my bed. It will be much better if there are two of us to cope with—whatever—

Jean: What, darling? [*sleepily*]

Consul: Jean! There's a very odd person in this room. Standing there at the foot of my bed.

Jean: Darling. Do try to get some sleep. We must attempt to set standards. We must discipline ourselves. We must not be afraid. We must be strong. We must be courageous. We must put up a noble front. It may be months before we are released. We must—[*she falls asleep*]

Consul: [*to figure*] I am a servant of Her Majesty's Government. I am in need of sleep. [*Falls back on pillow and pulls blanket over his face*]

[*Outside*]

1st Guard: Whatcher doing?

2nd Guard: Only watching them two.

1st Guard: What are they doing?

2nd Guard: It's real crazy. She's lying on the floor. He's on the bed. She's asleep. He's sitting straight up in bed like he's scared out of his wits.

1st Guard: What did you expect?

SCENE: GYMNASIUM. RED CHINA

[*Enter citizen's committee. Officials are in Mao uniforms.*]

Old Official: I seem to remember this place. [*looking around*]

Official: [*leans over and whispers in old one's ear*] We're in ancient conservatory of once Li Chieu private house. Hush. Worth your life.

Old Official: Memory has departed.

[Gymnasium Instructor *addresses three students who have entered the room. They have long black hair. The hair falls over their faces.*]

Old Official: Much hair. No pigtail.

Official: Hush. Much symbolism here.

Gymnasium Instructor: Down!

[*Three bow low, swinging their heads down*:] Mao!

Gym Instructor: Up!

Three [*lift up*]: Hair!

Gym Instructor: Down!

Three [*bend down*]: Mao!

Gym Instructor: Up!

Three [*stand up*]: Hair!

Gym Instructor: Sideways!

Three [*bend sideways*]: Mao!

Gym Instructor: Sideways again!

Three [*bend sideways*]: Hair!

Old Official: [*whispering*] Most instructive. We know *Mao* translate *Hair*. Why continue?

Official: For benefit of Western delegation. Very backward people. Do not understand Mao translate Hair.

Old Official: How long this continue?

Official: Perhaps long time. Until Western people understand many things.

Old Official: Ah. Many years.

Official: Many years. We have time. Much time.

Old Official: I don't.

Official: Sleep awhile old one.

Old Official: My years thank you. [*nods; sleeps*]

[*Now the gymnasium students are moving, as if in a trance. They have been performing for hours. The officials also appear to be in their own trance. There is slow Chinese difficult music and fast Chinese difficult music. Or there is Chinese rock. Everyone is in a trance.*]

Gymnasts: [*chant*] AIR MOUSE
SCARE HOUSE
WE SCARY GHOSTS
IN A TRUCE
THERE IS NO LOOSE FOR SCARE
WE FIND HAPPY HAIR
WE FIND NO SCARY HAIR
IN LOVING MAOING
LIKE CANOEING
ON PEACEFUL WATERS
WE SEND OUR DAUGHTERS
WITH SHORT HAIR
AND NO SCARE
LIKE BRIGHT MAO
SWIMS THE VOWEL
TO HAPPY CHINA

WE EMBRACE
FEARY FACE
MOST PORCELAIN GHOST
MOST HEAVENLY PLACE

Official: [*shakes himself*] I really don't know what this means.

Gym Instructor: This is not my plan, sir. For happy citizen celebration.

Official: I assumed it had been explained to you. [*groggily gets to his feet*] Poetry no longer part of Chinese culture.

Gym Instructor: Whole life I never read poetry. I physical man. I man of people.

Official: You will appear before the Central Citizen Penal Committee.

Old Official: [*wakes up*] Pleasant dream. Heard singing. Like young larks. Like old days in happy house. [*cackles, looks at the other two*] Trouble here?

SCENE: LONDON, 1890

[*Two men are sitting in the study of a house in London. Establish a sort of Sherlock Holmes atmosphere. Low fire. Horse hoofs on brick pavement outside. Fog.*]

1st Man: [*taking watch out of pocket, looks at it*] It's getting on. Must be taking myself off.

2nd Man: [*goes to window and pulls curtain back*] Quite a fog out. Have your man drive carefully. [*rings for butler who enters immediately*] Call Sir Andrew's carriage, Greaves. [*Exit butler*]

[*The two men smile at each other. They walk toward the door with their arms around each other's backs.*]

2nd Man: The next time I have a Chinese puzzle, I'll know whom to turn to.

1st Man: Nothing at all, my dear fellow. Any time. We have these problems every day at the museum.

2nd Man: Then you do consider the vase quite—quite.

1st Man: Consider! It is one of the finest specimens of the Dynasty!

2nd Man: Then I wasn't way out in paying that price?

1st Man: You have bought yourself one of the greatest bargains in the field. Any time you wish to hand that vase over to us at the museum, our grateful paws shall be outstretched.

2nd Man: And I assure you that given my few remaining years, your museum will be an early recipient.

1st Man: Enjoy the vase. It is very beautiful and very authentic.

[*Butler enters and announces carriage. The two friends say goodnight. Sound of horse hoofs on pavement, etc. Lights flicker.*]

2nd Man: Blast this electric light. Invented nonsense.

Butler: Shall you want anything else, sir?

2nd Man: No, no. I'll be taking myself off to bed. [*He exits, then butler lowers lights and exits.*]

[*Now we are in a silent room. Figures begin to step off a Chinese vase. Man fishing. Maidens with fans. Two men playing ancient Chinese chess game. Any sort of Chinese vase action. Opportunity for actors to improvise whimsical and delicate sort of mine. Probably in atmosphere a little like an old-fashioned ballet of toys in toy shops after the toymaker is asleep.*]

[*The last episode is taken from the Book of the poet, Tu Fu, who writes of his dream of the poet, Li Po. Li Po had been dead from the beginning of the first night, although Tu Fu had not known this.*

I quote from Tu Fu in translation.]

In these two "Dreaming of Li Po" dreams Tu Fu ranges over three distinct and incompatible theories of dream interpretation without apparently being aware that he is doing so. In lines 5–6:

Old friend entered my dream
Makes-clear I always think-of-him

He says that the dream apparition shows that Li Po has been on his mind a lot: a perfectly rational, psychological explanation. He immediately follows this, however, by expressing the view that it is Li Po's soul which has visited him, and he continues to assume this throughout the rest of the poem.

You are now in net (net is law—dream logic, meaning
how did you get here? I thought
you were in prison)
How have-got feather wings

Afraid is-not living soul
Road far cannot-be measured

Tu Fu means that Li Po's soul would be unable to make the journey there and back while he slept, because of the distance, such a great distance that the journey through the passes was made at night.

Soul come maple-woods green
Soul return passes dark
Sinking moon fills roof-beams
Still doubtful shine-on your face
Water deep waves broad
Don't let water-dragons get.

When Tu Fu woke he saw the whole room bathed in moonlight. He looked around half- expecting the moonlight to reveal Li Po still standing in one of its corners.

Then the 2nd Poem, "Dreaming of Li Po":

Three nights repeatedly dream-of you
Kindly concern your mind

Take leave always flurried
Ruefully say Come not easy

River-lakes much wind-waves
Boat-oars fear lose-sink

Go-out door scratch white head
As-if disappointed in life time ambition

Official fill capital city
This man alone is wretched

Who says net wide-meshed
Growing old body yet in trouble

Thousand autumn myriad year name
Forlorn post-mortem affair

Reviews

Frank O'Hara's "Hôtel Transylvanie"

The first clue to the meaning of the poem is the title, "Hôtel Transylvanie."* A nineteenth-century title. Transylvania belonged once to the Austro-Hungarian empire. It belonged once to Romania. It is in the Carpathian Mountains where Count Dracula comes from. Although we note O'Hara does not mention this bloodthirsty Count.

The country of Transylvania is wild and beautiful. William Penn once considered Transylvania as a name for the lovely countryside of the land he settled; instead it was named for him, Pennsylvania. There are no dark stories about this land in the New World.

The nineteenth century became fascinated by the Carpathians, reading of Count Dracula, a story written by Bram Stoker, who did his explorative work in the British Museum and wrote a story of a Count thirsty for the blood of humans.

In our times, the Carpathians have been a refuge for those fleeing the Communist regimes of Romania and Hungary. It is just possible that this hotel with the haunted name may have been noted by O'Hara on his walks in Paris, and that his imagination lent to it a sinister aspect, even in accord with a rumored place of political refuge, as much as with Count Dracula.

If the "Hôtel Transylvanie" were staged, and the poem is theatrical as are many of O'Hara's poems with their spill of emotive drama, the hotel guests would wear masks. Disguise is a theme of the poem.

Another level of the poem is about Chance. Chance has a role in gambling and poetry. In a place like the Hôtel Transylvanie they may speak of political duels, and again there is mention by the poet of "rigging the deck" (of cards). These guests have escaped from a sinister regime; they may be in disguise, in order to live.

* O'Hara uses the French spelling for the hotel name. It is possible that on one of his trips to Paris he may have seen the hotel. MS, dated 1959.

it will take them a long time to know who I am / why I came there /
and why I am and made to happen

The first stanza has introduced the idea of Fortune as a dark card that blindfolded one seizes. There is a Mallarméan possibility of chance on a night when the companions of Carpathia are stirring and making their rounds.

A charming word, surprising, is used by O'Hara; it may refer to someone of title, the Count,

chevalier, change your expression! the wind is sweeping over
the gaming tables ruffling the cards

"chevalier" is tossed so lightly on our path, as if afterward the poet turned aside, placing his weight on his toes like a dancer, then tiptoed away. In real life O'Hara often used this method of exit. Dramatic footwork is frequent in his poetry.

The residents of the Hôtel believe in chance which may help them to survive while gambling with cards and with life.

O *hôtel*, you should be merely a bed
surrounded by walls where two souls should meet . . . but not as
cheaters at cards have something to win

O'Hara is wishing there were not the false note, that the poem would not be forced to obey the omens, the music of the poem be less forbidding. In this sort of hotel, faces wear a mask; O'Hara puts on his mask as the poem gradually edges toward the zones of danger. The poem is now about surface disequilibrium. The setting of the poem begins to wobble as the inhabitants of the hotel hide in their dominos, hissing, "Shall we win at love or shall we lose . . . but not as cheaters at cards have something to win": their dubious origin and employment suggests itself as a "sublime moment of dishonest hope."

This is a moment of melodrama, and one asks why, but the poet is leading us through his own sense of the dramatic, or melodramatic. He is aware that he will write something any minute that will both puzzle and frighten the reader. It will not be about the hotel, but about his own life. O'Hara has been readying himself for this explosion about himself, the mask he wears. He chooses now to take off his mask and addresses himself:

you will continue to sing on trying to cheer everyone up
and they will know as they listen with excessive pleasure that you're
    dead
        and they will not mind that they have let you entertain
at the expense of the only thing you want in the world[!]

This is a Shelleyan moment in O'Hara's writing, the admitted loss of poetic power. His time has been spent trying "to cheer everyone up." It is not that this poem is one of his triumphs. In this poem he achieves what he has always attempted. Poetry had presented him with fictions and too much reliance on his genius. He has betrayed his abilities through pleasure and power. It has eluded him until now, the icy experience of the fleetingness of poetry, the possible loss, even when addressed, of the poetic moment. Now he confronts himself in a moment of testing, and knows he experienced the loss he wrote about, the loss of poetic power, and through this moment of recognition regains it.

We realize his continued addressing of the hotel is due to an identification with it in all its disguises, and the final disguise is the hotel as the personification of himself when he urges:

hôtel

you have only to be
as you are being, as you must be, as you always are . . .
no matter what fate deals you or imagination discards like a tyrant

A World by Dennis Phillips

A World combines the strategy of film with the properties of myth. Montage shifts the scenes as they overlap and dissolve. This gives the poetry of Dennis Phillips a stance of controlled momentum. Shards are thrown to the surface. Pressure shoots us upward through the veils of myth, a control discharges us depthward into the organs of myth through which we move into poetic areas of violence or grace.

A continuation of Phillips's earlier book, *The Hero Is Nothing* (Berkeley: Kajun Press, 1985), there is less reliance on a sympathetic internal search, less of an ego in search of cohesiveness, or the revealing frankness in which the struggling hero cried: "The air is thick in a way never known."

A World wraps itself around zones of conflict. The former heroic gentleness has been dropped, or rearranged. The *Hero* was a man of inner conflict, sensitive to deconstruction, he was delicate of ear, a poet. In *A World* he moves into an arena of disparate action, faced with impersonal attitudes towards a disintegrating fabric. He is a collector of shards. He turns to myth, which is initiated in its violent Homeric apparel, and fastens it onto a contemporary structure.

Rather than a series of poems divided into sections—and the section titles indicate the abstract signs that govern the poetry, "On Dry Entry," "Illium of Protection," "Alone Than Night"—the book can be read as one poem stretched upon a superstructure. The superstructure is weighted on each end by poetry of polemics and poetry of myth; they share an arena.

Women are blown into this arena and they bring the shadow of death as did the goddesses in the Trojan War. Powerful, frustrated women appear, veiled. Women and men from the Moorish world intermingle with the Judaic world and the Black, cast into struggle with adrenaline in their veins, hurtling through gravity. Their interjection surprises us. As we confront damaged Greek temples, there intrudes a poem, "My Mosque."

A sudden break and the poems are not cohesive; we are allowed a shift into other brooding worlds. Only a poet with a strong sense of control such as Phillips possesses would venture into these optimal margins.

It is the uneasy, toughened stride of his diction that both calms and shakes us, and his unhesitant grasp of the malleable, demanding form he has selected. The poems, formed under "pressure," indicate a struggle both internal and external, and from moment to quick moment we are perilously alone as the poems move in their febrile, inelastic charge. Phillips is fleet of mind.

Yet he intends to rescue us. His method is to transform both his tone and subject matter from hermetic asides into a lyrical obedience. Phillips is a lyric poet when he chooses. I suspect he rather takes his lyricism for granted and prefers to introduce his other eutectic selves, the politically controlled persona withdrawn from sea and cloud, and the mirror persona of nature. In this book he favors political intensity, which can turn into abstractions:

> no limbs allowed or needed
> only the fantasy of danger an
> old vestige losing strength a quieter dictum
> covering over.

There is an internal acrid vertical underneath the polemical poems which is made to contrast with the horizontal of the perpetuating observant sea.

> But a delta, finger of cocktip a new
> gravity where things stand, press against
> venicals.

The *Iliad* is surrounded by the sea and floats in it. The sea claims our eyes, even when we stand on the blood-drenched, celebratory beaches. In the sea sequences of Phillips's poems the Iliadic world meets *A World*, even as the specter fog disperses the more condensed ideate of his poetry. As at Troy, the poet of *A World* watches from the shore, examines the particles that float toward him, turns his back on the city:

> Saw one dashed by cruel waves
> saw tanks of air saw hotels

saw walkways leading to popular museums
unrated but stringy arms (mine) . . .
* * *
Dark storm day but hot
dark noon grey, sea grey.

Any calm disrupted ions
charged or pressure dropping . . .
* * *
Looked so long it vanished.
Using the word "named" instead.
A declamation devoutly to be wished.
Force of Helios powering upwards . . .
Upon a cloud—and lifeless bloundary . . .

Words emerge from Joyce: *seasilt*, *saltsick*, connecting the plot with Ulysses, who appears here in a long poem sequence. We are in the climate of a literature of sails, of remoteness, the death watch. The poet's conscience is the mold for these mythic models. We must remind ourselves that Phillips is not writing a book solely about Greeks or even the Attic world. The other half of the superstructure is the world today. Mythic people arise out of slum depths and wasted inclines of our civilization to disturb our conscience. The poems fill with adrenaline (a word of considerate power to Phillips) whenever they initiate a restive anxiety or explore the signals of contemporary failure that run parallel to the terrors of a former civilization. He adjures us to tend to our social awareness in a world that cuts itself off from societal beneficence.

You know the players
your pawns your rocky elements and barren
a place to seek vengeance
for a lifespark you claimed to taste
in this indelible fog.

Places and nature are damaged. *A World* makes note of damage even where nature is "damaged." Early into the poems there is a sequence which conveys the elegance of Phillips's stance, which will turn into an enhanced severity.

Damaged clouds.
An ovum clinging to ladened weather.

No fragment preserves silence.

In acceleration, in pregnant dark, clear.
Release is blurred, edges softened.

If I watch this long enough.

An idea in the form of a story
beginning with an ending, histrionic, sad,
a tragedy, inevitable, but false, a mirror
not false, not a mirror.

The severity takes several attitudes and one of them reveals itself in a sense of torment. Phillips tenants his book with fire and volcanic ash:

An older lesson, born of vulcanism:
Lava tubes pumping from the core
new extremities.

Don't look at me: If the fire escaped
even hope would vanish.

The poetry tends to take on an argumentative stance and the brunt of it can become dictatorial. "What voice we asked transmits orders?" This slight edge of harangue may be due to the ambition of *A World*, where even as they intermingle, current politics and past history have bituminous identities.

I suspect Phillips wishes to remove his vocabulary outside the idiom of *The Hero*, even as he argues that *A World* is a continuation of his hero's progress. He risks adding another kind of muscularity to the poetry, which may have metallic joints. Yet only a poet of finely honed spaces, as Phillips certainly is, can afford this risk. The difficulty is that the reader may tend to lose the scene, an important element in the book's structure, as it dissolves into abstractions. Phillips, to continue with the sense of his filmic direction, may require a camera lens of greater orbit to focus on the extant geographical regions into which he induces us in his formidable operative plan. That his continuing intelligence recognizes a need for a more revelatory scope is apparent in this sequence:

There's a place and it's a crater
malignant beyond chemicals and radium.

There's no incision to excise it.

And it's not just one side of an argument

Because the place breeds explosions
and murder and the home of the destroyed
breeds the next destruction.

Only a boat on a sea safe
steel waters, perpetual pacific

touch land, take water, set off

Adrift, lightless on black ocean.

The film moves very fast on multiple surfaces. Or slows down as the contemporary scene approaches and speeds as the poems assume the guise of the Hellenic war. The interior of the book becomes a labyrinth where there is a struggle to assimilate the congruence flowing between the past and present.

Phillips has made a bold move into the Yeatsian domain where we "Break bitter furies of complexity." The poetry of Phillips is abstruse, alchemic, equipped with transfiguring silver shears. Even in heated combat this poetry maintains a disciplined distance. A coolness directed by Phillips's verbal intensity throws a shelter over the "cities of the plain."

Susan Gevirtz's *Narrative's Journey*

I am excited by the method stunningly projected by Susan Gevirtz in her biography of Dorothy Richardson. I do not know if Gevirtz has used a post-structural method, or not! Her use of material widely differs from that of other biographers and presents an advanced non-conformism in the risky use of biographical material.

She has assembled an edifice which ventures into a new theory of biography. In part through her efforts in methodology, her biography of Dorothy Richardson becomes a writing of exploration, even as her subject survives as a notable innovator of the novel of the twentieth century.

In every successful biography, the biographer finds some point in which the subject becomes an extension of themselves, if only briefly. This

> enlargement of the scope of the field demands "empathy," a mysterious source. What Gevirtz and Dorothy Richardson share is an extending Modernity.

Along with James Joyce, Richardson is regarded as an initiator of the method known to us as "stream of consciousness." In *Pilgrimage*, Richardson's title for her series of separately titled novels, Miriam Henderson is the heroine. In the beginning Miriam is placed in the London of the early 1900s. Her world is of young secretaries and dental assistants, friends, who attend free lectures and musicales, who live in chill boarding houses in the city of London. The events in the novels are to be revealed solely through the eyes of Miriam. It is only through her perspective that emotional moments rise and fall. In this way the work of Richardson resembles that of James Joyce, and the figure of Bloom who is our guide to Dublin, as Miriam is our guide to London.

Toward the end of the novel sequence that extends into the 1930s, there is a possible falling off of the story line, as the author ages and is physically removed from the setting of her youth. Yet Richardson's projection of the

> stream of consciousness never lessens or hesitates. Her sensitive instrument, Miriam, will continue as our Virgil with a continued exposure to the hazards of enveloping time.

Gevirtz reminds us Richardson gave the title *Pilgrimage* to her series of novels. In Chaucer's time *Pilgrims went on Pilgrimmage.* They were on a *Quest.* Gevirtz writes that Richardson's *Pilgrimage is an allegory of allegory, or writing ABOUT WRITING.* This theme of a mystical journey to fulfillment and understanding of self will be reinforced throughout the novels with consistent allusions to Dante. This Dante parallel appears in the late novel *Interim*, when Miriam attends a Dante lecture and feels the absence of love in her being, *in her inability to feel humility in universal terms.*

Gevirtz explains that for Richardson WRITING is a means of participating in a sense of adventure, of producing a *joy that can then be reproduced in the reader, and by the reader. It is this longing for participation* that makes the whole process necessary.

What continues to excite us in the Gevirtz biography is not only the story of Dorothy Richardson as the exceptional Miriam, but the METHOD employed by Gevirtz. Our concentration on the method of Richardson will shift to her biographer now suspended in the process of making accountable the method of Richardson!

The idea of selectivity of method is strangely ignored by biographers whose choice is a linear one. In Gevirtz we witness the ingenuous, schematic, breaking of the stone of Biography. Her work is similar in effect to Richardson's "stream of consciousness" and with a shared iconoclasm.

For instance, the biographer, interested in film and seeking means for film to be useful in her writing, within the limitations of a page, includes notice of the reviews of films that Richardson wrote for the film magazine *Close Up*, published in the 1920s and 1930s, evoking a cinematic stroke on her page. Notice how cleverly she makes an assemblage of the *idea* of the Silver Screen attached to writing, itself. And she does this with music, another personal concern. Note how music fills and replenishes the pages of this book, as it also did in Richardson's novels.

And most importantly I wish to point out how immediate is Gevirtz's response to Richardson's idea of writing as participation, "the orchestral spectacle of the novel-chapters working *together*."

Tlooth, Harry Mathews

Harry Mathews has an energetic mind that bounces back and forth in time and geography. Peripatetic as a foreign agent from space, he descends on telescoped islands like Babar from his balloon. *Tlooth* is the story of the casuistry of dentistry, the maiming of the human body and mouth by various scoundrels and technicians, including loved ones. As a novel, it is, of course, more schematic than dentistry which can be absorbed as *Tlooth*'s metaphor.

The personae who fill the book as they enter the excited progression of the plot, chock-full of people, are caught in the malpractices of life. The method by which Mathews engages his characters in the misanthropies of their selection is that of an artful sequence of "surprises." "Where are we?" "Which way is out?" This stance, in which Mathews seems to rollick along with his wounded hero, is a way of teasing the reader into viewing his characters as personifications, and although these tactics reveal Mathews's emergence from surrealism, the novel is not content with the surreal.

Rather, there is an American air: bassoons thump on the bandstand, a climactic surface stirs like that in *Huckleberry Finn*. The hero, while engaging in self-destructive, oddball activities, manages to survive. Gradually we recognize that besides the fervid rompings there is an obstinate realism, like that underlying a comedy of errors, a place where everyone, not only the underdog, has a mistaken identity, a mistaken idealism.

Mathews's prevailing intellect with its hypersynchronization of science, medicine, art, music, poetry, and other savage activities, is not only energetic but occupied by a highly controlled fancy. With it we travel in peripheral space and light upon fictive landscape, invariably entering a hospital which is seldom a hospice (antiseptic Switzerland is an exception) because pain is one of the subjects of this book.

Finally we are permitted to view as "real" a Venice as the conspiratorial

Mathews will allow us, and which may be that of the Venetian, Casanova. Here orgiastic routines occupy Mathews, partly as subjects of parody, in an exercise of Joycean technique, but also, the reader guesses, because these genital sideshows entertain him. He introduces the atmosphere of Italian film of the 1960s (when *Tlooth* was published), and as we trudge through their ornamental fabrications we notice that this is not *La Dolce Vita*, but the entrance to "Dolce Morte." Even the accompanying music that from time to time should sound a refrain is mute; we do not hear it. The music belongs to its instruments, and they, like forceps of surgery, do not carry a melody; the musical notes are frightened away by the anxiety that pervades the novel and unsettles the reader.

This angst, like the plague, is transferred from hospitals to brothels, from grotesque landscape to the detailed orgasms of comedic lovers. Above the conceits, or beneath the parodic structure of his novel, we discover Harry Mathews with knotted forehead indicating a fierce determination to endure the spectacles he has secured from literature and the sophistries of life. *Tlooth* rightfully belongs among the distinguished excitements of literary exploration.

The Fiction of the Poet by Anna Balakian

On the page preceding the table of contents is printed this quotation from Mallarmé:

> To end up in a beautiful book / that is what the world was made for

and our clue to the dedicatory mind that directs *The Fiction of the Poet.*

Balakian selects five poets: Valéry, Rilke, Yeats, Stevens, Guillén. The basis of this selection is their relationship and debt to Symbolism. This is the ontology of a book bearing a joyfully confusing title.

In *The Fiction of the Poet* does she mean to discuss poets who write fiction, or the attachment of fiction to poetry, or is poetry the only "true fiction"? I believe she wishes to show us by her interpretation of texts poetry influenced by Symbolism maturing under the protectorate of Mallarmé and undergoing a removal from all mundanity until ionized it reaches the purity of fiction. That is as clearly as I can define her position.

I am impressed by how her exceptional intelligence—not intuition—hers is a practical mind—dignifies and gives weight to, even as it exalts, the poetic process.

Balakian's earlier book on André Breton proved to be an intensification of a progress through the mind of the poet. She did not present him as a poet maudit, a silly old fool, a lapsed Communist, or even a genius, she took on the difficult task of making him human. She really cares about the unenclosed world of modernism to which he was dedicated and which she is able to present as an enchanted world with all the difficulties of enchantment. Swedenborg, Voltaire, Mythology, an odd lot seen together, are tickets to this world we may see as a passing one, but not to Balakian, as her book so brilliantly confirms.

There is nothing ephemeral about her method. She views poets with a kind of abrupt practicality; they are not going to play any tricks on her, even as she reveres their presence. This attitude is assisted by her control of her material. There is certainty about everything Balakian offers us. She never nods and she takes the hurdles of her dislikes nobly.

And the 'no nonsenseisms': "long-winded like Valéry." Of the sacred cow, Rilke: "Perhaps if we could banish Nietzsche and Heidegger from his frame of reference we would reach the heart of Rilke's poetics more directly."

She is generous with her closeness to the poet's subject matter. Sometimes she comes to this subject matter in the guise of an inspired genie. She writes of Yeats's "The Second Coming": "we immediately become suspicious of the ready and obvious meaning of the title." She then proceeds to startle us with the remark that Yeats's poem is as powerful a poem about human failure as Mallarmé's "Le vierge, le vivace et le bel aujourd'hui." We learn that in the gyre, the labyrinth of self, the Falconer, the artist, twists, dreading his loss of control over his work, for when that happens: "the center cannot hold." She writes, "when the artist reaches that level of failure he has but one hope—the second change . . . second coming."

She cannot resist a return to Mallarmé. Nor should she, given the climate of her book. "Mallarmé thought of a work of art as an operation as painful and as risky as giving birth": "Noire, a l'aile saignante et pale, deplumee" [Black with a bleeding and pale wing, deplumed].

We are made aware that it is Symbolism that occupies the historical space in front of the poets she now approaches: its influence on these poets whether obscure or glaring. We are reminded that her field of honor is Symbolism.

In her chapter on Rilke she tells us that his Fourth Sonnet, about the unicorn, is "as total a model of poetic fiction as Mallarmé's Faun, Valéry's La Jeune Parque, and Yeats' golden bird of Byzantium." (Bringing together the poets of her book.) She reminds us that the dream of Mallarmé was "*to suggest and not to describe.*"

In her opinion, Stevens is a 'self-conscious poet.' And Balakian is so European she complains of, or perhaps one should more politely say notices, "the explicitly *national* quality of Stevens." For instance, she is annoyed with his decking out his poems with French words; she is not in sympathy with him, so she cannot interpret the cloak of Frenchness as a necessity to his poetry in search of a poetic fiction he could not locate in his natural environment. She neglects to take into consideration the Roquefort cheese and illicit wine in a suburban yard, those mediocre French paintings as patient devices to whittle away the Puritanic self. Balakian is possibly disturbed by the elevation of Stevens even as she hands over the American crown. On ornery terms with this book, she is nevertheless consistent in allowing Stevens, with his lien on Symbolism, into her iconoframe.

The Hero in this unravelling of heroics, as we now know, is Mallarmé. And it is well to read Balakian's book in particular for Balakian's study of his work: Mallarmé who told us "the true fiction is that of the poet." He also wrote and she quotes: "situated at the junctions of all the other arts, sprung from them and governing them, Fiction or Poetry . . ." She asks us to celebrate Mallarmé as the poet who "recognized and he opened up the process of creating that fiction."

Benjamin Constant's *Cécile*

Mr. Alfred Roulin in his introduction to this first publication in English of *Cécile* has placed the writing of the book in December of 1811. As many curious circumstances surround the manuscript, which was only recently located by the baron de Constant de Rebecque, and as Constant's friend Coulmann had never read *Cécile* and had reported a far different synopsis read to him by Constant, it is somewhat a matter of conjecture when the book was written. However, it does seem likely that in 1811 when Constant was settled with his wife—Charlotte von Hardenberg, the Cécile of this story, after the vicissitudes of a romance which had extended over a period of some thirteen years, and living in Schloss Hardenberg close to the Library of Gottingen where he wrote and rewrote his history of religion—there was undoubtedly the time and desire to recapitulate the events of the previous years. As he had once done so successfully with *Adolphe*, so now he continued his autobiography in the form of a novelette.

Constant confesses in his *Journal Intime* that, "I can only really love when I am absent, or feel gratitude, or feel pity," and thus provides the clue to his extraordinary behavior throughout *Cécile*; to a pattern of action which we had witnessed in *Adolphe*, of pursuit and disengagement, of complicated alliances and disalliances with women who were both necessary to his life and at the same time inordinately troublesome.

He first met Charlotte von Hardenberg, or Cécile, when he was in the service of the Duke of Brunswick as a gentleman of the bedchamber. She appears to us as a sweet, naive creature with a certain tenacity, as witness her reluctance to withdraw her hold on Constant even after many years of suffering and despite his reassurances with small hope of marriage. That she succeeded finally is more a tribute to her endurance than Constant's affection. Yet she would undoubtedly have continued her first marriage with an unfaithful husband had not Constant, his ego unhinged by his own wife's infidelity, attached himself to her. Two divorces ensued, but

Charlotte's family interfered, the marriage was postponed indefinitely, an arrangement which certainly suited Constant, and he was allowed to secure himself elsewhere with Mme. de Staël, or Mme. de Staël continued for fifteen years and produced one daughter, the Duchess de Broglie, or [the granddaughter] Mme. de Haussonville of Ingres's exquisite portrait. And yet it is almost exactly those years which concern his relationship with Cécile.

The element of "pity for women" certainly arouses those curious meetings with Cécile in small inns throughout Switzerland and again in Paris while she attempted to escape both her family and later a second marriage, and to tie herself finally with the ever-elusive Constant. This same pity is used to explain his attachment to Mme. de Staël, who is here described with nostalgia a few years after the liaison had been broken: "Her wit, the most widely ranging ever possessed by any woman, and perhaps by any man, was characterized, in all serious matters, by more strength than grace, and in all matters involving sensibility by a tinge of solemnity and affectation . . . her wit dazzled me, her gaiety enchanted me." Cécile represents a respite from the intense intellectualism and emotional energy of Mme. de Staël which both heightened Constant's intellectual powers and reduced his ability to further his own career. Cécile is the calm after the storm, a calm which later bored Constant yet forced him to his own powers of concentration which led in later years to the political tracts for which he was famous.

Confusion, indecision, self-torture, and a hectic dissimulation toward the two women who both attracted and repulsed him characterize the romance of *Cécile*. It is an extraordinary excursion conducted by Constant himself, into the regions of his personality. It is difficult, following the neurotic outline of these years, to remember that this is the Benjamin Constant whose lucidity in political affairs, whose insistence upon the practical rather than the emotional approach in politics led him to be recognized as one of the great Liberals of the nineteenth century. As Mr. Harold Nicolson has pointed out, it was he who emphasized to his colleagues and disciples that "there existed a middle line of thought between the ideologues of the Revolution and the hard efficient bureaucracy of the Napoleonic system."

In *Cécile*, Constant has revealed that this same attitude, no doubt agreeable to an intelligence which was "luminous, but did not emit warmth," and highly important to his political career, caused him innumerable personal difficulties on the uncompromising level of romance, which he perversely desired but was unequipped to sustain.

Dear Mei-mei, on the publication of *Empathy*

Your book arrived two days ago and I have been celebrating modernity, the contemporaneity and the advanced form of *Empathy*.

I congratulate you on your tenacity in clinging to your own idea of the way the book both in time and place should come together. And you have admitted your readers into the privacy of the work in an expert way by making us understand the design of your intentions. I like those bold numerals. And the poems don't admit a trace of struggle. It is all so mellifluous to read a poet who grasps the content of her own work.

I always loved "Alakanak"—I think it is a major performance, and I use that word because there is action in the poem that has nothing to do with audience, but is solely the acrobatics of nature.

And "Fog," because it appeals to my mystical sense without being mystical and because it is a little tragic. *Empathy* is so wise and formally triumphant. You permit us to view your mind and I treasure this, because we see the mind working within set movement. It is like "a honeycomb or geodesic dome turned inside out," and it wields the powers of the ethical and poetic world. It works out its own magnetism.

And what surprises me at each turn is the calm you gather out of storm. Perhaps you should never loosen your attachment to the far if it allows you this calm within your roaring mind. I don't believe one place could produce these poems and it didn't . . . yet tenacity needs light, the light you fix on your mind.

When poetry is marvelous there is absolutely nothing else like it, even those Renaissance painters, who were vastly concerned with calm when they were tearing up a painting, cannot give us the same pleasure. I am borrowing your "constant notation of parallel streams"––what a vast leaping expression—and I needed it, Swan, because I want to go on talking about "an order of impossibly beauty"—

Kenneth Koch's *Selected Poems: 1950–1982*

The publishers of one of the most important "Selected Poems" to appear in a decade, despite its unsolicited economy—we would have liked more poems—should be congratulating themselves and pushing Kenneth Koch buttons on the poetry machine.

We begin with the ebullient, ambitious young poet who brought us "Fresh Air," which in our silly, greedy fashion in the 1960s when this poem blew through the poetry works, we took it for granted and accepted it, as if Koch's air were free ozone and not air made freshly and expensively for us, unlike the warmed-over or overheated air circulating in the poetic climate. There is no one like Kenneth Koch. He carved a niche for himself leaving absolutely no space for anyone else with lesser credentials to crawl into. As we read the poems, the ambition they exude is staggering. The clusters of unexpected images ("little thrilled silence of snails"), the whole Graham Greene voyages, the railway trips over Koch construction, the harbors and farewells, these poems are not 'funny' or 'clever' or 'irreverent,' well, yes, they are that, thank goodness. This is American poetry wrought to a pitch from which it and the poet have probably never recovered.

I set forth one misted white day of June
Beneath the great Atlantic rainway, and heard:
"Honestly you smite worlds of truth, but
Lose your own trains of thought, like a pigeon.
Did you ride in Kenneth's machine?"
"Yes, I rode there, an old man in shorts, blind,
Who had lost his way in the filling station; Kenneth was kind."
"Did he fill your motionless ears with resonance and stain?"
"No, he spoke not as a critic, but as a man."
"Tell me, what did he say?" "He said,

'My eyes are the white sky, the gravel on the groundway my sad lament.'" . . .

And that is the Dantesque poem with which we are launched into "The Brassiere Factory" and "Desire for Spring" which begins with the teasing lines—"Calcium days, days when we feed our bones / Iron days, which enrich our blood," ending with "I want spring, I want to turn like a mobile in a new fresh air!" And that is the closest we can arrive at defining Koch. He is the Calder of poetry. (Not the e. e. cummings of jokey moralism.) Like Calder he is brighter than most of his contemporaries, more learned in the tricks of the French and more embracing of a visual world which bends under his parody.

The poems from which I quoted were from *Thank You*, written in 1962. It's all there at that moment. Kenneth, unlike many poets, found his grip at once, before Ashbery, even O'Hara, of whom there are fond soundings. He was replete and ecstatic and appeared very sure of himself, because being well educated and travelled he believed he could turn poetry around from its conservative narcissism. By way of doing so, he inadvertently inherited some of that narcissism, but never mind. The task of being unique, being all by yourself in what he believed was a fatigued literary scene, required stamina. There were the elders like Williams and Stevens, and Koch includes here his marvelous parody of Williams, together with love notes to Stevens who hovers outside the poems. Of his contemporaries, aside from those mentioned, there are few traces.

Today Koch has few imitators, perhaps Clark Coolidge and Ron Padgett come closest. Still his tracks are followed, if later abandoned by the susceptible; no alert younger poet can help picking up the trail. This in itself is exceptional in an age of the copyist, and one must consider Koch's unique position while reading the poems. With a sublime selfishness, the loneliness of the poet performs his acrobatic pauses while setting poetry on its ear. He is a *Pierrot Lunaire*. And the manic speed with which he constructed his geography!

I want to bear / My share of the anguish of being succinctly here.

We continue through a period of classicism beginning with *The Art of Love* (1972–1975), in which for the first time a strain can be detected on

Koch's apparently unlimited imagination. The selection concludes with the nostalgic *Days and Nights* (1982). Much of Koch is omitted, including the narrative poem, *Ko: or, A Season on Earth*, *The Duplications*, and the miraculous *When the Sun Tries to Go On*, which first appeared with a luminous collage cover by Larry Rivers, Koch's frequent poem-painting collaborator.

Any survey of poetry written between the years of this selection must consider paramount the work of Koch. He is the poet maverick who appears in many guises. Midway Koch turned to Byron (*Ko*), and Childe Koch descended upon us in perhaps his most natural form. This transmogrification is daring; the spirit of Byron is intact with inclusions of that poet's misanthropy, here a baseball tossed in the air.

Once the early Koch had been taped as surrealist in the '70s he changed his audience, becoming a spokesman out of academia, nudging aside Robert Fitzgerald's stale translation of the *Aeneid* with his Kochian deliberations on "The Art of Love" and "The Art of Poetry." Earlier, in "Fresh Air," Koch had castigated this academia in the ear-splitting:

> Until tomorrow, then, scum floating on the surface of poetry!
> goodbye for a moment, refuse that happens to land in poetry's
> boundaries! adieu, stale eggs teaching imbeciles poetry to bolster up your egos! adios, boring anomalies of these same stale
> eggs!
> . . . Oh GOODBYE, castrati of poetry! farewell, stale pale skunky
> pentameters (the only honest English meter! gloop, gloop!) . . .
>
> Hello, sea! good morning, sea! hello, clarity and excitement, you
> great expanse of green—

In his haste to follow his imagination, Koch is difficult to catch up with. This may be deliberate. There are so many Piranesi vistas with their references to the historiography of poetry, so much of the geography of poetry and the world is bestowed that swallowing these dollops may cause indigestion and even hysteria!

Koch once led us to modern-day Greece in what I believe is one of his most 'finished' poems, "The Departure from Hydra." Here he intimates the spiritual declimatization of exile, holding this anxiety at finger's length (again like Byron) while Koch marks the shadow in a series of flat statements:

For a human situation often leads
People to do things that they don't desire
At all, but they find that what they did desire
Has somehow led them to this situation
In which not to do that which is proposed
Seems inconsistent, hostile, or insane,
Though much more often very unfriendly; then too
Sometimes it chiefly is a lack of time
To explain how things have changed that leads one, waving
One's hands, aboard a ship that bodes one ill.

Finally in *Days and Nights* we enter the nostalgia of the poet as he remembers the life shared with his wife who has died. "With Janice" is a poem in which the memory of Janice is sublimated into the history of a poet's inspiration while the world which they cohabited is evoked. It in no way resembles any other 'In Memoriam' and as such is a remarkable isolated poem. I would like to quote from this poem at a point whose first sentences I consider to be of perfect mobility.

. . . Apollo, in some manner of time, lives on.
  Inside your mind
Things are being washed. Everything was docking
And we went down to see it. Memories of women made exactly
  the same
Kneeling down in the hot raft of daisies
It also got ragged for my walks. When are we going
To really have the time to have time?

Reading Koch's *Selected Poems* in an era of moderate poetry, how reassuring to discover *Permanently* ("until the destruction of the language") in aerated space the gyres of immoderation.

Anne Waldman, *Iovis: A Poem*

Iovis ("of Jove," "owned by Jove"), or as in a translation from Virgil, "*All is full of Jove*," Iovis omnia plena.

We must suspend our attention from the newly exhumed *Orlando*. The big O is *IOVIS* beside which Bloomsbury drags a mothy tale. How pecunious is Woolf with her ice floes, velvet doublets, and sexual masquerades beside the intensive and extensive world of *Iovis*.

Waldman creates a picaresque scene as filled with spectacle, danger, and humanity as Fielding. And like the author of the modern novel, this "autobiography" breaks the rules. And she does it advancing from poetics to prose with poppies and lotus blossom, taped interviews and cloud explosions. Swimming in and out of the Mahabharata, she is "Fast-Moving" in gender and form, without burdening the originality of her concept. She subsumes conventionality. Because Waldman lives outside the historical present, *Iovis* challenges with multiple sight (changing her Bull costume into a Star cloak) any precedent in poetic "autobiography."

Note the assurance with which toward the end of the book she includes a letter apparently from someone to whom she had sent her manuscript for criticism. Her inclusion of this letter is a very Fieldingian gesture wherein Tom Jones gets his comeuppance, but we continue to love him more for it. This letter incidentally proves how inapplicable criticism is to Waldman's book, how difficult it is to provide any sort of critical guide to what finally is a *document of an era*.

Beryl Barr-Sharrar Exhibitions

University Art Museum, SUNY Binghamton,
March 11–April 10, 1994

Palmer Museum of Art, The Pennsylvania State University,
June 21–August 21, 1994

In this recent exhibition, Barr-Sharrar separates herself from the classical Abstract Expressionism upon which her painting of the 1970s was based. She moves to a different format. These new pictures still retain the gesturalism of her previous work but it is used within the demanding format she now chooses. Within the set-up of seemingly astringent boundaries the new work consists of an interplay of vertical and horizontal in which bars of paper are laid horizontally upon the verticality of the paper.

These bars form panels each with an integral statement which establishes a relationship to the other panel, as a bar of music even while separating itself contains a relationship to the whole ensemble. So we have meaning inside the picture and meaning within the context of other paintings of the exhibition.

This "meaning" founded upon a gestural statement varies within the separate paintings. We move from sweet to solemn from dark to sunset and there is much inventiveness here mingled with an inevitable solemnity of purpose. In this exhibition there is no doubt that Barr-Sharrar is on to something new. Her approach is filled with possibilities. Now her painting exists in terms of a progression of sequences placed in time, sequences that emerge within a thoughtful and reflexive context.

She both complicates and uncomplicates herself, making use of the freedom of acrylics. She gives full expression to the natural energy of the gestural sweep begun in the earliest *Untitled* of 1985, painted as she mourned the death of her father.

In the more austere *Untitled* of 1993 we discover forms of intellectual selectivity. For instance, the daring size of the block of the top panel is softened in the middle lower ground as two similar blocks are excitingly reduced by brush strokes. The picture then balances itself at the bottom with one long rectangular strip. Yet this adding and reducing produces perhaps the most successful painting of the exhibition. It illustrates her concept of space within a conceit of ideas. We recognize she has presented us with the sprightly progress of several ideas within an intentionally self-sustaining format.

Everywhere there is a steady use of color forming decisions that in the cleared patches appear visibly in movement. She has a good eye for cloud effects when she wants to permit nature into her picture, but nature is not dominant. Ideas and emotive values command this innovative exhibition. With her pictorial inventiveness the painter has combined a wish to control the carefully allotted space and the decision to release it in gestural expansion.

December 1952

JOSEPH MEERT [Ganso] can perhaps be termed an Abstract Impressionist. Working from subconscious impressions, he then takes what he sees about him and transmogrifies it. *The Road and Beyond* is an example of this ability to transform landscape into a static and controlled space in which only color projects. In *Excursion with Color, No. 3*, form becomes relatively unnecessary and we witness the pure activity of color. Thus, although there is quality to the paint, and frequently also a kind of mosaic grouping of colors, the pictures tend to become metaphysical exercises and would move into poetry, rather than painting, were the artist not so extremely conscious of the variegated uses of color.

LILY SHUFF [Van Diemen-Lillienfeld] is a painter with two strong influences—French and American—which are sometimes opposed, but more often unite favorably and successfully prove that such a union is to be desired. Her figure grouping, when she does use the figure, is stylized in the manner of American art in the early '40s, and her color sense is extremely dependent on Rouault and his school. Working more frequently in a semi-abstract manner, she still does not seem to have arrived at a really strong and workable set of images and forms, although she is an experienced painter. Her still-lifes, in particular, have the air of "*morte*" about them which is not exactly pleasant and is perhaps just such a result of a strong color sense plus tendency to arrange the objects in a manner which is still changing.

STEPHEN ETNIER [Milch] still exhibits those light, graceful, and elegant paintings of the West Indies. And the blue skies and slender natives remain even though he has since moved his locale; many of the recent pictures are Maine landscapes, dark, heavy, and somber. It is difficult to determine whether or not this is a change for the better. His Maine pictures are more carefully American in tone, almost nineteenth century with their dark greens. At the same time, Etnier handles paint so well that it is highly probable he will later on develop his own genre of New England painting. Nostalgically, for this reviewer, *Shore Road*, a West Indian painting, spacious and lucid, is quite the best of the show.

RICHARD GUGGENHEIMER [Van Diemen-Lilienfeld], who teaches at Briarcliff, has his second show at this gallery of paintings of the sea and land which have a fine sense of texture to begin with, and move from there into a strong sense of atmosphere. *The Deeps* is simply the sea, or a wave, a single concentration in heavy oil in which the sea is painted simply for itself and then becomes, through a personal osmosis, water in its most terrifying degree. There is a painting of *Clouds*, nebulous, pink loaded with white, which is very beautiful, haunting, and is, moreover, an interesting exercise in technique. Guggenheimer is not afraid to simplify the object and from there to progress to the problem of painting itself.

CHILDE HASSAM [Milch] is seen in watercolors (of 1892–1926) which are amazingly fresh and illustrate how closely his paintings and watercolors are aligned. The pictures are all species of Americana, drawn with that particular intent of his to record settings and houses which made up the Eastern seaboard he knew so well; an intent which in a lesser craftsman might involve mere calligraphy, but in these watercolors revives immediately the tone and color of place which is neither sentimental nor merely topographical. There are the gardens of his friends wherein once again he can allow his Impressionism to run riot with the color of flowers. In *Rocks and Sea*, a drawing which is more completely in his middle style, Impressionism is laid over very thinly and there's a strong imprint of the northern coast of America with its blue which is not quite so cold as one usually expects, but as cold as Hassam could allow it to be. And *General Lee's House, Richmond*, where Hassam is determined that as a sketch-artist he will not allow this one to pass. One also notices in this group, particularly in *September Sky*, an indeterminism, a result of Hassam's recognition that, after all, the style of Impressionism was becoming rather dated, and that he must as a highly egotistical, vigorous artist, and one accustomed to fame, ride the new movements at all costs.

EYRE DE LANUX [Iolas] exhibits landscapes which look rather like blocks of sand in earth colors on which the outlines and dwellings of Pozzilli have been traced. The material for these landscapes appears first to have been dug up from the native soil, then baked in some archaic fashion, and then the designs of the houses traced on with a highly sophisticated intent to suggest the atmosphere and conditions of the surroundings. Whether or not this particular kind of mannerism is successful depends largely upon one's personal demands of painting. The landscapes are charming, yet for this reviewer more sensitivity than art appeared here.

RICHARD DE MENOCAL [Hugo] is a young painter who is having his first one-man show of exceedingly real still-lifes in watercolor. He has painted vegetables and fruits, *Lemons*, *Asparagus*, *Chestnuts* exactly as he sees them and they are not more real than life, nor more literal. There is, fortunately, no touch of magic realism here, nor are these watercolors merely pictorial or dramatic; they are simply objects of the vegetable and fruit kingdom as the artist sees them. Although his watercolors have the appearance, which is not consciously deceptive, of oils, one is anxious after seeing this exhibition to find out what De Menocal will do with oil. It might well mark the advent of a superior realist.

JEAN PAUL BRUSSER'S [Hugo] paintings of the city of Paris were exhibited as a kind of celebration by the French government both of the pleasures of its home city and the advent here in New York of the Barrault troupe. Brusser's paintings can thus be better viewed as illustrations of Paris, rather than chic and decorative comments on famous places. *Sacré-Coeur*, *Pont Royal*, etc., almost a personal assignment to convey the spirit and settling of Paris as he sees it. From this standpoint he can be permitted to escape the finer points of criticism and his paintings may be judged for the effect they have of nostalgia for a familiar locale, of certain atmospheric essences which he has perhaps caught and perhaps can be shared by Americans.

January 1953

RICHARD STANKIEWICZ [Hansa] is having his first one-man show of sculpture composed of aluminum and steel wires covered with white plaster, shredded rope, buttons, and bits of tubing. "Fantastic Creatures and Satirical Poses" are witty commentaries on the depravities and demeanors of insect and human life. This group of sculpture is somewhat academic and tight, and several "Poses," like *Tantrum*, remind one of Klee. His latest work is integrated on a much larger scale and moves from direct human experience and observation. *Mounted Man*, of aluminum, wire, screen, and plaster, is more brilliant; here he does not attempt to move us emotionally or intellectually, or merely to create a series of intricate designs, but succeeds in drawing us into a spectacle of the human caught in the minor complexities of his minor world. *Problem in Planes* clears out a good deal of unnecessary formula and is merely wire screen balanced on three levels. This small sculpture should mark the beginning of a development toward a pure and personal style on a high level.

T. MARKOE ROBERTSON [Ferargil] is a well-known New York architect who is also fond of architectural and locational reminiscences in watercolor. His watercolors of Southampton have a whimsical, Colonial air about them which goes well with the drawings of *Beach House* or *Dune Church* and should evoke nostalgia in the hearts of all lovers of that former spa. He has traveled and lived a good bit in fashionable settings of the West Indies and Mexico. *Band Stand, Cuernavaca, Harbor, Nassau* are painted from the rather romantic viewpoint of the cultivated and sensitive traveler.

LUDWIG BEMELMANS [Ferargil] is still the same knight errant progressing through the Europe he continues to adore in a manner which, despite all its charm and grace, has become (probably through a refusal to change in what he has recognized as a changing world) just a little aged. The same head waiters, the same Madame et Monsieur, the same enchanting harbor, this time Ischia, the same permanent landscape of the Riviera, Monte Carlo, remain what he knows and still cares to paint. The pictures are as good as possible, and still better than almost anyone else's who is interested in the same scenery, but the humor is slightly less divine.

JOHN WILDE'S [Hewitt] latest pictures, with the exception of his still-lifes, have a wise lewdness which appears to be characteristic of many Surrealists after they have been painting seriously in this manner for any length of time. *Surprise* allows us to look at a lovely red-haired lady, slightly pregnant, and beautifully painted from the viewpoint of sin triumphant; the victory of lively sin over morality is elsewhere predominant. *Radishes* and *Smelts* have all the exquisiteness of semi-historical painting, and, like Dalí, Wilde is a master of line and detail.

MALCOLM CASE [Copian], who has worked previously in watercolor, is now exhibiting his oils for the first time. The work is divided into two styles. An earlier group consists of squares in impasto against a flat yellow, red, white, or black background. These paintings are extremely flat, the squares of thick paint project only slightly from a one-dimensional background, and the content of the pictures seems to be made up of mostly arbitrary designs against an arbitrary color. His second style shows harlequin-like figures drawn in one continuous black line and flatly colored.

ETHEL MAGAFAN [Ganso] exhibits paintings which were done while she was on a Fulbright Fellowship in Greece. Thus all of the paintings consist of Grecian landscapes and towns and her colors have been changed by the light and color of Greece. She has a rather literal sense of landscape and paints directly from the scene. However this literalness becomes an asset in that she is quite objective about what she sees, with pleasant, direct economy.

ALEXANDER DOBKIN [A.C.A.] has been in Europe for the past four years and his present show consists in the main of paintings made from European backgrounds. *Poverty Against the Gates of Eternal Values* is the artist's interpretation of the Baroque cathedrals of Spain against which the figure of the poor with enlarged hand outstretched poses its problem, and *Boy from Salamanca* continues this same theme. Dobkin uses gold leaf and darkens his colors to convey the somberness which he has felt about the country. His New York *Subway Series* illustrates what he feels quite as much and are more fully developed and expressed.

BEERBOHM AND ROBINSON [American Academy of Arts and Letters] are shown across the court from one another and certainly no more opposing personalities could be collected within a smaller space. Sir Max Beerbohm is represented by caricatures, books and manuscripts borrowed from private libraries and estates; the organization of this show is pleasantly historical and nostalgic. One realizes, viewing these familiar drawings, the completely unique position Beerbohm occupies within his genre and how undated caricature can become when wisdom and humor dictate its aims. *The Poet's Corner* with "Mr. Yeats introducing George Moore to the Queen of the Fairies," "Byron Shaking the Dust of England from his Toes," or "Tennyson Reading 'In Memoriam' to his Sovereign," are pure and unsucceeded delights. And so are the benign caricature of "Il Pound" and the not so benign caricature of "Mr. Whistler." Passing into an entirely different set of attitudes, Boardman Robinson, the chronicler of the Harding era, begins the long and so far undeveloped reach of American caricature. These drawings are both political newspaper satire and attempts at the portraiture of character. Liberty and mayors, British personalities and war mongering are all rather violently expressed with a pen that now seems a little too sure of itself, a little too romantic, and at the same time willing to go along with the conventional attitudes of the day. The collection itself is excellent and includes several oils.

THEODORE STAMOS's [Parons] latest paintings continue to move from defined form into the realm of symbol. His paintings in black, ochers, grey, and white are nebulous incantations wherein somber forms evoke a series of magic formulas. *Long Island Sounds* has this quality of movement mysteriously hoarded and painted not so much for anyone as for another member of a cult. *Tea House*, 7 has another group of symbols; these are of the East, but still the East as seen by a member of a sect, not a layman or curious traveler, but one of a religious order. As such it is difficult to identify these pictures as they are outwardly constructed quite cohesively, and certainly the tendency of the uninitiated to find in them a kind of decoration may not be relative at all. But there are limitations to be found even within good painting, and here the aura about the pictures has gone too far beyond the ordinary.

February 1953

EDWARD JOHN STEVENS, JR. [Weyhe], has been traveling in Greece, Crete, and Italy and in his latest work has attempted to condense the historical past of these countries through symbolical characters and settings. Thus a gouache, *A Venetian Evening*, pictures a canal with an ancient craft, antique people, and a Byzantine city rising in the background. *Night Over Phaistos* shows a figure of antiquity from which stems the empty ruins of Greece. His technique is based on Persian and primitive painting, and frequently the painting is appealing and clever. Often his combinations of ancient methods, plus a washed Japanese-like background, come off as a tour-de-force, rather than actual painting.

DARREL AUSTIN'S [Perls] latest work continues along his familiar same lines. Bright tigers, forests of the night, ladies *sans merci*, magic spells are again there to enchant us. But it seems a pity that so much good painting should be wasted on such minor myth-making. The paintings take place at some point in the artist's night—all of the canvases are in deep blues and dark greens. *The Huntress*, a painting of a lady with a hoop stalking the forest with three tigers, her Renaissance hair the color of the tiger's mane, looks out at us compellingly as if we must understand the consequences of her actions and respond to the tiger's questioning glare. *Girl Casting a Spell* is again a painting of the night, and if here the legend ended, all might be well. But Austin continues with other ladies, wistful and evil, other beasts, until a certain weariness sets in. These figures do no cast a very big spell; they remain figments of a private dream.

ALLEN LEEPA [Artists Gallery], who has exhibited both in the United States and France and is now assistant professor of art at Michigan State College, exhibits largely in pastel and tempera. His abstractions are academic in the degree that they appear to have been worked out from a strongly conceived idea of exactly what a painting should contain, and there are certain mannerisms of color which in the end tend to appear decorative. He has carefully worked out his attempt to condense into a few elements of color and design a concept of the inner workings of painting.

FRENCH PAINTING [Coronet] includes work by Le Coadic, Cristellys, Gourjon, and Grandidier, contemporary painters of Parisian scenes and landscapes. Gourjon, whose manner is like that of Vlaminck—as Le Coadic is somewhat an imitator of Utrillo—is the best of this group which is more imitative than original.

HERMAN RAYMOND [Artists Gallery], a New Yorker who teaches drawing and painting in Colorado, exhibited work which was divided into two styles. Strings of thick paint in "jewel-tone" colors build up his early canvases of cities and landscapes which are heavily Impressionistic and attempt to reproduce too many elements of scene. *Early Morning* marks the beginning of his newer work and is perhaps his strongest and best-balanced painting. In his later work he has not yet condensed his attitudes, and appears to be groping for a much stronger, more lucid style—one in which superficialities do not dominate.

KERMAH KALLMAN [Salpeter] sculpts soft, rounded figures of people, nudes, cats, fish, all characterized by smooth surfaces and gentle contours. *The Reclining Nude*, in marble, and *Head*, in alabaster, have a serenity; execution is not forced or hard, and if most of the sculpture is conventional, there is a personal, human touch.

JOHN WHEAT'S [Grand Central] "paintings of New England" are clear, real depictions of barns, villages in snow, tobacco fields, and a seacoast which, in the winter, appears very far north. The winter scenes have the grey-green skies characteristic of this part of the country; *Shining Mountains* is snow-laden and chilling. Wheat paints meticulously and with an exactitude which refuses any trickery, and he has captured the remoteness of New England.

March 1953

MASTER DRAWINGS [J. Seligmann] coincides with the big museum drawing shows and brings together both well-known artists and those who are still relatively uncommon in America. Beginning with Antoine Caron and the sixteenth century, continuing through La Hyre, Le Sueur, Mellan, and Vouet, all of whose work illustrates the skill and accomplishment of drawing in a period in which artists were accepted as natural products of court life, a high point is reached in *Christ at Gethsemane* by Giandomenico Tiepolo—a somber, religious drawing in which there is an exquisite balance between landscape and the figures. The nineteenth century includes two drawings and a watercolor by Bonington; they are delicate, near-romantic, yet firmly controlled. *The Battle Field* by Géricault, in which space and color are handled in a highly beautiful and romantic manner, is perhaps the most unsuspected reward of the exhibition; and Gustave Moreau's almost difficult *Galatea* is a work to which a painter such as Rouault would turn—its heavily charged color and symbolism now seem almost Surrealist. The twentieth century is represented by a Léger *Diver* which has extraordinary mass movement in a small space, the figure plunging directly into the foreground; a classical *Pierrot* by Picasso; a Rajon, *Profile at Right*, in which an elaborate design to the far right of the drawing sets up a tension between the fragile, *spirituel* profile of a woman as seen dimly in a glass; and Seurat's *Bridge at Courbevoie*, a dark, thickly drawn sketch which might well be a painting.

PAUL BROSSEAU'S [Alphabet] calligraphic designs are exhibited for students and admirers of the simple and warm rhythms of his work. The designs are largely for commercial use and illustrate the varied and complex problems of graphic art which here have been solved in as individual a manner as possible.

SIMON LISSIM [Museum of Natural History] was born in Russia and worked there for many years as a painter, stage designer, and ceramist. Now associated with City College of New York, his exhibition included illustrations for folk and fairy tales, designs for vases and chinaware, and a series of *Sultan* pictures. Elephants, flowers, snakes, mythological creatures, and fishes form elaborate Oriental designs; the character of the exhibition is like an Arabian Nights story translated into Russian.

HENRY MITCHELL [Kraushaar], winner of a Fulbright Scholarship to Italy and student of Marini, exhibits sculpture that for all its European antecedents is surprisingly American in attitude. Subjects like *Paper Carriers*, *Chair Mender*, *Wash Women* convey a social realism that was prevalent here in the 1930s, despite his more modern, though certainly non-Marini, approach. He appears to be interested in subjects caught in their daily work or in off-guard moments of patent egotism, and as such the sculpture is pictorial. However, he avoids the static by a tensity which often is tempered by a sympathetic involvement with his subject matter.

CARL WUERMER [Grand Central] of New York celebrated his twenty-fifth year with this gallery with landscapes of the seasonal cycles of Vermont. He paints intimate, realist pictures of frozen ponds, lonely houses, village churches, and the hills which form a geography with which he is exceedingly familiar. *October Day*, *Frosty Morning*, *December Afternoon* are descriptive of exactly what appears before the artist's eye.

COLORED WOODCUTS [Truman] presents the work of three young artists who have attended the Philadelphia Museum's art school and subsequently taught there. Samuel Maitin is perhaps the most sophisticated, his woodcuts of *Europa and the Bull*, *Celebrants*, and the lovely *Nudes* take mythology as their point of departure, yet have, at the same time, a strong sense of the figure which gives them more interest than a mere interpretation of myth. Edward Cother's *The Dancers* and *Bird* are competent woodcuts, but their appeal is somewhat lessened by a stylism which appears to be a phase through which the artist is passing. Jerome Kaplan's woodcuts are more illustrative. *Court Martial*, in black and white, and *Rebbe Elimelech* are executed with a deliberate concentration on dramatic essences.

WILL BARNET [B. Senaefer] in his latest group of watercolors continues to paint the world as simply as possible. He gives formal meaning to ordinary actions, such as *Eating Oranges and Apples*, and clears away entire undergrowths of complexity to construct a landscape in which a garden is laid out for us and the path whereby we may follow it is imprinted with small blue footprints. His interpretations of human actions and reactions in *Following* and *Tumult* are almost watery and unsubstantial, their value consisting in the picture seen as an entity, or even as a lay analysis, without judgement. The only difficulty in these pictures is that once one has caught the clue, one has seen all; succeeding watercolors do not reveal more. Often the painting appears to be a formula, as if the spirit behind it could lay on one impression after another.

April 1953

ROLF NESCH [Serigraph], a Norwegian graphic artist, showed metal-cuts which take several points of departure, particularly from Klee and the folding screens of Japan. He has either very complicated designs of undersea configurations or he simplifies with a few dense objects—rock, heavy sand, flat sky. The work is intense and at the same time intellectual, quite conscious on several levels, and on these levels he succeeds admirably, if in a rather stylized and derivative manner.

LOUIS EVAN'S [A.F.I.] latest paintings continue with their architectural abstractions of the city and nature. He has also included two paintings of a very different genre, *March Sea* and *Way Down East*, somber nineteenth-century-type pictures, thickly painted and varnished. These interrupt the even flow of thinner paint, abstracted trees, and architecturally planned cities that make up this exhibition. Evan paints very directly from idea to canvas and there is little confusion between the artist and the viewer. He simplifies nature into three thin trees; he simplifies everything he sees, so that his greatest difficulty is not what he is going to paint, or how he is going to translate his subject, but the manner in which he is going to paint it. Frequently he is clumsy and overt in a good painting, and often his directness leads to over-simplification.

ABRAMSON AND LEVINE [Davis] are two young artists working in different mediums yet each arriving at a more conservative and conventional manner than one would expect. Arnold Abramson, who has been awarded a Tiffany grant, shows woodcuts, lithographs, drawings. His portraits, such as *Lois*, a clear, realistic drawing, are the best of his group. David Levine, who has studied with Hans Hofmann, might easily be a surprise of the year. His paintings are completely reminiscent of the turn of the century. The style of dress and hair of the women he paints, their particular poses, the handling of color and values, especially in *The Woman in the Red Chair* and *Horse in Field*, are startlingly similar to those late nineteenth- and early twentieth-century American paintings whose artists had passed through the School of Paris and returned to paint their native subjects. Working against contemporary influences, Levine has quite determinedly turned out paintings which will satisfy his own aesthetic values and as such can be regarded as nostalgic representations, or on the level of their considerable own merit.

SNORRE ANDERSON [Serigraph], a Norwegian painter, is having his first exhibition in the United States of recent paintings executed here. The smaller ones, on canvas-board, cut landscape to the size of its psychological aspects. He paints *New England Landscape* with only a few objects—a church, the hills, the snow—and the relationship of this scene to the Puritan culture it exemplifies is brought out. In *Sails*, a very simple picture consisting entirely of a few boats on water with a background sky, water is painted as loneliness. In each of his pictures, the objects or the landscape painted has little importance as a single view; it is the aspect of nostalgia or remoteness that is important.

May 1953

CHAIM GROSS [Jewish Museum] has traveled recently in Israel, and this offering of watercolors includes scenes of the people, countryside, and towns. Painting directly from what he sees, Gross appears to be interested mainly in portraying in a simple and realistic manner the life which is current now and which has also its mainstream in the past. Architectural motifs are heightened, and we absorb the distinct blend of architecture in half-opened buildings, sidewalk shops, and overall views of the city of Jerusalem.

TATSUO ARAI [Riverside Museum] exhibited a large group of paintings that divided themselves into several styles, progressing from the earlier Paris scenes and Paris influences and ending in semi-abstractions. Seen thus as a retrospective of 1933–52, the exhibition often displayed an uneasiness, an unsureness in each genre, almost a timidity. It was very seldom that the artist arrived at his own, personal forms; he appeared to be overshadowed by the influences surrounding him. *Ave Maria*, a semiabstraction, is a happier solution than most. Although still inclined to overcautious underpainting and brushstrokes, lately the artist appears to have become freer and more direct.

Summer 1953

NORWEGIAN SERIGRAPHS [Serigraph; to June 29] is a collection of the work of Norwegian graphic artists who, with the exception of Erling Merton, have never shown in this country before. Their serigraphs are much freer than the American work, more influenced by the Far East, and the color has a delicacy and a lightness which is not often attempted here. Erling Merton's style is the closest to his American contemporaries and he shows a controlled use of the medium. His *Speilegg* and *Tulipanen* are delightful still-lifes, somewhat derivative of Matisse, but the color is lighter and the composition is personal. *Klovnen* by Finn Christensen shows the serigraph technique used to approximate oils: extremely intricate and decorative motifs perpetuate a sense of fable or story and have a charm which is not belied by his novel use of the medium. Hanna Jessen's *Kergmiker* is possibly more clumsy and amateurish in the medium than would be allowed here, but there is an expression which manages to override any failure of technique. The exhibition is also an object lesson to Americans working with serigraphs who have perhaps lost their originality through too strict an adherence to the problems of craft.

GUNVOR BULL-TEILMAN [Serigraph] showed portraits, landscapes, and interpretations of legends. Always personal, whether interpreting a Norwegian myth or a landscape, much of her imagery appears to arise from the unconscious or from pure fantasy. When she is good, as in *In Ringtime*, a romantic painting of a legend, she slows charm and delicacy; when she is bad, she tends to crowd her pictures, to reveal a good deal more of the unconscious than is necessary, and she shows an arbitrary regard for color. Although her paintings of children are better than those of adults, her portraits are often clumsy and reveal little of the personality of the sitter, although they purport to be realistic.

WING HOWARD [Knoedler] shows watercolors of a vanishing America and a Paris evoked from the 1900s. Consistently conscious of the single elements of his nostalgic drama—the garden chair, the period dress, the carriage—Howard intrudes himself only as a visitor leaning from the atelier, overlooking the rooftops of Paris. These are pleasantly colored, nicely atmospheric watercolors, and if their sensibility verges on the obvious and thus lends itself to the chic and the fashionably romantic, still there is a modesty in his affection for the past.

LUBA GURDUS's [Stephen Wise Congress House] drawings were exhibited in commemoration of the tenth anniversary of the Battle of the Warsaw Ghetto. In her other drawings of the Maydaneck concentration camp, where she was interned, Miss Gurdus reminds us frequently of Kollwitz, her teacher, yet with less of the positive strength of Kollwitz's drawings. In these scenes there is only the relationship between the sketch-artist and what she is witnessing. She has avoided overt emotionalism to a remarkable degree and these drawings of the ghetto made during its final days are thus most moving as records of human betrayal and despair.

LUDWIG Y. WOLPERT [Jewish Museum], a teacher at the Bezalel School, Palestine, and the foremost Israeli craftsman, exhibits ritual art objects. Wolpert is unique among his fellow craftsmen in his use of Hebrew letters as architectural motifs. Thus in his crown for the Torah, Hebrew characters, changed so that each line is equal in width to the other, form a highly satisfactory design for the ancient crown. The effect is that of a simple yet dramatic cohesion between the past and the present. His work in silver and copper has an elegance which appears so natural that it is taken almost for granted until compared with the work of other craftsmen. There are several mezuzoth that have an unusual delicacy combined with a deliberate break with the more conventionally constructed objects, and this is true also of his Torah crowns.

October 1953

KARNIG NALBANDIAN's [Chapellier] latest paintings continue with their soft, wistful backgrounds onto which are laid the rapid, thin slices of "jewel-tones." His landscapes, particularly his most abstract one, *The Pool*, show more strength and interest, and it may well be that Nalbandian will emerge more successfully as an abstractionist, his symbology having worn rather thin. His drawings are always excellent, almost antique in their literature and expression, extremely delicate yet never fragmentary.

SAMUEL KOCH [Chapellier] recently showed bright and freshly colored paintings of village streets, Florida palms, and bays from the optimistic standpoint of the primitive painter happily adjusted to any landscape he happens on.

November 1953

SIDNEY ZIMMERMAN [Matrix; to Nov 17], young New York painter, worked at the Art Students League and has previously exhibited in Mexico. He is having his first one-man show here. His paintings organize color to create space and they move into depth as well as across surfaces; a system of painting away from Cubism and falling back toward Impressionism. His earlier Mexican pictures are painted on gesso in strong, deep colors. These are very good and lively and one would be satisfied had his show not more to offer. He is now organizing color in extremely rich areas reminiscent of the nineteenth-century French, yet the form is not arbitrary but entirely sensible to the color which poses it. Zimmerman has both strength and sensibility, and should produce, once he ages within his métier, some excellent painting.

MAX BAND [Jewish Museum] shows paintings of 1949–53 of Italy, France, and California. Trained in Paris, Band is a disciple of the school of French easel painting which always produces pleasant, well-executed if somewhat innocuous painting. *Place St. Germain-des-Prés* is a painting one has seen often before, and Band has done little to change one's previous conceptions. *Piazza San Marco* renders Venice in a curious green tone, rather heavy, yet at the same time the picture is more individualistic, as if the painter actually saw Venice in dark greens. *San Pedro, California* adds brighter colors, but the composition is conventional and the artist here appears, as in his other California paintings, to be seeking to convey the California colors, yet has been in some way interrupted by his visions of the South of France.

STANLEY, BOXER, EUGENE POWELL [Perdalma] exhibited two very different styles of painting, both of which were interesting for a kind of sureness of execution. Boxer, a student of the Art Students League, showed for the first time strangely tangled, arabesque interiors with the furniture and people hidden under the darkened colors in a Vuillard palette. His large interiors lack spontaneity, but his smaller ones, such as *Figures in Interior*, are very pleasing, the color controlling the figures and the figures giving strength to the color. A former Guggenheim Fellow, Powell shows abstract paintings which have a Japanese quality, a flatness of space and hue which frequently tends toward the decorative and the static, yet in *Scorched Landscape* there is less prescription and the painting moves freely revealing the painter's capabilities.

ARTHUR TIEGER [Artists' Gallery], young New York artist, is having his first one-man show of work accomplished over the past two years. Tieger is essentially a self-Expressionist; that is, the painting results from an explosion of his ego. This kind of work, when successful, as in *My Studio—a Winter Mood*, reaches toward the level of Van Gogh, and when it fails reveals a torment in the painter's temperament which is often difficult to witness. He uses strong, vibrant, large areas of color to show the artist standing beside his easel, or to paint a table, or a room. In *Color Storm in March* he has begun to break through into Expressionism, but the picture is nearly not finished.

WOLFGANG ROTH [Galerie Moderne], theatrical designer of the present production of *Porgy and Bess*, has been connected with the theater and with the circus a good part of his life. His paintings are of clowns, old actors, a *Greek Tragedy* (dedicated to Judith Anderson), and a setting for *Porgy and Bess*. Roth is primarily a draftsman, not a colorist, and he is interested in the interpretation of character by black line against a strong white or earth color, to state his attitude toward *Jimmy Savo* or Shakespeare's *Grumio*.

HAROLD PARIS [Galerie Moderne], who has been awarded a Guggenheim Fellowship for a project of graphics, *Eternal Judgement*, exhibits a series of pictures related to this work, but in the medium of paint. He has developed his own technique of waxes and paper rubbings which produce the curious effect of an image much tinted over, almost nebulous. He has a series of faces, *Moloch*, *Agnostic*, and *Neutral*, strange shapes and distortions arranged in his own fantasy of the world of the ancients and the world of the present. There is irony, bitterness, and almost a disappointment in humanity in these series, broken only by the romantic *Lullaby River* and *Twilight in a Strange Garden.*

GABOR PETERDI [Borgenicht] is preoccupied with the beginnings and endings of things, the birth of minutiae and their conflagrant end. As such, his paintings are explosive, interpretive, and flamboyant in color. Frequently they tend toward the gigantic illustrations of civilizations bursting in flames seen in popular magazines; again, as in *Silver Spawning*, the coloring and the softly moving forms convince one that if painting is itself an act of interpretation, that if through the evolution of the canvas, thought can move and change, then Peterdi has correctly stated his theme. His graphics, however, show him more at ease within a medium which can satisfy indirectly through execution; here black on white makes no demands on the artist as a colorist, or as one working with the spaces provided by a large canvas.

EDMUND CASARELLA [Korman] is a young painter who has been on a Fulbright fellowship in Italy and has returned with many pictures influenced by the present Italian school. He has painted or drawn in black lines the landscape and the ruins of the cities he has seen, such as *Pink Ruins*, which looks like a rather elegant Italian rendering of the Colosseum at sunset, or *Neapolitan Street Vendor.* He also traveled to Greece. These slim, black, elegantly abstracted lines have changed somewhat in a more solid picture, *Rugged Balance*, and in a degree it is more interesting.

ARTIST'S CHOICE [Serigraph] is a collection selected by the artists themselves. Mary van Blarcom, who died recently, is represented by *The Beast*, an excellent serigraph selected by her husband. It shows most clearly the possibilities of this technique and the extent to which it can be developed in the hands of such a resourceful artist. Robert Kiley's work is extremely good, as well as Blackburn's *Slumber* and Marion Huse's *The Park.* Other artists are not so well represented, and a certain facility and lack of content betrays itself throughout the show.

LEE MULLICAN [Willard] has begun to show a surprising change from the careful, topographical settings of his past work and is now moving rapidly into more intense colors and shapes. One senses with Mullican that he is more sure of himself as a painter, there is more of a professional ease, and he is freer to experiment. Some of these new paintings are successful, others are not. *Cannon of the Dragon* [A.N., Oct. 1953], a much stronger declaration of New World imagery, is a vivid and dynamic picture, as is *Frame of the City*, a horizontal with which he has previously worked so well. *Asia Minor* is confused and may mark a position in transit. He has ceased commenting, however, and has begun to express more direct feelings about and within his paintings.

RUTH HAGEMANN [Artist's Gallery] is having her first one-man show which illustrates very clearly the problem of combining naturalist forms in abstract paintings. Here the artist has chosen plants, trees, a garden. She is lyrical, yet repetitive. Three paintings of flowers might almost make the same painting; *Geraniums* has a tedium which exists because the space is not filled with enough form or enough color and might even be said to fall into mere floral painting, a danger which this artist should not even be aware of as she is obviously a competent abstractionist. *New Year's Wish* is more clearly in the genre of abstraction and is the best painting of the show.

NINETEENTH-CENTURY AMERICAN PAINTERS [Chapellier] is a delightful gathering of well-known, little-known, and anonymous artists. All of the works, with the exception of a primitive portrait, are of nature, of the American landscape which at that time was stronger than the city and was the concern of Dangerfield in his *Forest Scene*, Blakelock in *Indian Encampment at Night*, Moran with *Mexico*, Durand's *Sunrise*. It is nature at its mysterious best, dominating the technique and personal standards. The two outstanding pictures are *Cranberry Picking*, attributed to Winslow Homer, which shows two figures on a sloping hill, a small and moving painting, and *Pasture*, by an unknown, which is merely cows in a field, but which carries the entire music and moodiness of a little-settled land.

GUSTAV WOLF [Jacobi], a German painter and engraver who took asylum in this country from the Nazi regime and died while a teacher in Northfield, Mass., was given a memorial exhibition of his work. His paintings and woodcuts are expressive of the spiritual reconciliation felt by so many artists in the Germany of his period. Distorted forms, angels, strange galaxies make up the chaotic worlds of his woodcuts and engravings for the books of Psalms and Genesis. And in his oil painting, also, the work is not primarily painting for its own sake, but to find a meaning in the universe. The total concept is one of personal intensity which makes itself felt most clearly in the prints where the work is technically of a very high order.

December 1953

NEW YORK SOCIETY OF WOMEN ARTISTS [Riverside Museum] recently had their annual exhibition. Most of the work was contemporaneous and this attitude gave the collection a sparkle which is frequently missing from such large groupings. Also, the direct femininity of the painting was less apparent than is usual and could be detected only in a tendency which most of the painters had to catch a particular moment in time, or to portray the particular atmosphere of a setting. And this sort of sensitivity, of course, is feminine and gave an additional aura to such paintings as *Kentucky Spring* by Ann Cole Phillips, *Remembered Moments* by Sylvia Carewe. *Fugue* by Lily Shuff and Frances Avery's *Vernal Patch* were two paintings of interest, as was *Summer Storm* by Grace Borgenicht, whose work is very delicate, yet still a little too mannered. The sculpture was much duller, with the exception of Louise Nevelson's *Head of a Distant Relative*, reminiscent of Barbara Hepworth.

SCHOOL OF PARIS [Janis] brings again to New York work which has hitherto been screened from the public eye by private collectors, and furnishes new evidences of the work-in-progress of various masters. Possibly the belle of the ball is an *Odalisque* by Miró, painted in 1918, which startles with its ripe and riotous Oriental decor reminiscent of Matisse, yet, despite birds and flowers and a Cubistically ripened female, points toward this artist's later abstraction. There are also two Cubist paintings by Herbin and Metzinger, the Herbin surprisingly romantic, and the Metzinger, *Woman with Fan*, serene and at ease amid its planes. Léger is represented by *Girl with Ladder*, of the same period as his *Bicyclists*. Other highlights are a 1914 Juan Gris collage and an earlier Severini of a timid yet lucid distinction. From the Stein Collection appears a 1906 Matisse. A 1913 de Chirico, owned by the late Paul Éluard, shows de Chirico unusually blunt and harsh, with frontal boxings of space, so that the disappearing background appears less as an escape, more as an exit.

LEONID [Durlacher], concentrating on the sea and those who earn their living by it, again pictorializes space into man, horizon, sky, and water. These paintings over the past two years reaffirm his position as an inheritor of the Baroque and animator of Surrealist themes. His ability (without perversity) to analyze the affinity between beach and horizon, his regard for all the details of color and light which produce in his work a "quality" which is not fashionably admitted elsewhere, have placed him in the position of one outside current dogma, yet nearer, perhaps, the center of painting itself. It is true that the American scenery does not seem to lend itself so well to his approach, because for some reason it is not important that so delicate a balance be preserved in this country between the scene and the painter. It may perhaps be that here the very drama of the coastline refuses the subtlety of which Leonid has made himself a master.

ROBERT COOK [Sculpture center], previously awarded Tiffany and Fulbright grants, has spent the past five years in Italy. His earlier work, such as *Bather*, shows strong, naturalistic tendencies which he has now broken into concave lines of bronze, belting his *Bronco Buster* and cording in areas of space. He still evidences a regard for the conventions of physiognomy, but the sculpture now moves both upward and outward. Curious also is his strictly American choice of subject matter, yet at the same time the Italian influence can be found in a greater elegance, a lyricism which removes a *Circus Rider* from its American tent into larger dimensions.

BERNARD REDER [Borgenicht; to Dec. 12] exhibits a series of monoprints cut in wood, titled *Comédie Humaine*. These are difficult to categorize as they move from what at times may be called a Renaissance head into the slight distortion which could extend itself into Surrealism. They are portraits of frailties and of beauties, *Head of a Girl Strangely Adorned* or *Head of a Lady*, all of these personages of the tragi-comic pattern of life, half-human and half-divine, yet recognizable. What Reder has done is to equivocate the mystery of his apparitions with a complicated technique, and one guesses that the process of the printing has evoked all of his strength and skill. Here, too, is a series of much larger prints. *Prayer* treats of rabbis and personages of an intense Jewish world—their personal background and history.

JOHN ALTOON [Artists' Gallery] is a young painter, winner of several awards in California, who is having his second one-man show. There are two styles of painting here, one in which the scenes, *Androcles and the Lion*, *Chicken Thief*, *Mother and Child with Birds*, are carefully worked out in composition and color. Altoon uses a lot of paint, and later supersedes layer in cautiously blocked-out areas of color. He has also a facility which assures the painting of a technical weight, but this same ease causes him to fall into certain art-school clichés. Lately, however, he has turned from what has been styled "easel painting," to the use of plasterer's tools, and the surfaces of *Nudes*, *Tired*, *Hungry and Lean* are rough and cement-like. These later works are more interesting, not only because they are more adventurous, but also because they show the artist's personality asserting itself abruptly.

ELMER EZRIEL SPIEGEL [Crespi] of Los Angeles appears to be seeking form through abstraction, but is at times overcome by the unconscious, so that one is never sure where the picture begins or ends. His colors are somber and the pictures attain neither height nor depth, but merely unroll, frequently in a lurid manner. His etchings are much better.

BERTRAND GOODMAN [Artisans] exhibits paintings and drawings which give a retrospective glance over his past work and bring it up to the present. His former painting is almost overtly professional, with a skillful grouping of figures caught in theatrical movement, the colors bright to garish and in style reminiscent of the '30s. Later, however, he tends to elongate his figures and the draftsmanship, which is quite good, is content to lose itself in a distortion which changes the scene and gives the pictures, now only dimly colored, a strangeness and poetic quality which formerly did not appear.

January 1954

AMERICAN NORTHWEST INDIAN ART [Carlebach], mostly from the nineteenth century, includes masks, totems, a Chilbah (1920), all simply executed, showing the use these peoples made of any material at hand. One mask is inlaid with abalone shells that glisten in the dark. Another quite beautiful mask, made in human proportions by the Taimshian tribe, shows the high level on which this tribe worked as compared to the simpler ones of the Tinglit, who used very large colored masks as decoration or as symbols of the wealth of their owner.

FRANK PACK [Creative], who served in Europe in the war, continues his paintings of stricken people in stricken war areas. Debris, rubble, mutilations, painted in cold blues, greens and violets fill his canvas with an emotional recording of the era, yet leave one wondering when Pack will leave off this preoccupation with the war to find more resources within his canvas.

CLEMENT REINHOLD [Argent] exhibits paintings which he calls *Faces of the Mind*. These are portraits of *G. B. Shaw*, *Gandhiji*, and others, together with landscapes, painted thickly in rapid slices of color in an Expressionistic manner.

FRANK DI GIOIA [Milch] continues his "Little Italy" series of paintings depicting the life of the Italian section of New York in all the aspects that are familiar to the artist. People, single faces of children, an elderly couple, all engaged in the eager business of living and survival, make up these humorous and touching paintings. There is very little of human content that Di Gioia has missed, and his pictures have also the effect of fast sketches, of movement crossing faces that must be immediately caught and set down so that he may go onto the next group, so that "Little Italy" itself may be recorded before it passes away. *Playtime* shows dozens of riotous children clambering over a "jungle," heightened by bright color, the impact and tumble recorded. A larger painting, *Wedding Feast* is here a conclusive compliment to the customs of the Italians. Nothing is missing from this picture: the orchestra, the bridal couple, even the photographer. What is so impressive about Di Gioia's painting goes beyond a technique which is certainly not unique, even subject to clichés of drawing and color, but his immediate sense of life, his ability to make his pictures move as Italian life moves, turbulent and expressively. He has refused to change with fashion and has quite consciously dedicated himself to what he believes to be his talent—the simple fashioning of a certain group of people onto canvas. And this dedication calls forth its own particular respect.

ANN RYAN [Parsons], well known for her collages—her work is a direct continuation of Schwitters's—now shows, together with new collages, some oil paintings. She has managed to break clearly away from the rules of her collage and in three large paintings, *Numbers 1, 2,* and *10*, has expressed the art of the sudden wish. This is wish-fulfillment brought clearly from all that she has known about painting into a revelatory style in which the preconceived idea is never present; everything takes place directly before us on the canvas, by accident, by the inner wish to relate what can be found in the interior. The thin colors move intuitively, a small triangle is sketched inadvertently and then suddenly a dark line precedes from technique overtly used, but discovered almost by chance. Her collages are now much larger, more open, yet it must be admitted that, good as they are, they do not always satisfy as did her smaller ones. An exception is *Number 3, White Collage*, whose purity admits any amount of space and has the architecture of the mind embedded in the palest of colors, the firmest of space.

FRED HAUCKE [Creative] has invented horrors of nude and wandering women caught in giant traps, or has exchanged for the symbols of the dream certain images whose interpretation is difficult, if not questionable. One regrets here the waste of talent within the morass of subject matter.

FERDINAND SPRINGER [Wittenborn], who studied with Bissière, is now living in Paris and is represented in many collections both here and in Europe. He exhibits recent engravings. His sharp, shortened lines abstract setting and convey in a Chinese way, a concept of scene, of life, which is intellectual and formal. *Field* again is Chinese scenery, and this engraving illustrates very well how carefully Springer has balanced the technique of the East with its philosophy; idea and concept coalesce here on an equal level. This formalizing of his medium brings to his engravings an abruptness, a coldness in which everything is contained in an orderly fashion.

ALFONSO OSSORIO'S [Parsons] large show of recent paintings held several surprises. Not only were there many pictures of his vegetable, mineral, and unconscious world, darkened and thinned, remote and complicated, but very new, brightly colored paintings wherein form was brought from the unconscious straight into the light of day. These new works mark a change in his style. It is as if everything that had gone before was suddenly clarified—the whole multiple world of his art had found a direct meaning. His pictures had never wandered intangibly in their aura, but now they explode with a control that is quite delightful to witness, and with color which appears to be the reverse image of the color he had previously used. *Numbers 10* and *12* are large, direct statements of where the artist is at this point. Yet Ossorio's forms never appear arbitrary, but decisive; color precedes directly from light and the two combine in painting which leaves one alert to its further development.

February 1954

THE AMERICAN SCHOOL [Hirschl, Adler] can be found not only at the Metropolitan, but in this exhibition which ranges from such primitives as Hicks, through Wollaston, Copley, West, Innes, Eakins, and Sloan. Notable are two paintings of the Holmes brothers: one painted in Charleston by Wollaston, the other in Boston by Copley. They are brought together for the first time in two hundred years, and their reunion lends a poignancy to the skill of the portraits. *Mrs. Samuel Murray* by Eakins is an excellent portrait which, oddly enough, could very well resemble a painting of Virginia Woolf by Sickert. A still-life by Harnett, *Young Girl at the Piano* by Mather Brown, a portrait of Lincoln painted shortly before his death by Joseph Ames are a few of the other outstanding pictures.

KARL ENGREN [Gallery 47a], a New York painter who has studied at the League, is having his first one-man show. These oil paintings on wood present certain difficulties; they are both good and bad. Clichés appear and then are destroyed by an intuitive grasp of painting, by the appearance of what can only be called innate talent. A few earlier pictures are abstract patterns, darkened and obscured and not successful. Later he has painted city scenes, a figure disappearing down a sidewalk, a young man lolling against a building.

MARTIN NELSON [RoKo], taking the Tarot cards as a point of departure, has developed a series of paintings in heavy oil, turning dark over light and into light again. The paintings gather an intensity through this use of thick paint, yet elsewhere skillfully contrive to appear mysterious and haunting. *The Empress* and *Masquerade* impress us with the symbols which they represent, even more than the technique through which we are made aware of them. This is romantic, symbolic painting, yet at the same time it is extremely conscious of its effect on the viewer.

ILIYA SCHOR [Salpeter], who is also a metal worker, exhibits paintings, many of them of the Hebrew world which he inhabits and chooses, religiously, to paint. There is a highly personal quality in his work which is apparent not only in his pictures of people, but in *Landscape* and *Still-Life with Black Chair*, which appears to spring from a strong inner life. Schor's work has a Chagall-like quality which never quite falls into poetry, but has taken its manner from a direct and strong feeling about the aspects of orthodox Jewish life.

MOURA CHABOR [Galerie Moderne], who has studied and painted in Paris, is showing here for the first time. Much admired by Bourdelle and influenced by Valadon, her painting has both inventiveness and charm, with neither quality lessening the other. Her color is that of the city, transplanted with only the relativity of time onto canvas: nothing else, no school or genre, has intervened. *L'Opera* appears just as it would to the practiced eye of one who views it suddenly, for the first time, at exactly the moment for which he has been prepared. It is perhaps this kind of realism which has never quite presented itself in American painting, realism which is fictional as well as representational, that separates her work from her other painters of the Paris scene.

MAXIM KOPF [Heller], who has recently returned from the South Sea, exhibits paintings of a part of the world where the light falls quite differently. *Around Tahiti* is a simple and lovely painting which reflects not only the colors of Tahiti, but conveys an immediate sense of the locale. His figures have a vitality, almost a human competitiveness against the languor of the setting. Opposed to these South Sea pictures are earlier paintings of Spain which are somber and romantic, with darker colors and small, black figures who, unlike the direct, strong personalities of his South Sea natives, are lost within the landscape.

JOHN GROTH [Art Students League] took a year's leave of absence from his classes at the League in 1951 to travel in Korea and the Far East. He is exhibiting drawings which give us a direct, visual report of what is happening in that area. Hospitals, geisha houses, a midwife, battlefields, American nurses make up the background of his quick sketches of a somber world which he has managed to make tangible. One realizes from this show how much better drawing-on-the-spot is than photography, and how Groth appears to have been everywhere at once so that he might convey to us his very accurate and disturbing memoranda of the Korean catastrophe.

ROUAULT PRINTS [Town] from *Misserere et Guerre*, the work commissioned by Wollard and only released after his death, the *Père Ubu* series and *Cirque* woodcuts, form a grandiloquent tribute to one of the masters of the medium in this gallery's effort to introduce and popularize graphics of all countries.

KARL ZERBE [Alan] has recently returned to city landscapes. *Columbus Castles* marks the beginning of this subject change, yet here one has only to recall the former still-lifes and flash them back upon the painting, as a montage, to receive the effect of his former work. Color and form are still sliced horizontally so that the diesel engine or the cityscape remain rigidly within the same pattern. There is the same formal color control and areas still continue to build closely to one another. At times the paintings become pictures within pictures, mirror-scoped. Yet in *The Building* a final solution seems to have been found. Here Zerbe has executed his new scheme with little extraneous variation, so that the building can have no other nomenclature; the pattern is retained without ambivalent imagery, and the controls are few and simple.

ENRICO DONATI [Parons] continues his post-Surrealist experiments with roughened, velour-like surfaces, still somber in greys, blacks, and white, with an occasional earth color to brighten the scene. *Moonscape Black and Black* is indeed a trip to the moon, here a blackened crater. *Composition in Grey* contains several surfaces, heavy against light, and this painting in which there is breath and more uncontrolled atmosphere is perhaps the most successful of the group.

EINAR JOLIN [St. Etienne], represented in many museums in his native Sweden, has his first American showing. Stockholm is the setting for his landscapes, both the old and new city, and it is within this environment that Jolin is most secure. The setting is flat, cold, and Northern. There are many small figures, people walking, careful drawings of cars and busses, a boat, a fountain, a public building. Everything here is static, caught as before a camera, yet detached as in a dream. His paintings, for all their semblance of reality, have no motion. One almost doubts their probability until finally in *Old Stockholm*, where everything is several centuries removed, a kind of documentary awareness, as of a folk saga, is achieved. His still-lifes are conventional and often surprisingly bad. Yet his earlier portraits, while derivative of French painting, evince the talent which, curious and remote as it is, has located him among the foremost Swedish painters.

RICHARD LINDNER [Parsons], a German-born painter who lived for some time in Paris and now teaches at the Pratt Institute, has his first one-man show in America. These paintings, looking back upon the Surrealist symbols, have a separate style, personally derived from the painter's own memories and concept of life. They contain the silence of the transfigured moment which is arrived at within Surrealist painting, yet they move backwards and forwards in time which is not static, but moves as the emotions themselves change. Having spent his childhood in a mediaeval city, Lindner places mediaeval rooms upon his canvas, closed rooms with low ceilings wherein appear, in *Entre-Acte*, the King of Bavaria seated upon a stool, the artist as a boy in a sailor suit, his aunt in early century dress, two friends inhabiting a space with which they are unfamiliar, yet made at ease by their position within the picture; this, his latest painting, has the strength of intuition brought to its most mature stage. *Proust* and *Verlaine* are painted with a sympathy which does not go beyond the private atmosphere of these artists, and thus the pictures affect us as memoirs in which personal fictions can be completely understood.

March 1954

ABSTRACTIONS IN AFRICAN ART [Segy] selects those aspects which have become identified with modern art. Tribal masks with their simplified plasticity—the large eyes, the nose which is a line, the use, as in the Adoumas tribe, of concave and convex—have been seized upon by the Cubists and later abstractionists. If by now one is accustomed to seeing African masks only in relation to modern art, this exhibit is an excellent selective reference. Of particular note are the Baholoholo masks and a lovely Bakota funerary mask which contains singularly within its abstraction a modeling which is almost classical.

REALISM AND ROMANTICISM [Gallery East] juxtaposes the more academic, realist work of two painters, Milosh Cundrich and Haim Mendelson, beside the Romanticism of Joel Boxer and William Ekgren. Cundrich, who learned to paint while imprisoned by the Nazis, shows a very good *Still-Life* and even better drawings. He is a modest, sympathetic painter who appears to be limiting himself to his present medium thoroughly to learn his craft and the reaches of his expression. Mendelson is a competent painter whose *Self-Portrait* is unoriginal yet modest and his work within its restrictions is quite successful. Ekgren, a Scandinavian, exhibits fantastic portraits and still-lifes in shrill curlicues of color, a method which can be disturbing. Boxer, the most Romantic of the group, leans toward a contemporary Pre-Raphaelitism in *The Lady of the Italians.* Another large abstract canvas is somewhat literary and interpretive, a little English in approach; he has read and looked at Blake and a good bit of the mystic is here. If Boxer has a tendency to use his ideas as decorations, his decor is suggestive and fluent.

CUNO AMIET [St. Etienne], Swiss artist known there as the "painter of Sunny Life," has his first exhibition in America. Studying in Paris in 1888 under Bouguereau, he was later influenced by Bernard and Sérusier who brought him into contact with the work of Gauguin and Van Gogh. This exhibition, with the exception of an early picture, *Red Earth*, 1924, contains the work of recent years. Surprisingly enough, little change seems to have appeared. He is an Impressionist in *Still-life with Apples. Pasture*, 1949, closely resembles the Gauguin-like *Red Earth*. Quality and interest vary tremendously, yet the pictures are successful in a simplified way. He is indeed sunny; there are no problems. It appears that once one has mastered the technique of the 1890s, as Amiet did, an unlimited amount of canvases may be produced. Viewing this painting as the work of a Swiss, a good bit of this tranquility and satisfaction may be understood. It is the work of a man who carried his knowledge with him from Paris, and then proceeded to paint in isolation.

GILBERTA D. GOODWIN [Argent], in her first New York show, exhibits skillful, schooled paintings in a semi-Cubist manner. *Green Bowl and Ferns* is a stronger example of this manner, and *Green Bowl 1* more gentle, less Cubistic and perhaps more individual. She is a judicious painter and if there is little that is explosive or overtly original in her work, there are also few mistakes.

ALICE, IRENE, LILI GROSS [Wellons] are three sisters who exhibit sculpture and oils. The simple, naturalistic sculpture in terra cotta consists of figures molded in a somewhat amateurish manner. Irene Gross is a more skillful painter, her realism containing dramatic elements, and all of her pictures evince a professionalism which should become more apparent as her scope broadens. Lili Gross paints ordinary life in the small town; her work is limited yet honest and careful.

JAY ROBINSON [Milch] shows rather unclassifiable paintings on wood, real Kentucky wood no doubt, with the outlines of his figures carved, or burned in, and color added here and there whenever a mountain or cabin or kinsfolk demands it. He has also a fondness for copper backgrounds with sturdy male heads attached, or even mosaic (real stone) backgrounds. There is an atmosphere of the American musical, locale Kentucky, about this exhibition which has its humorous moments and certainly does not lack variety.

GRACE TREADWELL [Barbizon], who has been exhibiting and teaching for many years, shows lively and refreshing watercolors. She has both a taste and a kind of muscular control which lends to even the simplest New Hampshire setting the touch of the veteran and professional painter. Interested in the design formed by clouds, by the earth, design found anywhere, she does not permit it to overcome or overbalance the picture. *The Blow* is a painting which has been allowed to find itself through the guidance of a firm hand; it is almost an abstraction.

BEN ISQUITH [Tanager] is having his second one-man show. He is an abstract colorist who uses color only to convey form and subject. This type of painting abstracts from art history, as here from Tiepolo or Tintoretto, simply the use of color, and applies the rules of the contemporary New York School. Many of Isquith's pictures are Rococo, some are classical. They become abstractions of the aesthetic, of the beautiful. The difficulty is that much depends upon the painter's understanding of past painting, and also his color sense must be faultless. Isquith succeeds several times: *Black Painting*, wherein layers of black, heavy and thin, form a finished painting and black is not the absence of color, but quite the opposite, as light or as dark as he wishes; *Silver-White* again is nothing but paint, yet still it is a painting; in *Dark Grey Painting* he clearly shows the influence of the New York School—for the first time there is roughness, struggle and activity; *Blue Square Painting* is his latest picture and here we see him heading into abstraction reminiscent of Rollin Crampton, a not unnatural conclusion in a genre which seeks to deny all means of self-expression but one.

April 1954

ART OF THE AMERICAS [Sudamericana] brings together styles in painting now current in Latin America, Mexico, Jamaica, and Haiti. There is the Indian idiom formalized and popularized by Orozco and represented here by Del Prado, a Bolivian who showed for Bolivia at the São Paulo Biennial. The decorative, non-primitive, slightly fancy-dress style based on primitive motifs is seen in Lucner Lazard of Haiti, and the decadent, elegant, pseudo-European painting, in Antonio Gattorno, a pioneer of modern Cuban painting. A primitive manner is used by Francisca Moya in charming and rather threatening paintings of gardens. Fernandez Ponce de Leon, a Cuban, is very Spanish in his Goyaesque *Silver Fish.* Fernando de Szyszlo, a Peruvian now living in Paris, offers abstractions. These paintings do have the air of the New World; even the European influences appear somewhat trained and isolated to the degree of having been transported and, in the distance, losing their original opportunities.

LOPEZ-REY [Eggleston] paints bulls and matadors with a competent professionalism. *Banderillas Seated in the Chair* depicts the delight of a Spanish crowd viewing with macabre humor the matador and the charging bull. In *Silence* he has distilled the dramatic moment of the bullfight in Spanish shadows.

May 1954

MIRIAM SOMMERBERG [Kaufmann] shows sculpture, oils, watercolors, and prints. Sculpture is her natural medium and these large and small wooden studies work through an Expressionism into an almost mystic interpretation of the figure. She cuts tall, vertical figures who appear to be reaching upward toward solutions, to the meaning of "being," as in *Oneness*, *Dream*, *Creation*. The unique aspect of this work is that the figures do soar as in the early Gothic.

SCULPTURE GROUP [Clapp] brings together varied styles. Arnold Geissbuhler shows *Bird* and *Figure I* in a late Cubistic manner which has recently turned to institutional décor and somewhat detracts from the real craftsmanship of his bronzes. Rhys Caparn shows *The Withdrawal* and

Cat curiously structured with an intense abstraction of detail. *Echo*, a large sculpture by Koren der Wasey's very simple and handsome *Goose*, and Blanche Philip's *Mother and Child* are successful entries.

LOUIS BOUCHÉ [Kraushaar] proves that formula of color and design can continue to produce competent, professional painting. These paintings appear automatic in their lack of surprise, their diluted pleasure, and their fulfillment of the artist's means. Nature is a tool rather than a power, light refines color rather than heightening it, the human figure is either design or illustration rather than contour or muscle. This show also illustrates the ability of the painter with a limited imagination to exert his control over a canvas so that the will existing *a priori* can produce the picture.

DOUGLAS LOCKWOOD [Willard] is a painter of nature, which he sees as mysterious and elliptical. In short, tense lines he abstracts the landscape as in *Marsh* into both its natural appearance and the atmospheres which hover about the land and are visible to the mystic. In *Falling Star*, febrile heavens appear, the upper reaches which are to this painter beyond the grasp of realism and are conveyable only through a fine spray of light.

LUCILLE PARISH, MELVIN BUCKNER [Creative] show separate styles of painting. Parish uses a thin, bisected line, tense and concentrated. Buckner has several styles, ranging from that of stained glass as in *The Bird* through the religious configurations of Rouault into romantic Cubism.

N.A. ANNUAL EXHIBITION [National Academy of Design] of oils, sculpture, graphic art, and watercolors managed to run a conspicuously safe course. Among the more progressive paintings, including, most happily, Louis Bosa and Joseph Floch, the first and second Benjamin Altman Landscape Prizes went to William Thon's *Seabirds #2* and Edward Betts's *Nightmood Monhegan*. In a more venturesome gathering these two paintings might well have been unnoticed, but here their merits were undeniable. Raphael Soyer's *The Dressmaker's Shop*, a skillful and atmospheric picture like an early O'Henry story, and *The Big Sea* by Joseph De Martini certainly deserve mention, as does Keith Finch's *Family Group* and some of the gayer pictures in this truly sombre gathering, Dong Kingman's *17-mile Drive, California*. The sculpture was extremely limited, as was the watercolor and graphic art section. The exhibition appeared to have been cautiously chosen and apparently—with a selectivity leaning on favorites such as John Carroll, who won a prize for an innocuous *Mother and Child*—was unwilling to admit any of the untamed influences roaming the wilds of America and occasionally sipping the honeys of Fifty-Seventh Street.

GOODWIN, KERNS, MARKELL [Pen and Brush], award winners of this club, are given separate, although simultaneous exhibitions. Gilberta O. Goodwin, who teaches at the Centenary Junior College in New Jersey, shows watercolors. Her work, as in *Salt Marshes* and in *Green Bowl #1 and #2*, is influenced both by the Cubists and Impressionists, yet is individual in its use of color, its soft yet controlled line. Maude I. Kerns, from Oregon, is a non-objective painter who has a facility in her mellifluous use of color which shows a strong, almost academic training at work. Isabella B. Markell shows etchings of the upper East River and competent colored woodcuts.

LOUISE NEVELSON [Clapp] showed recent sculpture in terra cotta, wood, and marble. She has constructed, with several pieces of terra cotta joined together by a cylinder, sophisticated primitives who are capable of movement and even appear prepared to speak. *Mountain Woman* in aluminum has the planes and abbreviations of Cubism—as to a degree does all her work—and *River* in terra cotta proves that even Maillol can be abbreviated without a lessening of power or beauty. In *Twilight Figure* she has chosen marble to render a figure in mysterious contemplation, cubed and curved, and here her sense of deletion is apparent where after many choices only the essential plane is allowed to appear. This sculpture is one of varied and shaded meaning of half-tones, ironic and beautiful.

ALFRED LESLIE [de Nagy] has left behind those startling still-life abstractions of his last show and following the current trend exhibits paintings of the figure. What remains is still a sudden use of carmine, of bright green falling from the shadows of his blacks, greys, and madders. What is left behind is a virtuosity and daring which are his real forte, an ease and looseness which carry him out of the threatening monotony of this present show into the foreground of artistry. These pictures are all studies with many slashing stokes to remove any static possibility. In *The Black Stockings*, *The Black Shadow*, we find thus a series of virtuoso experiences on canvas, but we do not have the seated female figure. She moves from picture to picture farther outside the painter's reach, so that finally one wonders where the original intent existed. Leslie appears to have been doing several things at once, with one eye on the figure and the other fixed on his mobile attitude toward art itself, a difficult separation. This often leads, as here, to painting about painting where the real experience never quite comes off. Extremely successful is a series of brilliant floral pictures, probably the best by a contemporary now on view in New York.

Summer 1954

SUMMER EXHIBITION [Milch] is one of the more pleasant renderings of the season. Leion Kroll shows *Normandy Beachhead*, one of those expertly arranged and romanticized paintings wherein the real scene is never quite lost despite the Greco-Roman trappings. Hobson Pittman gives us another painting of the romantic American house, *Storage Room*, and here again it is not so much what he arranges pictorially, although that is done very nicely for us, but his awareness of light and his strict attention to color values. In *Lido, Venice*, Louis Bosa is again himself, in strict command of his picturesque and clownly antics.

CONGER METCALF'S [Karnig] paintings of Italian street boys and nostalgic groups of girls with antique vases hovering in the background recall the Italy of Browning and William Dean Howells. Deliberately antiquated, the paper used here looks as if it might have been found in the drawer of an old desk. Metcalf is a good draftsman, but not essentially an interesting one, and these portraits and drawings recall a past which may not altogether be his, but whose nostalgic recall is entertaining.

CLARA MCDONALD WILLIAMSON [Alan] is another discovery among American primitives. Although she has had some formal training, this elderly Texas lady relies on her memory of frontier days to re-create a past in a way which has little to do with the rules of art schools. Her pictures are of cowboys and cattle, as in *Old Chisholm Trail*, and of religious camp meetings, such as *Standing in the Need of Prayer.* These pictures are unlike any paintings of the Far West any of us has ever seen—there is no noble savage, no lone cowboy. They are intensely and warmly human, and turning from painting to painting is like turning the leaves of an old-fashioned photograph album.

CLARKE, RAGER, WARHOL [Loft] are members of this new gallery who exhibited in different styles. Allan Hugh Clarke showed large, crowded, colorful, cubed paintings in which all he knew and could assemble about the scene and art was allowed to appear. Ed Rager can be a very good painter when he wishes, as in *Twilight in Connecticut*, where the very ordinariness of the subject causes one to look for those qualities in the artist which will supersede, and here do supersede, his objectified aim. Andy Warhol has developed an original style of line drawing and a willingness to obligate himself to that narrow horizon on which appear attractive and demanding young men involved in the business of being as much like Truman Capote or his heroes as possible. His technique has the effect of the reverse side of a negative, although his lines are broken and the spaces not clouded.

ANDUJAR, ESTELLA [Coeval] are two abstract painters who work in different styles. Claudia H. Andujar is primarily interested in color, which she uses riotously and in heavy impasto. All this color does not necessarily distribute form nor add anything to the picture. Her work, like that of Ramon A. Estella, who uses arbitrary shapes, although sometimes abstracted from reality, has a nebulous, unfinished air about it as if the picture were merely work in progress and not the completed idea.

NACHUM GUTMAN [Heller], who lives in Israel, exhibits watercolors which are whimsical, imaginative renderings of the Israeli scene. He is also an illustrator and these pictures might well be shown in storybook form. Light, amusing, the houses and beaches have the atmosphere of a fairy tale which may be quite real to the occupants of the land. There is a holiday or holy day spirit present in these pictures—he has removed any somber reminders of the past or future.

GORDON PRESS [Coeval] is a young New York artist who recently had his first one-man show. He has a colorful, loose style which tends to be too easy and at times decorative. *The Princeton Killer*, a painting of a football player, is an example of this rapid portrayal of subject which goes no deeper than the surface of the canvas. There are many unguarded areas in his pictures which require solidifying, and at present his talent appears fragmentarily.

YOUNGER AMERICAN AND EUROPEAN PAINTERS [Jackson] is a refreshing exhibition made up of the work of painters who have been introduced previously in New York shows. The outstanding painters for this reviewer are William Scott and Lawrence Calcagno. Scott, an Englishman, whose work at first glance looks like that of New York painters shown recently at the large Stable Gallery gathering, separates himself by certain European mannerisms and methods of applying paint, and, despite his entirely different style, his most subtle relationship is to the English painters Surtherland and Bacon. Calcagno, an American who now lives in Paris, shows *Red Painting*, an abstraction whose merit depends to a large degree on the artist's excellent color values and his understanding of spatial composition. Hultberg is an abstractionist with powerful compositional drives which perform here most favorably in *Sea Journey*. Trukes, well known in Germany, shows several idioms, one remarkably like the present French abstractionist style derived from Impressionism and another, strictly German in its formal shapes and linear design.

NOVELLE PARIGINI [Karnig] paints the kind of pictures one expects to see and frequently does find in Hollywood. Her ladies are either young and glamorous in the Roman manner of lanky dark hair, eyes slanted as far upward as possible, or blonde Hollywood stars who create quite a contrast with their full-blooming faces and the look of greedy intensity that frequently arrives with stardom. There is not much to say about the quality of the paintings, which appear to have been dashed off any old remembered how, but there is an impression of personal daring by the artist.

Notes

Abbreviations

FI: *Forces of Imagination: Writing on Writing*, Kelsey Street Press, 2003

DW: *Dürer in the Window*, Roof Books, 2003

GP: Barbara Guest Papers, Yale University's Beinecke Rare Book & Manuscript Library

Mysteriously Defining the Mysterious: Byzantine Proposals of Poetry: There are three distinct versions of this essay. The first was a talk delivered at St. Mark's Poetry Project in either March or June of 1986, with the title "Mysteriously Speaking of the Mysterious: Byzantine Proposals of the Poem." The recording exists. The second and unpublished version had removed roughly four full paragraphs, had slightly revised other areas, and had the subtitle, "Byzantine Proposals of Poetry." A third further trimmed the second. When this third, minimal version was published in Kathleen Fraser's journal *HOW(ever)* 3 no. 3 (San Francisco: October 1986), it was described as "excerpts" from the St. Mark's talk. Those "excerpts" were reprinted in *Jubilat* (Fall 2002), ed. Peter Gizzi, and republished in FI. The second version, of which there are typed copies in GP for copytext, is made available here.

The four full paragraphs cut from the St. Mark's talk have been transcribed by this editor and shared below. The first was the introductory remark. Two other paragraphs comprised what Guest duly called "an aside," and readers can see now how they were inserted. The fourth paragraph below was the conclusion for that St. Mark's talk.

> On this subject of "Mysteriously Speaking of the Mysterious: Byzantine Proposals of the Poem," I wrote a little. I started to write Eileen a poem about architecture, because she said something once about my poems are

like architecture. And the poem didn't work, but I ended up with four lines which I'll start this with:

poets under Byzantine persuasion
donate their sanguine feathers
to merciless corridors
to golden domes and purple birds

. . .

And if that were so, I wouldn't need to present my Byzantine proposal.

As an aside, I would like to discuss an article I read in the *New York Times* on deconstructivism. My secret belief is that this method, deconstruction, found its niche at Yale because professors of English were very tired of being called professors of English and wished to attain the more lofty title of humanist. Deconstructivism offered them this choice. In the *Times* article we are given a brief excerpt, demeaning in its brevity, from one of the greatest poems in the English language, *Paradise Lost*. Then follows a deconstructionist reading of the poem. Now, in the first place, I am astonished that Jacques Derrida of the École Normale Supérieure, the founder of deconstruction, could pretend to understand, I almost said "underrate," a foreign language to the extent that he could comprehend one of the most difficult poems in the English language. I don't think any of us here could possibly understand a similar French poem. This goes, in the article, unremarked. In the absence of Mr. Derrida, a deconstructivist attempt is made to perform acrobatics on this selection from the poem. The passage here, we are told, is one of extraordinary beauty. One that "has both moved and troubled many readers"—for "many readers" read clergymen—an example of "the luxuriance of Milton's poetic power." All this, God who is invoked knows.

Now, nowhere is the potential, inherent poetic mystery of the poem mentioned. Their stated job is to find the meaning inherent in Milton, but no one attempts to find his marvelous abilities. The mysterious qualities which absolutely glisten in the poem, the degree of struggle whereby Milton attains his greatness. The skimpy selection is about Eve: "Shee as a vail down to the slender waist, / Her unadorned golden tresses wore / Disshevell'd, but in wanton ringlets wav'd / As the Vine curles her tendrils, which impli'd / Subjection . . ." Subjection is what troubles them and they feast on it. Is she or is she not subject to subjection? It might well be a feminist question, but it is not. It's not a question at all. These people give us the answer of "yes" and "no." And they are attempting to understand, mind you, a poem luxuriant with troubling mystery which is what life is all about. Troubling mystery wrapped up in sound. Poets as disparate as Eliot and Keats were enriched by this work and what they discovered in *Paradise Lost* was the mystery of imaginative process invoked here by Milton. Auden said, "every poem is rooted in imaginative awe." And Marianne Moore said that what must be present in poetry is an impassioned interest in life's creative secret. We have the adjectives "imaginative," "impassioned," "creative," connected to all in "secret."

. . .

Finally we can turn to the Chinese artists who in their definition of a painting of plum blossoms agree. The idea must always, however, be rooted in the object that inspired it. There is no conflict between realism and imagination. In painting, it can be noticed that the paintings are clearly representational and clearly imaginary. If there is any difference: clearly abstract and clearly concrete at the same time. If there is any difference of opinion here between East and West it may have to do with our different concepts of time. I personally am devoted to the idea of *at the same time*. Now we have arrived at the borders of other things. I quoted from painters to illustrate what can be called the time-space sense of a poem, its fallibility and its ardent silence, its arrival and departure. And these essences are summoned by the serious owls of the inner sound until the region mysterious to the poet and painter mysteriously opened and there the poem or plum blossom bursts into flower.

Gothic Elevation: Separate document included with essays in GP, used as copytext. Dated December 16, 1996. There are two copies with "JOAN!" written above as a title but crossed out in pen in one copy. Titled here by editor.

Sympathy with Ovid: This piece was adapted from a letter Guest wrote to Etel Adnan in the late 1990s. Guest extracted, edited, and typed these lines into a separate reflection, of which there are two drafts filed with her other essays. Among other small changes made in her drafts, two copies have "Etel," which was previously only at the top of the letter, now inserted into the passage as "Remember, Etel"; yet one copy has that inserted "Etel" crossed out with pen, rendering a more general poetic piece. Titled here by editor.

Radical Poetics and Conservative Poetry: A talk presented at the St. Mark's Poetry Project, New York City, May 5, 1990, as one of four lectures on "Poetry 1990: The State of the Art." Final draft in GP. FI used as copytext.

A Talk on "Startling Maneuvers": Talk delivered at The Jack Kerouac School of Disembodied Poetics, Summer Writing Program, 1998. Transcribed by Cole Swensen and published in *Poetry Project* newsletter 172 (December/January 1998/9): 8–10. Publication used as copytext. The poem, "Startling Maneuvers," was published as "A Reverie On the Making of a Poem" in *American Letters & Commentary* no. 10.

Art in America: The Nineteen Fifties and Sixties (Viewed in 1999): Three final drafts are in GP. The one most thoroughly proofed used as copytext. Written in 1999.

Kant Sees: Final draft in GP. FI used as copytext.

Preface for *A Portfolio of Poetry: Selected by Barbara Guest*: "A Portfolio of Poetry," *Chelsea* 57 (1994): 20–88. Copytext.

Anarchy of the Emotions: Document found among essays in GP and used as copytext. Titled by editor.

Shifting Persona: Published in *Poetics Journal* 9 (1990), eds. Lyn Hejinian and Barrett Watten; reprinted in the *American Poetry Review* (September/October 2002), ed. Arthur Vogelsang. It was published again in FI, but, due to a few punctuation and spelling typos in FI, the version from the *American Poetry Review* used as copytext.

Prague Walking: An undated and ostensibly finished essay in GP used as copytext. Internal references suggest it was written in the late 1960s.

Forces of Imagination: A talk delivered in April 1999 at Guest's award ceremony for the Robert Frost Medal for Lifetime Achievement in Poetry by the Poetry Society of America. Published in the *American Poetry Review* (September/October 2002), ed. Arthur Vogelsang. Final draft in GP. FI used as copytext.

An Inconsiderate Preface: Final draft of "An Inconsiderate Preface" is in GP. FI used as copytext. The first four paragraphs of this essay were part of a drafted essay titled "Translation" in GP. That "Translation" is undated, but references to the apartment and overheard Portuguese resonate with *Seeking Air* (1978), since those dynamics inform the novel's penultimate scene.

The Shadow of Surrealism: Talk delivered at the Kouros Gallery, New York City, 1986. Published in *PEN American Center Newsletter*, no. 2 (1987); and in *Women's Studies* 30, no. 1 (2001). Final drafts in GP. FI used as copytext.

Poetry the True Fiction: Talk delivered at the State University of New York, Buffalo, April 1992. Published in *Carcanet*, 1995, ed. Michael Schmidt; and in *Exact Change Yearbook*, 1995, ed. Peter Gizzi. Parts of this essay were also copied and reworked into a smaller piece in FI, "Vision and Mundanity." Final draft of "Poetry the True Fiction" in GP. FI used as copytext.

Imagism: Final draft in GP. FI used as copytext.

A Reason for Poetics: Published in *Ironwood* 24 (1984), ed. Michael Cuddihy. Final draft in GP. FI used as copytext.

Invisible Architecture: Published in *INPRINT* (November 2002), eds. Dorothy Terry and Maureen Michaels. Final draft in GP. FI used as copytext.

Wounded Joy: Published in the *American Poetry Review* 31, no. 5 (September/October, 2002), ed. Arthur Vogelsang. Final draft in GP. FI used as copytext.

"The Work" in *Goodnough*: Published in *Goodnough* by Barbara Guest and B. H. Friedman (Paris: The Pocket Museum, Editions George, 1962). Copytext.

The Vuillard of Us: James Schuyler: This essay was published in a special issue on James Schuyler, *Denver Quarterly* 24 (Spring 1990), ed. Donald Revell. A one-page version was read on February 18, 1999, at New College for an education on James Schuyler. The final draft of that longer published piece used as copytext.

Why has Louise Bourgeois finally become the Artist of the Moment?: Published in *Denver Quarterly* 28, no. 1 (1993): 72–76. The title is a reply to an August 1992 *New York Times* article by Michael Kimmelman, "ART; After Many a Summer, A Sculptor Comes to Age," where Kimmelman stated, "Ms. Bourgeois's work suddenly seems very much of the moment." There is a copy of this essay reprinted in DW, but that version has deleted an introductory passage and added male pronouns into the concluding quotation. That version also contains differences in punctuation, different phrasing for titles, some altered clauses, and numerous typos. It's likely that, despite citing the original article, Guest added changes but it wasn't perfectly proofed. For these reasons, and the sake of variety, the original from *Denver Quarterly* is used here as copytext. However, one comma was added by this editor to complete the clause, "*Fallen Woman* (1981), compared to the puzzled figures clinging to their personalities of the 1940s, is like a shower of Narcisse Noir," and the written title of a Bourgeois piece in that article, "Brother and Sister," was changed to the more historically accurate *Brother & Sister*.

For Celebration of Allen Ginsberg's 60th Birthday: Essay in GP used as copytext. Presumably written in the summer of 1986 when Ginsberg turned sixty.

Robert Duncan, As Once I Viewed Him: Essay in GP used as copytext. Dated February 5, 1998.

The Story of Bryher (A Proposal): Copy in GP used as copytext. This book proposal was likely written soon after completing *Herself Defined: The Poet H.D. and Her World* (New York: Doubleday & Company, Inc., 1984), but the project was ultimately abandoned.

Dorothy Richardson: A Letter from Cornwall: Published in *HOW(ever)* 3, no. 2 (1986): 13–14. Copytext.

An Evening with Charles Olson: Document in GP used as copytext. Undated.

Jeanne Reynal: Published in *Craft Horizons* 31, no. 3 (June 1971): 40–43. Copytext.

Nell Blaine at Yaddo in the 1950s: Document among essays in GP used as copytext. Written for the Memorial Tribute to Nell Blaine, Tibor de Nagy Gallery, January 8, 1997.

Robert de Niro in the 1950s and '60s: There are two versions of this 1998 essay in GP. This version is longer by a few sentences.

Helen Frankenthaler: The Moment & The Distance: Published in *Arts Magazine* 49 (April 1975): 58–59. Used as copytext. This publication is significantly longer and more detailed than the version printed later in DW.

Piet Mondrian: Written in 2000. Version in DW used as copytext; except Hans "Hoffman" in DW is changed to "Hofmann" here. The "Piet Mondrian" essay is itself a combination of two different pieces: that titled "Survival" in *Forces of Imagination* and an anecdote Guest drafted separately several times.

The Color Green in the Art Work of Richard Tuttle: Written in 2000. DW used as copytext.

Jean Arp: From a talk at Poet's House, New York, November 1989. A shorter version of this essay was first published in Poet's House's *Passwords: Poets on Poets*, November 30, 1990. A second, of which there are final drafts in GP, was printed in DW. But since the graphics and formatting of this essay in DW could not be duplicated, the format of the same essay in GP was used as copytext.

Leatrice Rose: Published in *Arts Magazine* (Summer 1985). DW used as copytext.

June Felter: Published in *Art in America* 79 (March 1991). DW used as copytext.

Memorial Service for Tibor de Nagy: In GP. A talk prepared for a memorial service for Tibor de Nagy at the Tibor de Nagy Gallery, May 1994. The word "Memorial" was added to the title by this editor for clarity.

Mary Abbott: DW used as copytext. However, DW states *Honey or Wine?* resides at the National Gallery of Art in Washington, DC, but the Smithsonian American Art Museum in D.C. currently has it filed in their collection.

The Intimacy of Biography: Published in *The Iowa Review* 16, no. 3, "H.D. Centennial Issue" (Fall 1986): 58–71. Copytext.

"PART FIVE" of *Herself Defined*: "Part Five" consists of these two chapters, "Lausanne-Lugano 1947–53" and "The Bryher Path." The first edition of this book, *Herself Defined: The Poet H.D. and Her World* (New York: Doubleday & Company, Inc., 1984), 281–301, was used as copytext (rather than later editions published by the press of John Schaffner and H.D.'s daughter, Perdita Macpherson Schaffner). In this edition, "Schmideberg" [*sic*] is kept and refers to Dr. Walter Schmiedeberg. And yet I have added the bracketed "[Macpherson]" to the first mention of "Kenneth" in "The Bryher Path" for possibly needed context here.

H.D. and the Conflict of Imagism: A paper read at the Voice Box Festival,

London, April 26, 1992, in celebration of the "Centennial of Imagism." Published in *Sagetrieb* 15, no. 1/3 (Spring and Fall, 1996). DW used as copytext.

On *Richard Aldington & H.D.: The Early Years in Letters*: Review dated June, 1992, of *Richard Aldington & H.D.: The Early Years in Letters*, ed. Caroline Zilboorg (Bloomington: Indiana University Press, 1992). In GP. Copytext.

A Review: H.D.'s *Ion, a play after Euripides*; H.D.'s *Nights*: Review published in *Conjunctions* 11 (1988), 280–83. Copytext. A review of H.D., *Ion, a play after Euripides* (Redding Ridge: Black Swan Books, 1986); H.D., *Nights* [by John Helforth] (New York: New Directions, 1986).

Letter from Barbara Guest to Susan Gevirtz: Published in *HOW(ever)* 4, no. 4, 1988. Copytext.

***Seeking Air* [Dedication, Epigraph, Preface, & Chapters 1-10]:** Two existing editions of the novel were consulted and used: *Seeking Air* (Black Sparrow Press, 1978) and *Seeking Air* (Grand Iota, 2021). In the first edition, the word "witholding" in the preface has one "h" but is spelled correctly in the Grand Iota edition. Yet, in the Grand Iota edition, there is not a period between "bookshelf But" in the Preface, while there is a period in the first edition. In chapter five of the Grand Iota edition, there is a typo where "she" should be capitalized, as in the Black Sparrow edition, "young wards. She was . . ." Therefore, the version printed here has opted for the correct spelling and punctuation in either case.

***Foreheads*, with Joe Brainard:** "Foreheads," *C Comics*, no. 2, 1964. Scanned copies obtained from the Brainard Papers at University of California, San Diego.

The Influence of Music on the Work of George Eliot, as recalled by George Henry Lewes: Published in *Conjunctions* 16, The Music Issue (1991), 233–36. Copytext.

Motion Pictures: Published in the *American Poetry Review* 26, no. 1 (January/February, 1997): 20–22. Copytext. This is an early look at what would become *The Confetti Trees: Motion Picture Stories* (Los Angeles: Sun & Moon, 1999).

Chinese Ghost Restaurant: Written in 1967. There are several drafts of this unpublished, unstaged play in GP. This appears to be the final draft.

Frank O'Hara's "Hôtel Transylvanie": In GP. O'Hara's poem was written December 9, 1959, while Guest's essay is undated.

***A World* by Dennis Phillips:** Published in *Temblor* 10 (1989): 31–32. Copytext. Dennis Phillips, *A World* (Los Angeles: Sun & Moon, 1989).

Susan Gevirtz's *Narrative's Journey*: Review published in *Sulfur* 40 (Spring 1997): 186–88. Copytext. Susan Gevirtz, *Narrative's Journey: The Fiction and Film Writing of Dorothy Richardson* (New York: Peter Lang, 1996).

***Tlooth*, Harry Mathews:** Published in *The Review of Contemporary Fiction* 7, no. 3 (1987): 117–18. Copytext. Harry Mathews, *Tlooth* (Paris Review Editions, Doubleday, 1966).

The Fiction of the Poet **by Anna Balakian**: Published in *Sulfur* no. 34 (Spring 1994): 223–25. Copytext. Anna Balakian, *The Fiction of the Poet* (Princeton: Princeton University Press, 1992). Review written February 1993.

Benjamin Constant's *Cécile*: In GP. Review of Benjamin Constant, *Cécile*, trans. Norman Cameron, ed. Alfred Roulin (New York: New Directions, 1951).

Dear Mei-mei, on the publication of *Empathy*: A letter to Mei-mei Berssenbrugge, titled "On the publication of *Empathy*," is in GP. Mei-Mei Berssenbrugge, *Empathy* (Station Hill Press, 1989).

Kenneth Koch's *Selected Poems: 1950–1982*: In GP but written for the *East Hampton Star*. Kenneth Koch, *Selected Poems: 1950–1982* (New York: Vintage Books, Random House, 1985).

Anne Waldman, "Iovis: A Poem": In GP. Anne Waldman, *Iovis: A Poem* (Minneapolis: Coffee House Press, 1993).

Beryl Barr-Sharrar Exhibitions: In GP. Titled by editor.

Notable Omissions

A complete collection that would include all of Guest's plays and the entirety of her novel *Seeking Air*, and the biography *Herself Defined: H.D. and Her World*, would have required a multivolume set unsought by the publisher and editor.

Two short stories written in the mid-1950s ("Carolina Moon," rejected by *The New Yorker* in 1956, and "The White Alsatian," rejected by *Partisan Review* in 1957), were thought to be unpolished by reviewers and voted out.

Guest's one-paragraph "Homage to O'Hara" was published in *Homage to Frank O'Hara*, edited by Joe LeSueur and Bill Berkson in 1988, but this remembrance was, like her one-paragraph "Introduction to a Reading by Etel Adnan" in 1997, comparatively informal, short and light.

The two shorter comic strips written with Joe Brainard, reprinted in *Dürer in the Window*, are not duplicated here but represented by Guest's and Brainard's longer comic *Foreheads*.

A number of Guest's briefer poetic reflections were kept exclusively within *Forces of Imagination*: "Walter Benjamin in a Museum," "The Element of Surprise," "Survival," "Green Shoots," "Consider," "Allow Yourself," "Splendor Falls," "Poetic Creation," "The Voice of the Poem," "The Beautiful Voyage," "Why They Are Called Tales," "Early Days of a Poet," "On the value of criticism from painters, rather than writers," and "The Desire for Sensationalism in Literary Culture."

About the Authors and Editor

Barbara Guest (1920–2006) published over twenty volumes of poetry and earned numerous awards, including the Robert Frost Medal for Distinguished Lifetime Achievement from the Poetry Society of America.

Joseph Shafer teaches at the University of Marburg and publishes on American poetry, critical theory, and aesthetics. His books include *Appearing Beside Text: Uprisings of Indifference in Post-1945 American Poetry* and he is coediting a new *Selected Poems of Barbara Guest.*

Marjorie Welish is a poet, painter, and art critic. She taught modern art history at Pratt Institute before holding the Madelon Leventhal Rand Endowed Chair in Literature at Brooklyn College. Her arts practice was the subject of the book, *Of the Diagram: The Work of Marjorie Welish.*